ASPECTS OF
RELIGIOUS PROPAGANDA IN
JUDAISM AND EARLY CHRISTIANITY

UNIVERSITY OF NOTRE DAME
CENTER FOR THE STUDY OF
JUDAISM AND CHRISTIANITY
IN ANTIQUITY
Number 2

Aspects of
Religious Propaganda in
Judaism and Early Christianity

ELISABETH SCHÜSSLER FIORENZA
editor

UNIVERSITY OF NOTRE DAME PRESS
NOTRE DAME   LONDON

Library of Congress Cataloging in Publication Data
Main entry under title:

Aspects of religious propaganda in Judaism and
early Christianity.
"Essays . . . originally delivered as lectures in
a series of Apologetics and mission in Judaism and
early Christianity."
Bibliography: p.
1. Apologetics—Early church, ca. 30-600—Addresses, essays, lectures. 2. Heroes—Addresses,
essays, lectures. 3. Magic—History—Addresses,
essays, lectures. 4. Miracles—History—Addresses,
essays, lectures. 5. Judaism—History—Post-exilic
period, 586 B.C.-210 A.D.—Addresses, essays, lectures. I. Fiorenza, Elisabeth Schüssler, 1938
BT1110.A84   239'.1   74-27890
ISBN 0-268-00578-8

Contents

v

Acknowledgments

THE ESSAYS OF THIS VOLUME WERE ORIGINALLY DE-livered as lectures in a seminar on Apologetics and Mission in Judaism and Early Christianity sponsored by the Department of Theology of the University of Notre Dame. I am particularly grateful to the chairperson of the department, Father David B. Burrell, C.S.C., for his interest and support in planning and preparing the seminar. Special thanks are due to the donors of the Rosenstiel fund for the support of the seminar and the book. I wish also to thank Ms. Barbara Cullom Bondi, Ms. Ann Rice, and Mr. Bruce Fingerhut of Notre Dame Press for their help in editing the volume as well as Dr. Richard Sturm for his assistance during my stay at Union Theological Seminary in New York.

My hope is that these essays not only further the understanding of the Jewish and Christian missionary endeavor in the Greco-Roman world but that they also provoke new research in this area.

Elisabeth Schüssler Fiorenza

Contributors

DR. PAUL J. ACHTEMEIER
Union Theological Seminary, Richmond, Virginia

DR. HANS DIETER BETZ
Claremont Graduate School of Theology

DR. LOUIS H. FELDMAN
Yeshiva College, New York

DR. ELISABETH SCHÜSSLER FIORENZA
Department of Theology, University of Notre Dame

DR. DIETER GEORGI
The Divinity School, Harvard University

DR. JUDAH GOLDIN
Department of Oriental Studies, University of Pennsylvania

DR. WAYNE A. MEEKS
Department of Religious Studies, Yale University

1: Miracles, Mission, and Apologetics: An Introduction

Elisabeth Schüssler Fiorenza

EXEGETICAL INQUIRY OFTEN DEPENDS UPON THE THEO-
logical and cultural presuppositions with which it
approaches its texts. Historical scholarship therefore judges
the past from the perspective of its own concepts and
values. Since for various reasons religious propaganda, mission, and apologetics are not very fashionable topics in the
contemporary theological scene, these issues have also
been widely neglected in New Testament scholarship.
Many exegetes do not presently perceive the history of
early Christianity as the history of a propagandistic-
missionary endeavor. Instead they consider the New
Testament writings primarily as documents of an inner-
Christian doctrinal struggle and they understand early
Christian history mainly as a "confessional" history, as a
struggle between different Christian parties and theologies.
With the exception of D. Georgi's work,[1] studies on the
"opponents" in various New Testament writings have concentrated upon the presence of theological conflict within
the early Christian communities. These factions, parties, or
groups are defined primarily by their creed or confession
but not by their cultural and societal setting. Likewise the
New Testament writings, especially the Gospels, are defined as products of doctrinal, especially christological,
controversy rather than as missionary literature[2] written in

order to promote the Christian movement and to proclaim Jesus Christ in the propagandistic language and pattern of the time. The public-societal dimension of Christian literature is thus absorbed into a congregational-confessional framework. This public-societal dimension of the New Testament problems and writings could be regained, however, if the cultural-religious milieu of the Greco-Roman world would no longer be considered solely as "background" material for the New Testament writings. Instead the early Christian movement and its literature should be viewed as rooted in the attempt to attract and to convince persons of the Hellenistic world, be they already Christians, Jews, or pagans.

Judaism[3] as well as Christianity[4] had a period of great expansion at the beginning of our era. Jews as well as Christians appealed to the Greco-Roman world and used the means and methods of Hellenistic religious propaganda. They stressed the antiquity of their faith, gathered followers in small, private communities, attracted people through their worship, painted the great figures of their religion as heroes and demi-gods, exhibited the miraculous, magic, and ecstatic powers of their religion, and proved that their religious associations and customs were beneficial and accepted by the political power of the time. The appropriation of such missionary-propagandistic forms was necessary if Judaism as well as Christianity were to succeed in the face of competition from other religions, especially those of Oriental origin,[5] as well as competition from the philosophical movements[6] of the time. The cultural and political situation was very propitious for such a propagandistic attempt. The spread of Hellenism had torn down many barriers separating people from people, culture from culture, and religion from religion, and the political unification in the Roman Empire made traveling and cultural-religious exchange very easy.

Judaism had confronted this propagandistic task at least three centuries before the origin of Christianity. Hellenistic cultural and religious thought had permeated the Judaism not only of the Dispersion but also of Palestine. Recent scholarly investigations have proven that a clear separation between Palestinian Judaism and Hellenistic Judaism, often presupposed by historians of primitive Christianity, never existed.[7] Indeed over an extended period of time, Judaism had not only been spreading progressively throughout the Greco-Roman world, but the success of Jewish propaganda and the strange character of Jewish religious and moral custom and praxis provoked the bitter reaction of anti-Semitism in antiquity.[8] To answer the needs of the rapid expansion as well as to counteract the slanderous attacks, Judaism had produced a body of propagandistic literature written in Greek.[9] In such literature it developed a sophisticated apologetics to strengthen its own members and to convince its gentile readers of the truth of the Jewish faith. Whereas apologetics answered the criticism leveled against Judaism, missionary propaganda put the Jewish cause in positive form in order to win over the gentile audience. Thus apologetics and missionary propaganda functioned like two sides of the same coin.[10] The success of this Jewish missionary propaganda was so great that Philo in his *Life of Moses* could state: "They [the laws of Moses] attract and win the attention of all: of Barbarians, of Greeks, of dwellers on the mainland and islands, of nations of the east and of the west, of Europe and Asia, of the whole inhabited world from end to end" (2.4.20).[11] Therefore, it is surprising that in the past thirty to forty years, scholars have paid very little attention to the phenomenon of Jewish missionary and apologetic propaganda in the so-called intertestamental period. No recent in-depth study of this phenomenon exists, and recent study of early Christian mission pays but little attention to its heritage of religious propaganda from Judaism.[12] It does not investigate in what ways the early Christian movement learned from the Jewish missionary propaganda nor how it distanced itself critically from this heritage.

Especially in German New Testament scholarship the

study of early Christian mission has received renewed interest in recent years. However this interest is not directed toward the forms and themes of religious propaganda nor its setting in the Greco-Roman world, but rather it concentrates on the origin of early Christian missionary activity and its theological legitimization.[13] Present-day exegetical discussion addresses the question almost solely as an inner-Christian phenomenon and theological problem. Jewish apocalypticism is the only contemporary movement which comes into view in this discussion.[14]

Debate centers around the question of whether or not Jesus extended his ministry to the Gentiles or whether he hoped for their conversion as an eschatological act. Did Jesus initiate a gentile mission, or did he explicitly limit his preaching to Israel because of his eschatological expectation?[15] Also at stake, then, is the question of whether the early Christian mission derived its theological legitimization from the historical Jesus or from the commandment of the resurrected Lord.[16] Connected with these theological concerns are more explicitly historical questions. Did the gentile mission start in Jerusalem, Galilee, or Antioch? Did Jesus himself[17] or did the so-called Hellenists[18] initiate the gentile mission? Or does the suggestion of Acts that the Apostles and Paul were the initiators[19] reflect more the historical reality?

It is interesting to note that in this exegetical discussion missionary activity and proclamation is seen mainly as addressing the gentile world. This understanding of early Christian mission rests upon the dichotomy between inside and outside. It fails to perceive that the self-identity of the missionary community is intertwined with its understanding of its mission and the formulation of its propaganda, and it fails to recognize that communication is possible only where common conceptuality and common language can be presupposed. Any adequate discussion of the early Christian movement must consider both the relationship of the early Christian movement to the Jewish propagandistic movement, on the one hand, and the impact of the Greco-

Roman religious and cultural environment on both movements, on the other hand. The exegetical interest in the
origins of the gentile mission in recent scholarly discussion
appears to have kept scholars from recognizing the inter-
play between early Christian missionary and apologetic
activity and the religious propaganda of the Greco-Roman
world.

The six essays of this volume attempt to elucidate in
various ways and approaches the interdependence of Jewish and early Christian missionary activity and apologetics
with the culture of the time. These essays were originally
delivered as lectures in a series on "Apologetics and Mission in Judaism and Early Christianity." Although the
various lecturers were asked to speak on a topic as broad as
this, they chose, independently of each other, to concen-
trate upon the role and function of the charismatic figure
and the related topic of miracles and magic in the ancient
world. Their reflections contribute to the present scholarly
discussion on aretalogy as well as on miracles and magic. In
relating to the wider topic of religious propaganda in the
Greco-Roman world, they bring to the fore the public-
societal dimension of these issues.

In the initial essay, D. Georgi places the question of the
origin and meaning of the figure of the "divine man"
within the context of the urbanized culture of the Hellenistic period. A person was proclaimed and recognized as a
divine man not because of some abstract theological interest but rather for the sake of demonstrating the presence of divine power for the well-being of a city and its
inhabitants. Whereas modern missionary propaganda often
stresses the personal significance of religion for the sake of
the individual's soul, in the Hellenistic world missionary
activities centered on public issues and societal interests.

The articles of W.A. Meeks and L.H. Feldman center on
one expression of the "divine man" figure, the divine king
and messenger. The idea of the divine king is operative
both in Philo's description of Moses as in Josephus' depiction of Solomon. Meeks compares the divine king in

Philo's portrait of Moses with the Fourth Gospel's image of Jesus and in so doing he shows how the same theological motifs can function differently in a different context. Whereas Philo employs the image of Moses in a broad cultural-political struggle, the Fourth Gospel uses the image of Jesus as heavenly messenger first in its discussion with Judaism and then in a narrowing sectarian controversy. The cultural-political element of Jewish apologetics is also underlined in the essay by L.H. Feldman. Josephus' characterization of Solomon reveals the extent to which he had modeled Solomon after the image of King Oedipus and has touched it up with Stoic overtones. Josephus thereby sought to counter the Hellenistic charge that the Jews had failed to produce any great man, such as a political genius, a powerful king, a great initiator of arts and crafts, or an eminent sage or wise man.

Apologetics as the "art of persuasion" has its original place in the rhetoric of the lawcourts. It is true that in its attempt to persuade and convince, apologetics is often in danger of manipulating its materials and information, but its appeal to reason and common cultural-religious tenets nevertheless indicates a willingness to stand publicly accountable for one's religious convictions. In his essay, H.D. Betz argues that Paul in his letter to the Galatians employed both sides of apologetics for his defense. In order to be taken seriously Paul appeals on the one hand to the Galatians' common ecstatic experience and on the other hand he employs magical features. Since belief in the power of magic was all-pervasive in the Greco-Roman world, it would be surprising if it had not also influenced the Christians of the time.

The notion of magic and the miraculous is the topic of the last two articles. J. Goldin carefully traces the notion of magic and superstition in Jewish and especially rabbinic literature. His essay serves to underline the universality of magic in antiquity, to point out the close relationship between magic and religion, and to acknowledge the dependency and interrelationship between magic and the "authorities." In the final article, P.J. Achtemeier places the early Christian interest in the miraculous and magical in the wider context of Christian apolgetics and mission of the second and third century, A.D. Achtemeier points out that, with the exception of the infancy narratives, the stories about the miraculous activity of Jesus did not substantially increase in the apocryphal gospel literature but that the miracles and great deeds of the Apostles did multiply rapidly in the apocryphal Acts. It is clear that the apocryphal Acts literature does not intend to fill the miracle-gaps in the canonical traditions about Jesus but that it evidences the desire to outperform other magicians and miracle workers of the time in the example of the Christian apostles and missionaries. Since the miraculous and magical was part of the cultural world which Jews and Christians shared, the Christian missionary propaganda had to increase beyond any doubt the miraculous power and capacity of the apostles. It is important to notice that the apocryphal Acts literature is patterned after the popular Hellenistic romance literature of the time, which, in distinction to the philosophical literature, was very much interested in the miraculous.

Both the apocryphal Acts of the Apostles and the canonical book of Acts should be studied in the light of the Hellenistic popular and religious propaganda of the time. Unfortunately, recent studies of Acts have not sufficiently emphasized the aims and means of the missionary propaganda and apologetics that the author of Acts has employed.[20] The study of E. Plümacher[21] is an exception since he does point out that the author of Acts, Luke, employed literary techniques, forms, and motifs of Hellenistic literature in order to address the educated Hellenistic reader. Nevertheless, even this study fails to understand these literary motifs and techniques as functions of the author's missionary apologetic interests; instead Plümacher considers them to be an expression of Luke's theological concern with the disappearance of the imminent expectation of the Parousia. Yet, it does not seem probable that

Luke's reason for using Hellenistic literature was oc-
casioned by the delay of the Parousia, but it is understandable that he would resort to Hellenistic literature and
language if he wished to convince and persuade his Hellenistic readers, be they Christian or not. How then does
Luke view and depict the Christian missionary and his
Hellenistic audience? An answer to this question might
also provide the concrete frame of reference in which the
different aspects of missionary apologetics and propaganda
developed in the several articles of the present collection
could telescope into a clearer picture of early Christian
mission and religious propaganda in the Greco-Roman
world.

A cursory reading of Acts makes it obvious that for
Luke the Christian missionary possesses magic powers and
exhibits miraculous capabilities which prove to be greater
than those of the competition. Yet not only miraculous
gifts, but also powerful speech and ecstatic experiences
characterize the Christian apostle and missionary. Moreover, we also find motifs of apologetics, as, for example,
the defense of Christianity before the political powers, the
polemics against idol worship and the concern with leading
figures and persons of the time—all of which are very
familiar from the apologetic literature of Judaism.

Acts 19

According to E. Haenchen a comprehensive picture of
Paul, the missionary *par excellence,* and his propagandistic
activities is drawn in chapter 19 of Acts.[22] Here the
activities of Paul are situated in Ephesus, the missionary
center of the Roman province of Asia. The whole chapter
of Acts 19 can be divided into seven scenes which are
grouped into three main sections or parts. The first part
defines Christianity in relation to Judaism (19:1-10). The
opening scene, 19:1-7,[23] points out what the mark of the

true Christian is which distinguishes the Christian disciples from those of all other Jewish sects (like the fellowship of John the Baptizer for example).[24] This decisive Christian mark is belief in Jesus as well as ecstatic speech and prophecy. The following scene, 19:8–10, stresses at first that Paul followed Jewish missionary practice when he preached in the synagogue. However, after some slanderous attacks and opposition from the side of the Jews, Paul separated the Christians from the synagogue and thus established an independent Christian congregation. The new place for the Christian assembly was no longer the synagogue but the hall of Tyrannus. This new locale served to foster the image of the Christian community as a philosophical school[25] and to depict Paul as a teacher in dialogue with not only the Jews but also the Greeks. The story reflects both the symbiosis in which the first Christian missionary endeavor existed alongside the Jewish synagogue and also the eventual separation of the Christian from the Jewish community. Paul is here pictured as initiating and authorizing the abolition of the fellowship with the Jewish community and the subsequent establishment of the Christian community as an independent religious group. The first part of Acts 19 thus portrays the differentiating process which separated the Christian group from other Jewish sects and from the synagogue itself, which was the missionary center in Hellenistic Judaism.[26] It summarizes the early Christian development which Luke describes from the very first chapters of the Book of Acts.

The second part of Acts 19 exhibits the miraculous powers of the Christian missionary (19:11–20). After a summary of Paul's healing miracles (19:11–12) there follows a scene describing the competition of Jewish exorcists (19:13–17). This scene concludes with the description of the burning of the books of magic and sorcery (19:18–20). The second part of the chapter stresses that the Christian miraculous powers and magical endowments are recognized and utilized by the Jewish competition.

Finally, the third part of Acts 19 further develops this theme of competition. The focus here, however, is the relationship of the Christian religion, not to Judaism, but to the main pagan religion and the chief deity of Ephesus (19:21–40). Following a general reference to Paul's plans to visit missionary fields (19:21f.) is a well composed scene which both emphasizes the threat of the Christian mission to the Hellenistic divinities and also gives a public defense for the Christian religion and its missionaries (19:23–40). Since this collection of essays is primarily concerned with the miraculous and magical elements of Christian mission, the relationship to Jewish mission and apologetics as well as to the Hellenistic religious propaganda, and lastly with the public dimensions of Christian mission and apologetics, a closer examination of Acts 19 in its setting in the wider context of the book might provide us with an exemplary text of New Testament literature where all these elements converge.[27]

Christian Mission and Miracles

The summary statement in Acts 19:11f. underlines Paul's extraordinary miraculous powers and highlights their magical efficaciousness. In the Greco-Roman world the wandering preachers and missionaries sought to attract the attention of their audience and to demonstrate the exceptional character of their message by miraculous deeds and powerful speech. Since the miraculous powers exhibited by the missionaries extended clearly into the realm of the supernatural and the divine, the audience tended to regard them as god-men, demi-gods, or gods.[28] For the propaganda of a religion it was especially important to show that its founder or leading figure had such miraculous, divine capacities. For instance, the literature of Jewish apologetics and propaganda therefore expanded the miracles of the Exodus in order to prove that Moses was such a divine miracle worker and charismatic figure.[29]

The connection between the miraculous power exhibited and a pagan audience's veneration of the miracle worker as divine is clearly made by Luke in Acts 14:8–18 and Acts 28:6. The section 14:8–18 is especially important since in it Luke shows Christian missionaries encountering for the first time in Acts a purely pagan audience. The heroes of the section are Paul and Barnabas, who were chosen and sent out by the Holy Spirit through the community of Antioch to preach the gospel (13:1ff.). In Lystra Paul healed a cripple. The miracle impressed the Lystrans so much that they confessed: "The gods have come down to us in the likeness of men." They identified Barnabas as Zeus and his companion Paul as Hermes. Not only the common people but even the official cultic functionaries, the priests of Zeus, intended to pay Barnabas and Paul cultic honors. In his *Alexander, the False Prophet* (13), Lucian of Samosata reports the same reaction of the people of Abunoteichos toward Alexander, the successful prophet and miracle worker. They believed him to be "the god visible" (ἐναργῆ τοῦ θεοῦ) and therefore began to pray to him and to worship him.[30] Jewish apologetic writings evidence the same motifs as Acts when they show that the great leaders in the history of the Jews, especially Moses, were highly honored and even deified by the non-Jews whom they met. For example, the Jewish apologist Artapanus presents Moses in direct competition with the traditional Egyptian benefactors. The Egyptian priests not only regarded Moses as worthy of being honored like a god, but also called him Hermes because of his interpretation of the sacred letters.[31]

The speech in which Paul rejects the cultic veneration of the Lystrans differs in structure and content from those speeches to a Jewish audience. Moreover, this speech has only one other parallel in Acts: Paul's speech on the Areopagus (17:22–31). The content of the speech to the Lystrans corresponds to a much cherished topos of Jewish missionary apologetics. As did the Jewish apologetic writers, Paul urged his listeners to turn from vain idols to the living God who has shown his goodness in the works of nature.[32] The Areopagus speech, the second discourse of Acts addressed to Gentiles uses basically the same theological argument, even though it is much more elaborate and complex. In his speech before the Athenians Paul addressed not the common Hellenistic populace, as in 14:8–18, but competed with the leading philosophical schools of the time, the Epicureans and Stoic philosophers. They evaluated Paul as a chatterer and babbler (σπερμολόγος), a missionary of foreign divinities, namely Jesus and his consort Anastasis.[33] They ridiculed Paul in the same manner as Aristophanes had ridiculed Socratic philosophy. Moreover, they hurled at Paul the very charge with which Socrates was condemned to death.[34] In Acts, however, the Epicureans and Stoics were confronted by a man who knew the secret which Socrates did not know or want to reveal. Socrates had taught the Athenians to seek the full knowledge of God, who was unknown to them, and in his preaching Paul now revealed precisely this "unknown God."[35] It is important to note that Luke does not mention a miracle at the end of the scene in Athens. The two speeches before Gentiles in Acts thus appear to reflect the religious-theological interests of the two Hellenistic audiences. They appeal as well to the interests of the common people who were fascinated by miracles, magic, and the display of extraordinary, divine powers, as to the interests of the more educated circles who were critical of magic and polytheism but interested in philosophy as a way of life. The strong emphasis of Acts on miracles and extraordinary appearances indicates, however, that Luke attempts to picture the Christian missionaries and apostles more as miracle workers than as itinerant philosophers of the time.[36]

Christian Mission and Jewish Magic

In ancient literature it is very difficult to distinguish the category of miracle from that of magic. They go hand in hand.[37] In Acts 19:11–20 Luke links miracles and magic closely to each other. His summary statement about the great miraculous powers of Paul includes magical elements (19:11f.). The following scene of the encounter of the seven sons of Sceva with an evil spirit reflects the great reputation of the Jews for magical practices (19:13–17). The whole section is concluded with the statement that many of the Christians rejected the practice of magic and therefore burned their books of magic and witchcraft (19:18–20). Superhuman powers are thus attributed to the Christian missionary and mission, and they are portrayed as being far greater than those of Jewish and Hellenistic magic.

Hellenistic magic was in constant search for magical names. The greatest contribution of the Jews to the magic of the Greco-Roman world was the name of the Jewish God: "Iao," which is found in many magical papyri.[38] It appears that at a very early stage the name of Jesus was included in the repertoires of the professional magicians. With the story of the seven sons of the high priest Sceva, Luke stresses that the name of Jesus was so powerful that even Jewish exorcists used it. Itinerant Jewish missionaries and magicians who knew what was supposed to be a powerful magical name, that of their own God, are thereby shown to usurp for their exorcism and magical performances an even more powerful name, that of Jesus. Nevertheless, the evil spirit recognized the fraud of the Jewish competition, for he knew Jesus and acknowledged the missionary Paul but not the Jewish exorcists.[39] Quite the contrary, the evil spirit overpowered them and badly wounded them. According to Luke, then, the success of the Christian mission is based upon the powerful name of Jesus. As a man of his time, Luke does not hesitate to conceive of this power partly in magical terms. For him the outcome is decisive: Jewish as well as Greek residents of Ephesus acknowledged and extolled the powerful name of Jesus. The climax of the whole section is the summary which points out that all those Christians who had previously practised magic and sorcery confessed their practices

and burnt their manuals of magic and witchcraft.[40] Thus
the power of the name of Jesus and the Christian mission
is unrivaled. It overcomes all Jewish and Hellenistic and
Christian magic and sorcery.

Luke is also concerned with the question of magic and
magical powers in his first account of Christian missionary
activity. In Acts 8:4—25, he combines two seemingly
different stories, the story about the great success of the
first Christian missionary, Philip (8:4—13), and the account
of the converted magician Simon, who aspires to buy the
power of the Holy Spirit from the Apostles Peter and John
(8:14—25). The historical problems behind this whole section of 8:5—25 are very complicated, and the redactional
intention is still very much debated.[41]

The first story is easy to understand. Luke ascribes the
beginning of the Christian mission outside Judea to Philip,
one of the seven so-called Hellenists. He characterizes
Philip as a very effective miracle worker, exorcist and
preacher who invoked the powerful name of Jesus Christ.
Philip's greatest missionary success in Samaria is shown to
be the conversion of the former great magician Simon.
Simon had amazed the people with many magical events
and he had presented himself "to be a great one." As Luke
underlines, not only the Samaritans but even this sorcerer
Simon believed the missionary proclamation of Philip and
became a member of the Christian community. After his
conversion, Simon remained at Philip's side and closely
observed him and his deeds. The concluding verse 13
stresses the major point of the story: the signs and
wonders of the first Christian missionary, Philip, were able
to overwhelm even such a great magician as Simon. Thus
Simon's conversion forcefully demonstrates the superiority
of the Christian missionary propaganda.

The second story in 8:14—25 is much more difficult to
understand. Two motifs appear to be governing Luke's
description. *First*: Luke wants to stress that the Apostles
in Jerusalem are responsible for the whole of Christian
mission. He subordinates the traditions of Philip as an
independent missionary to his own concept of the develop-

NO

NO

ment of early Christianity and early Christian mission, in which the Jerusalem church is given primary significance. *Second*: Luke probably intends to emphasize in this story that the most important factor in Christian mission is the power to transmit the Spirit. Luke understands the Spirit, as ecstatic Spirit, to be the driving force behind the Christian missionary endeavors. It is important to note that Simon did not want to buy the gift of the Spirit for himself but the capacity to transfer it to others. Only this power over the Spirit could make him an equal to the Christian apostles. He who was a great magician before his conversion now wished to buy the power behind the Christian missionary activity. The story thus underlines: the power behind the Christian mission cannot be bought[42] or manipulated. It is entrusted to the apostles, whom the concluding sentence depicts as itinerant missionaries preaching the gospel (8:25).

The third passage in Acts which deals with magic is the story about the encounter of Paul with the Jewish magician Bar-Jesus or Elymas, in the Cyprian city of Paphos (13:6–12).[43] According to Luke this Jewish sorcerer and false prophet appears to be the court theologian and astrologer of the proconsul Sergius Paulus. Sergius Paulus had become interested in the Christian missionary preaching and had consequently summoned Barnabas and Paul before him. Under these circumstances, the Jewish court theologian naturally perceived the two Apostles as a threat to his influence and therefore attempted to divert the proconsul from the Christian message. Paul therefore opposed him and called him "son of the devil," an ironical word-play on the man's name, "Bar-Jesus." Elymas is "son of the devil" because he attempted to counteract the Christian missionary influence. In order to prove that the Christian missionary propaganda is the more powerful, Paul, as the messenger of God, proclaimed divine judgment over him: for a "certain" span of time Elymas was struck blind. This punitive miracle impressed the proconsul so much that he came to have faith.

The story clearly reveals the competition between the

Christian missionary and the Jewish court theologian. Jewish as well as Christian missionary propaganda sought to
win over the most important political figure of the Roman
province, Cyprus. As we know from Josephus, Jewish
missionary propaganda addressed especially those who
were influential in their society.[44] Luke's account of the
Christian missionary appeal evidences the same propagandistic praxis. It is no accident that according to Acts the
first gentile convert was the Roman officer, Cornelius. It is
likewise no accident that the first convert of Paul was the
highest political authority of a Roman province. Especially
the second part of Acts attempts to give an apology of the
Christian faith and mission before a Roman audience.[45]
Since the early Christian mission attempted to address all
people and their religious interests, it had to be public and
political in a society in which religion and politics could
not be separated.

Christian Mission and Pagan Religion

This public dimension of Christian mission comes also
to the fore in the major section of Acts 19. The passage
Acts 19:23–40 deals with the threatening competition of
the early Christian mission to the pagan religion. As this
story about the riot of Demetrius demonstrates, such competition implied not only a religious threat but an economic and political one as well.

If one reads the story as a historical account one
encounters many difficulties and historical improbabilities.
The whole section can be divided into three parts, wherein
each of the first two parts ends with the acclamation:
"Great is Artemis of the Ephesians" (vv. 28 and 34).
Despite this twofold public affirmation of the mother
goddess Artemis, it is the success of the Christian religious
propaganda which represents the focal point of the story.
It was not a Christian, however, but the enemy of the
Christian missionary endeavor, Demetrius, who proclaimed

this success. The competition acknowledged the danger which the Christian mission posed for the native cult. The Christian missionary preaching has turned many people away from the religion of Artemis, not only in Ephesus but in all of Asia Minor. As was the case with Jewish missionary apologetics, this missionary preaching attacked polytheism: there are no gods who are made with hands. According to Demetrius this preaching not only harmed the business of craftsmen, who derived their livelihood from the cult of Artemis, but it also afflicted the temple and cult of the great goddess herself. Because of the success of the Christian religious propaganda the goddess who is now worshiped by the whole province of Asia will be forgotten and neglected. These accusations against the Christian mission incensed the crowd so much that it responded with the affirming cry: "Great is Artemis of Ephesus."

The second part of the story (19:29–34) demonstrates the support of the Asiarchs,[47] the cultic officials of the Roman civil religion in Asia Minor, for the Christian missionary, Paul. Luke's point is quite clear: a sect, whose leader had such friends, cannot at all be dangerous to the Roman Empire. The following interlude of the defense of Judaism by someone with the name of Alexander indicates on the one hand that in pagan eyes Jewish and Christian mission were still identical and that because of the success of the Christian mission the Jews had to defend themselves. On the other hand, this interlude gives Luke the occasion to repeat the acclamation of Artemis.

After this in the third section, the story takes an unexpected turn. The γραμματεύς of the city, whose duty it was to execute the decrees of the popular assembly and to control, together with the στρατηγοί the administration of the city, suddenly stood up to defend the Christian missionaries. He argued that, since Ephesus is well known as the city of Artemis, the cult of the great goddess cannot be in danger. The Christian missionaries have neither robbed her temple nor offended the goddess herself. The representative of the city's civil authorities himself rejected the accusation that the Christian missionary propaganda is a threat to the cult of Artemis. Luke thereby shows that the religious as well as the civil leaders of Ephesus are on the side of the Christians. Not the Christians but Demetrius and the rioting crowd disturbed the order of the city. Any accusation against the Christians has to be dealt with properly. The law demands that the issue be brought to court, but it does not permit tumultous lynch-proceedings of a mob against the Christians. The opponents of Paul and of the Christian missionary propaganda are indicted, whereas Paul and the Christian movement are exonerated. Luke succeeds in giving the impression that the Christian religious propaganda does not at all threaten the great goddess of Ephesus and her cult.[48]

If we read the story as an apology for the Christian faith and mission to the Greco-Roman public, then the historical improbabilities make perfect sense. Luke does not aim to give an historical report of the riot in Ephesus, but to show that the rioting Ephesians, and not the Christians, disturbed the public order and peace. Not a Christian missionary but the official of the city's authorities testified to this. We find this apologetic interest from the very beginning of the story. It is important to note that not the cultic officials of the temple of Artemis, the priests, but only Demetrius and his guild protested against the Christian religious propaganda and its success. Thus in the eyes of Luke's readers the religious issue becomes an issue of economic self-interest. Moreover, the Asiarchs, the representatives of the Roman imperial cult, are not disturbed by the success of the Christian mission, instead they worry only about Paul's safety. The officials of the Roman Empire are Paul's true friends.

There are other astonishing features. Luke introduces a startling fact, when suddenly a Jew named Alexander intends to make a speech in defense of Judaism. No one until now had attacked the Jewish religion, but rather only the Christian mission. It is also puzzling that Demetrius no longer appears on the scene after he and his followers reach the theater and the time for action has come. Finally, the city's official appears on the stage and attempts to appease the crowd. His speech does not answer the accusation that Christians consider the great goddess as nothing or as an idol. Rather his speech succeeds in giving the impression that on the one hand the Christian propagandistic endeavors are not as dangerous as Demetrius claims and that, on the other hand, the Christian missionaries cannot do any harm to the goddess and her cult.

On this note of public justification, Luke's apology of the Christian missionary propaganda in Acts 19 comes to an end. The Christian missionary praxis is presented as not only superior to the miraculous and magical means of the Jewish missionary propaganda but also as very successful before a Hellenistic audience. Moreover, the official public cults of the state need not feel threatened by the Christian missionaries and their propaganda, for the Christians do not disturb the public order and they even have friends among the leading political and religious figures of the Roman Empire.

In conclusion: According to Lucian's *On Writing History* (34) the two primary requisites of good historiography are "an understanding of society" and the "capacity to interpret." This introduction attempted to point out how much an understanding of the Hellenistic society and its cultural, religious, and political aspects furthers the interpretation of Acts and the comprehension of the history of the early Christian missionary endeavor. Moreover, early Christian missionary propaganda and apologetics cannot be understood apart from Jewish missionary propaganda and apologetic literature. However, Luke's account of the missionary preaching before the Gentiles shows not only themes also found in the Jewish religious propaganda literature, it also incorporates motifs of the philosophical as well as the popular Hellenistic religious propaganda.

Finally, religious propaganda in the Greco-Roman world is very much a public-political issue. A defense of Judaism as well as Christianity had to present its arguments before a public-political forum. The publication of this collection of essays hopefully will show that the history of the early Christian movement cannot be understood solely as a sectarian struggle. It has to be seen in the context of the Hellenistic and Jewish religious propaganda and its public dimensions.

NOTES

1. D. Georgi, *Die Gegner des Paulus im 2. Korintherbrief* (WMANT, 11; Neukirchen-Vluyn: Neukirchener Verlag, 1964).

2. The suggestion of C.W. Votaw, *The Gospels and Contemporary Biographies in the Greco-Roman World* (fb. Bibl. Ser., 27; Philadelphia: Fortress Press, 1970), pp. 2–11 is that the Gospels are written as "evangelistic tracts to promote the Christian movement." As the biographies of the Greek and Roman intellectual leaders were primarily written in order to exhibit their teaching, so the Gospels were written to commend Jesus Christ to the Mediterranean world. Recently D. Georgi has again opened the discussion. Cf. his article "The Records of Jesus in Light of Ancient Accounts of Revered Men," in *Society of Biblical Literature Proceedings of the 108th Annual Meeting,* 2 vols. (Philadelphia: SBL, 1972), II, 527–542.

3. Cf. S.W. Baron, *A Social and Religious History of the Jews,* 8 vols. 2nd ed. (New York: Columbia University Press, 1952), I, 170; J. Juster, *Les Juifs dans l'Empire romain,* 2 vols. (Paris: P. Geuthner, 1914), I, 179–212; V. Tcherikover, *Hellenistic Civilization and the Jews,* trans. S. Applebaum (1959; repr. New York: Atheneum, 1970), pp. 288–295.

4. Cf. M. Hengel, "Die Ursprünge der christlichen Mission," *New Testament Studies* 18 (1971/72), pp. 16f.; A. Harnack, *The Mission and Expansion of Christianity in the First Three Centuries,* trans. J. Pelikan (New York: Harper Torchbook, 1962).

5. Cf. A.D. Nock, *Conversion: The Old and the New in Religion from Alexander the Great to Augustin of Hippo* (London: Oxford University Press, 1961), pp. 48–137; C. Clemen, "Die Missionstätigkeit der nichtchristlichen Religionen," *Zeitschrift für Missionskunde und Religionswissenschaft* 44 (1929), 225–233.

6. P. Wendland, *Die hellenistisch-römische Kultur in ihren Be-*

ziehungen zu Judentum und Christentum (HNT I, 2; Tübingen: JCB Mohr, 1907), pp. 39–53. Cf. also K. Prümm, S.J., *Religionsgeschichtliches Handbuch für den Raum der altchristlichen Umwelt* (Rome: Päpstliches Bibelinstitut, 1954).

7. Cf. M. Smith, "Palestinian Judaism in the First Century," in M. Davis, ed., *Israel: Its Role in Civilization* (New York: Harper, 1956), pp. 67–81; M. Hengel, *Judentum und Hellenismus* (WUNT, 10; Tübingen: JCB Mohr, 1969), pp. 453–463.

8. I. Heinemann, "Antisemitismus," in Pauly-Wissowa-Kroll, ed., *Realencyclopädie der classischen Altertumswissenschaft* (Stuttgart: Metzlersche Verlagsbuchhandlung, 1931), Suppl. V, pp. 3–43.

9. Cf. M. Friedländer, *Geschichte der jüdischen Apologetik als Vorgeschichte des Christentums* (Zurich: Verlag v. Caesar Schmidt, 1903); K. Axenfeld, "Die jüdische Propaganda als Vorläuferin der urchristlichen Mission," *Missionswissenschaftliche Studien* (Festschrift Warneck; Berlin: Berliner evagelische Missionsgesellschaft, 1904), pp. 1–80; A. Causse, "La propaganda juive et l'hellenisme," *Revue de Histoire et de Philosophie Religieuses* 3 (1923), 397–414; E. Schürer, *The Literature of the Jewish People in the Time of Jesus* (New York: Schocken Books, 1972); C. Schneider, *Kulturgeschichte des Hellenismus,* 2 vols. (Munich: C.H. Beck, 1967), I, 881–898.

10. P. Derwacter, *Preparing the Way for Paul: The Proselyte Movement in Later Judaism* (New York: Macmillan, 1930), pp. 15–32.

11. Cf. also Fl. Josephus, *Against Apion* 2. 281–284.

12. The short summary treatments of the Jewish mission by F. Hahn and H. Kasting are in no way sufficient. Cf. F. Hahn, *Mission in the New Testament* (Bibl. Theol., 47; London: SCM Press, 1965), pp. 21–25; H. Kasting, *Die Anfänge der urchristlichen Mission* (BevTh, 55; Munich: Chr. Kaiser Verlag, 1969), pp. 11–32.

13. See M. Hengel, "Die Ursprünge," pp. 15–38 and G. Schille, "Anfänge der christlichen Mission," *Kerygma und Dogma* 15 (1969), 320–339; E. Neuhäusler, "Exegese und Mission," *Zeitschrift für Missionswissenschaft und Religionswissenschaft* 42 (1958), 56–63.

14. O. Cullmann, "Eschatology and Mission in the New Testament," in W.D. Davies and D. Daube, eds., *The Background of the New Testament and Its Eschatology: In Honour of C.H. Dodd* (Cambridge: University Press, 1956), pp. 409–421.

15. Cf. the review of scholarly opinions by S.G. Wilson, *The Gentiles and the Gentile Mission in Luke-Acts* (Cambridge: University Press, 1973), pp. 1–28.

16. Cf. H. Kasting, pp. 52 and 82ff.; A. Harnack and F. Hahn,

however, see the universal mission of the early church rooted in the universal message of Jesus.

17. See F. Spitta, *Jesus und die Heidenmission* (Giessen: Töpelmann, 1909), p. 81; G. Schille, pp. 336–339.

18. See M. Hengel, pp. 26–30.

19. Cf. M. Meinertz, "Zum Ursprung der Heidenmission," *Biblica* 40 (1959), 762–777; H. Schlier, "Die Entscheidung für die Heidenmission in der Urchristenheit," in *Die Zeit der Kirche* (Freiburg: Herder, 1956), pp. 90–107.

20. The most recent investigation of the problem by S.G. Wilson does not even allude to the issue.

21. E. Plümacher, *Lukas als hellenistischer Schriftsteller* (StUNT, 9; Göttingen: Vandenhoeck & Ruprecht, 1972). Idem, "Lukas als griechischer Historiker," in Pauly-Wissowa-Kroll-Ziegler, Realencycolpädie der classischen Altertumswissenschaft (Munich: A. Druckmüller, 1974), Suppl. XIV, pp. 235–246. For a review of contemporary scholarly tendencies cf. W.C. van Unnik, "Luke-Acts, A Stormcenter in Contemporary Scholarship," in E. Keck and J.L. Martyn, eds., *Studies in Luke-Acts: Festschrift P. Schubert* (Nashville: Abingdon, 1966), pp. 15–32.

22. E. Haenchen, *The Acts of the Apostles,* trans. R. McL. Wilson (Philadelphia: Westminster Press, 1971), p. 558.

23. Haenchen does not include verses 1–7 in his chapter on "Paul's Work in Ephesus" even though the episode of Acts 19:1–7 is located in Ephesus and portrays Paul.

24. Cf. E. Käsemann, "The Disciples of John the Baptist in Ephesus," in *Essays on New Testament Themes* (Philadelphia: Fortress Press, 1964), pp. 136–149.

25. Paul is imagined as an itinerant philosopher cf. H. Conzelmann, *Die Apostelgeschichte* (HNT, 7; Tübingen: JCB Mohr, 1963), p. 111. For the influence of philosophical schools and ideals upon Judaic culture, see H. A. Fischel, *Rabbinic Literature and Greco-Roman Philosophy* (Studia Postbiblica, 41; Leiden: Brill, 1973).

26. See D. Georgi, *Die Gegner,* pp. 87–113.

27. G. Klein, "Der Synkretismus als Theologisches Problem," in *Rekonstruktion und Interpretation* (BevTh, 50; Munich: Kaiser Verlag, 1969), pp. 262–301 argues that Luke is here more concerned with the illegitimate usurpation of Christian motives by Jewish and pagan syncretists. Yet it is doubtful whether Luke intends to develop a "theory about syncretism" (ibid., p. 301).

28. Cf. D. Georgi, "Forms of Religious Propaganda," in H.J. Schultz, ed., *Jesus in His Time* (Philadelphia: Fortress Press, 1971), pp. 124–131.

29. See Philo, *De Vita Mosis* 1.156–158; Josephus, *Antiquities* 2. 272–280; Artapanus in Eusebius, *Praeparatio Evangelica* 9.27 cf. W.N. Stearns, *Fragments from Graeco-Jewish Writers* (Chicago: University Press, 1908), pp. 46–56.

30. Cf. A.D. Nock, *Conversion*, pp. 93ff.

31. "For these reasons, therefore, Mousos was beloved of the masses. And because he was regarded by the priests as worthy of being honored like a god, he was called Hermes because of his interpretation of the sacred letters." Cf. Eusebius, *Praep. Ev.* 6, translated by D.L. Tiede, *The Charismatic Figure as Miracle Worker* (SBL Diss. Ser., 1; Missoula: University of Montana, 1972), p. 318 (appendix II). The account which Artapanus gives of Moses miraculous release from prison is very similar to the first two accounts of miraculous releases in Acts 5:18ff. and 12:5–10.

32. See P. Dalbert, *Die Theologie der hellenistisch-jüdischen Missionsliteratur unter Ausschluss von Philo und Josephus* (Theol. Forschung, 4; Hamburg: Herbert Reich, 1954), pp. 124–130; G. Schneider, "Urchristliche Gottesverkündigung in hellenistischer Umwelt," *Biblische Zeitschrift* 13 (1969), 59–75; C. Bussmann, *Themen der Paulinischen Missionspredigt auf dem Hintergrund der spätjüdisch-hellenistischen Missionsliteratur* (Europ. Hochschulschriften, XXIII, 3; Bern: H. Lang, 1971), pp. 39–81.

33. This interpretation was first given by Chrysostom (Hom. in Act 38.1).

34. Xenophon, *Memorabilia* 1.1.1.; Plato, *Apologia* 24b. See K.Lake and H.J.Cadbury, *The Beginnings of Christianity*, 5 vols. (London: Macmillan, 1933), IV, 212.

35. Cf. E. Norden, *Agnostos Theos* (1913; repr. Darmstadt: Wissenschaftliche Buchgesellschaft, 1956), pp. 31–56; K. Lake, "The Unknown God," in *The Beginnings of Christianity*, V, 240–246. Cf. however the conclusion of M.Dibelius, *Studies in the Acts of the Apostles* (London: SCM Press, 1956), p.42: "Thus the first notion of the speech rests upon Old Testament ideas, expressed in modernized hellenistic language."

36. At the same time Luke takes care to portray Paul as the "true Socrates." He and the other Christian missionaries are not charlatans and impostors. For Paul's own defense along these lines cf. H.D.Betz, *Der Apostel Paulus und die sokratische Tradition*

(BhTh, 45; Tübingen: JCB Mohr, 1972), pp. 18–39. For a socio-cultural analysis of the situation and of the types of early Christian missionaries cf. G. Theissen, "Legitimation und Lebensunterhalt: Ein Beitrag zur Soziologie urchristlicher Missionäre," *New Testament Studies* 21 (1975), 192–221.

37. J.M. Hull, *Hellenistic Magic and the Synoptic Tradition* (Stud. in Bibl. Theol., 28; London: SCM Press, 1974), pp. 45–72. Exorcism and magic were especially associated with Ephesus; cf. *The Beginnings of Christianity*, IV, 240. For an analysis of the social functions of ancient magic and miracles see G. Theissen, *Urchristliche Wundergeschichten* (StNT, 8; Gütersloh: Mohr, 1974), pp. 229–261.

38. J.M. Hull, p. 31f.; cf. also M. Smith, *Clement of Alexandria and a Secret Gospel of Mark* (Cambridge: Harvard University Press, 1973), p. 233, n. 10. The name of Moses was also considered a magical name; see J.G. Gager, *Moses in Greco-Roman Paganism* (SBL Monograph Ser., 16; Nashville: Abingdon Press, 1972), pp. 155–161.

39. According to Mark 9:38f. an exorcist who was not a Christian cast out demons in the name of Jesus Christ. The Gospel of Mark as well as that of Luke (9:49f.) describes Jesus as being tolerant of such a use of his name. Since in his Gospel Luke does not correct Mark's point of view, it is improbable that he uses this story of Acts to demonstrate an illegitimate usurpation of the name of Jesus but only to confront the Jewish exorcists with the great miracle worker and exorcist Paul (against G.Klein, pp. 276–279).

40. G. Klein, p.297, n. 193 correctly stresses that the subjects of verses 18 and 19 are not identical. If this is the case then Acts 19:19–20 demonstrates that a clear and absolute division between insiders and outsiders is not justified. All, Jews, Greeks, and Christians, live in the same milieu and culture.

41. See E. Haenchen, pp. 30ff.

42. Luke also stresses that the Apostles are not religious charlatans who would make money from their main religious power. For such an attitude cf. H.D. Betz, pp. 114f.

43. A.D. Nock, "Paul and the Magus," in *Essays on Religion and the Ancient World* (Cambridge: Harvard University Press, 1972), pp. 308–330.

44. Fl. Josephus, *Antiquities* 20.34–54; 18.65–84.

45. See J.Weiss, *Über die Absicht und den literarischen Charakter der Apostelgeschichte* (Göttingen: Vandenhoeck & Ruprecht, 1897),

pp. 54–60; J.C.O'Neill, *The Theology of Acts: In Its Historical Setting* (London: S.P.C.K., 1961), pp.153–157.

46. Lily Ross Taylor, "Artemis of Ephesus," in *Beginnings of Christianity,* V, 251–256.

47. D. Magie, *Roman Rule in Asia Minor,* 2 vols. (Princeton: University Press, 1950), I, 449f. and II, 1298ff.

48. For a similar attempt to defend the Jews who were accused of having contempt for foreign gods see Fl. Josephus, *Antiquities* 4.207 and *Against Apion* 2.236, 291. Cf. also G. Delling, "Josephus und die heidnischen Religionen," in *Studien zum Neuen Testament und zum hellenistischen Judentum* (Göttingen: Vandenhoeck & Ruprecht, 1970), pp. 45–52.

2: Socioeconomic Reasons for the "Divine Man" as a Propagandistic Pattern

Dieter Georgi

THE FOURTH CENTURY B.C.E. IS COMMONLY SEEN AS THE period of the final decline of the Greek "polis," that is, of the Greek city not only as state but as an institution. But the many scholars who share this view are only the latest victims of the propaganda of the Athenian imperialism of Pericles' time, usually presented as the classical period of Greek culture. The very fact that several hundred "Greek" cities were founded in Asia, Africa, and even Europe during the next 300 years would speak against that scholarly assumption and put it into the area of fairy-tales. Moreover, Roman cities were another version of the Greek city. Athenian imperialism had claimed that Athens was the one and only real city, but it had done so at the expense of many other cities it had subjugated. They were brutally forced to pay the price for what we now call classical Greece, namely Athens' fame—economically, socially, and culturally. At best they were reduced to satellites and were not allowed to become or to remain cities like Athens.

The Greek city as a form of life did not collapse during the fourth century. The struggles taking place between 430 and 330 simply reflect the birth-pangs of the Greek city coming to its true mission as a center of trade, industry, and culture. They were labor pains preparing for the explosive spread of cities under Alexander the Great and his successors. Such an expansion would be unthinkable without assuming that the Greeks were ready for it and had prepared for it by a hundred years of hard work and experience.

The Greek city had come to realize that it could not be a state. In that role it had proven to be a very costly and unwieldy instrument, practically an unworkable one. The imperialism, first of Athens, then of Sparta, Thebes, and Syracuse, had shown that in each case the "state" had killed the "city," turned it into a rather parochial phenomenon. The cities, most of all Athens during the classical period, could not have survived on their own. They needed the resources of other cities which they freely exploited, and they were heavily dependent on the energy of immigrants, traders, craftsmen, artisans, etc., from other cities, even of philosophers like Aristotle. Although these strangers contributed enormously to the well-being and fame of the "host"-city, they were not integrated and duly respected. In Athens these "immigrants" were denied citizenship by a law that Pericles himself had introduced in 451 which allowed citizenship only to those whose father *and* mother had been citizens of Attica before. The Greek city encouraged specialization of skills and functions, and the discovery of the individual was only a philosophical accompaniment of the economic fact of this growing specialization, which showed also in the arts. The cities burst with diversified energy. But they could not handle it through the instruments and institutions of the collective consciousness of the archaic period. Nor was the Athenian democracy an answer. It left out many immigrants and denizens despite heavy dependency upon them, and it methodically disrespected other cities.

The cities encouraged not only skill, but extreme, even monumental accomplishments by individuals. But the cities could not handle this individual greatness which they elicited and produced. Everywhere the divine was seen and presented in individual human form; the society called for great individuals who reflected in their work the divine and thus were rising by definition above the ordinary. But when these individuals did excel they were punished, exiled, or executed. While the city as culture created "divine men," the city as state could not handle them. In Athens, for instance, Themistocles, Kimon, Phidias, Alcibiades, Thucydides and many more were exiled; Miltiades and Socrates were killed.

This tendency to remove extraordinary persons was perverted recognition of the fact that these persons (by the very instigation of the society they lived in) rose above their native or host city and transcended into an urban culture at large—the Hellenistic culture, a thoroughly urban culture of a universal kind with the Greek language as its instrument of communication. This culture already existed many decades before Alexander, although in the disguise of the imperialistic as well as parochial city-states. Trade had already turned into world-trade. A world-currency was in the making. The need for world traffic by sea and land was seen and partly responded to by the Persians. Lifestyle and cultural expressions had become similar. Ideologically, the idea of one world and of one humankind became conceptualized. The need for a universal humanism dawned on the philosophers slowly. To describe all this as decomposition and disintegration seems to me highly inappropriate, and those modern scholars who judge the period before Alexander in this fashion are too quickly following the party line of certain critics who happened to live at that time, with Thucydides as their most influential spokesman.

The common talk that religion broke up in those days again reflects more contemporary party opinions than historical fact. It is sure that the *Homeric* religion did not survive very well, but there was a rather positive and constructive reason for this. Homeric religion was basically feudal and could not provide the necessary infrastructure for the urban society, i.e., a society calling for interaction of cities and their citizens and experimenting with the oneness of world and humankind in praxis and in theory.

The Homeric religious potential had been finally destroyed by Athens' attempt to ursurp the pan-Hellenic piety of the Persian wars. Pericles' attempt to unify Greek culture and religion under Athens' leadership did not succeed because it proved to be an imperialistic program.

The humanizing of gods had not been foreign to Homeric religion but in the fifth and fourth century the kinship between gods and men became more consciously emphasized. It found expression in epic, lyric, drama, in sculpture and painting and then especially in philosophy. Despite the continuation of other more archaic forms of religion, the urban society concentrated on this more aesthetic form of religion. The ancient gods on the whole remained associated with their traditional locals. They stretched only reluctantly beyond that (mostly via "interpretatio Graeca"). The new humanistic religion found its base easily beyond the confines of the native city. It conquered the world.

It is noticeable that Dionysus, who still had a sort of human—i.e., a heroic—past and was understood as the most mobile, received increased attention in the period described. Euripides offered his services to Dionysus, the missionary, in his rather propagandistic play the *Bacchae,* composed not in Athens but at the royal court of Macedonia. Just as Heracles had expressed the cultural aspirations of the Greek colonists between 750-550, so Dionysus accompanied the explosive expansion from 330 onward. Alexander the Great himself took Heracles, the alleged ancestor of his house, as his guide and protector as he moved beyond the border of his father's empire, first to the north and then into Asia and Africa. Dionysus also was seen as precursor, guardian, and model for Alexander's invasion of Asia, either by the young king himself or by his admirers immediately after his death.[1]

The third hero who caught general attention at that time was Asclepius. He later was transformed into a full god, but he still was seen as somebody who knew of the predicaments of the human race, through his own fate and

that of his sons. He became *the* healer-god of the Hellenistic age, and his importance was still growing in the
Roman imperial period. The successful oracular and medi-
cal practices at his temples were major factors in the
ancient world's belief in the reality of miracles.

Of major importance for the growing urban society were
the diversified availability and swift mobility of the divine.
The cities realized that they could not afford to remain
self-contained. They needed to be open for the extraordinary, whatever it was and wherever it came from. They
needed to let people come and go, to stir up energy and to
invite talent. The imperialistic failure taught the city that
openness was the best protection, because it served best
the interest in a free flow of resources—human resources as
well as material and ideal goods. These cities lived on, and
for, greatness, and they invited extraordinary, "divine,"
achievements.[2] Already the architectural appearance of
the city was prestigious, and most of the other expressions
of city life followed suit. The most economic way of
utilizing the necessary talent was to share it on a wide
geographical scale.

The ancient city-state was very much dependent on
lavish voluntary contributions by its well-to-do people to
cover the expensive outlays which the monumental
achievements of the city demanded. Enforced contributions from conquered cities later were supposed to allevi-
ate that, yet when this had turned out to be a failure, the
cities again had to look for benefactors. Taxation would
not have been sufficient. While to various degrees voluntary benefactors were still found in their own midst, a great
portion of support was expected from the outside. Mother-
cities occasionally helped, but substantial help frequently
came from the strong men of those days—generals and, most
of all, kings, especially after Alexander. It may surprise modern people to learn that even in America today cities and
towns do not possess the degree of freedom from state and
central governments that the Hellenistic cities had. Even in
Ptolemaic Egypt, the most centralized system in the Hel-

lenistic world, the city of Alexandria had a relatively high degree of independence. It is surprising how much central governments in the Hellenistic and Roman world minded their own business, which was that of the royal court, of the central bureaucracy, the military and foreign affairs. There was, of course, always the temptation to interfere with the cities for extra revenues, better control of trade and political correction. The cities' being open made them very vulnerable. But one way for cities to check those temptations was to lure sovereigns and other strong and rich men into some beneficial action and then by vote of the people to acknowledge them through statements, acts and even monuments of public gratitude, the gifts of the benefactor (χάρις) being responded to in the εὐχαριστία of the people. The expressed gratefulness of cities amounted to at least an increase in reputation for the strong man. Anything, matter or action, which could be considered beneficial to the city could be counted here, the alleviation of financial burdens (tributes and taxes), financial contributions, rendering of commodities, providing of public buildings or streets, etc. The stronger the benefactor, the more he could also be counted on for interference against internal and external adversaries by way of protective force. The most spectacular actions of that kind were the acts of military deliverance from oppression; the restitution of autonomy of the city and of the original rights, with granting of new rights, usually issued after that. In these cases of emergency-protection the cities were most willing to vote recognition of this act as a divine act, perhaps even to establish cultic worship in gratitude for it. This worship might vary from occasional to perennial cultic exercises, the erection of statues in temples and elsewhere, the building of temples, institution of games, naming of months after benefactors, etc.[3] Cultic honors were the most dramatic and public form of the recognition of "divine men" in the ancient world. Whether or not this worship related at all to the dynastic worship requested by the Hellenistic monarchs is still much debated. In any case, dynastic worship seems of little importance for our topic. The cult of benefactors in Hellenistic cities had much more impact on ordinary life and it was more intricately related to expressions and forms of urban life.

We have already seen that the borderline between the human and the divine was rather fluid in those days.[4] It was a matter of taste as well as of political sensitivity and shrewdness to single out certain actions as dramatic and extraordinary enough to justify gratitude in the form of cultic worship. The establishment of worship implied a degree of commitment which could prove embarrassing in the case of a change of policy, or even a shift of political power and sovereigns.

But against Habicht, I would hold that the growing transparency between divine and human actions and between clearly extraordinary deeds and more ordinary assistance applied not only to monarchs or, at best, major generals. If there was any distinction between the beneficial deeds of rulers and those of other people it did not last very long. Mott has shown more definitely than Habicht that cultic honor as response to acts of benevolence could be conferred on lesser people than kings: for example, generals, statesmen, or administrators. Acts 14:7–13 (18) gives a good example. In this narrative a healing miracle exercised in Lystra by Barnabas and Paul makes people of the town discover in them Zeus and Hermes. The priest of Zeus is about to bring them sacrifices. The humorous tone of the story betrays belittling criticism by the narrator. However the pattern is clear. Another New Testament equivalent for this public recognition of "divine" visitation is found in the so-called "Chor-schlüsse" in miracle stories of the synoptic Gospels, i.e., the praise of the miracle worker by the people who were present at the miracle or who were informed about it.[5] Although we do not see here that the city's official political machinery acts by way of voting, we very frequently see that the public of the village or the town did react in an honorific manner. The miracle worker is not made divine by that acclamation any more than the voting of cultic honors confers deity on the benefactor so honored. Rather the vote or the simple acclamation states that the public has experienced divine action through a benefactor, perhaps even a divine visitation. And this is not an expression of abstract interest in divine essence, but only the pragmatic question of the demonstration of divine power and its public recognition and ratification. The fact that this public recognition became an established feature of miracle stories, both on the level of folklore and of popular literature, speaks for its firm ground in public life and expectation.

The question of the origin and meaning of the concept of the "divine man"[6] must be seen in the context of the wholly urbanized system of Hellenistic culture. It cannot be treated as a separate issue. It is also an important segment in the complex infrastructure of cultic, religious, philosophical, artistic and trade-associations so characteristic of Hellenistic urban life. These groups created many additional connections to people of other cities which bore on the public life of a city.

This urban infrastructure provided and guaranteed the flow of resources relating to the health, wealth, and vitality of each city. Each hoped for as many extraordinary contributions as possible, especially from outside sources, because all cities lived close to the limits of their means, if not beyond them. Every city hoped for an increase in reputation in order to attract more attention, which in turn meant the chance for more contributions, gifts, talents, trade, etc. In this context we can define the "divine man" pattern as an ideological expression (a) of the dependence of cities on extraordinary contributions, and (b) of the fact that essential contributions came from outside. This could also imply (c) mobility as a necessary element of the "divine man" pattern.

Thus far I have spoken more or less about the relationship of cities to one another and to governmental institutions. What about religion? The infrastructure of beneficial relationships described above supplemented and often even replaced the relationship to local deities as benefactors. In former times the local gods and the cults provided a major source of well-being for the city, not only spiritually but also materially. As public religion changed, the role of the gods changed too. A deity now could be of real help if he or she attracted attention from the outside. This had been true already in classical Greece, but there—for example in Athens—imperialistic measures brought about these outside attentions, by means of military and economic force. Now more voluntary means were looked for.

Even foreign cults and new religions gained the eyes, ears, and, finally, hearts of Hellenistic citizens, because they proved to be of benefit for the public as well as for the individual. The most sensational example of the fact that foreign cults were introduced for the well-being of a city was the transfer of cult-objects and priests of the cult of the Great Mother from Asia Minor to Rome during the time of the Second Punic War. But this was by no means the only instance of that kind of public recognition. The most consequential case of public recognition of a "foreign" religion was that of Christianity under Constantine. This meant an open acknowledgment that the persecution of Christians had done damage to the state and its people, and that the acceptance of Christianity would be for the common good. The Christian apologists had worked toward this goal of public recognition for the sake of the state's and of humanity's well-being. And the Christian apologists had only imitated the idea, intent, and technique of the Jewish apologists. Most missionary religions meant well for the public—at least in the understanding of the missionary—in their venture, which was usually somewhat inaccurately described as "apologetic."[7] The works of Jewish apologists, the Acts of Luke, and the pastoral Epistles are good demonstrations of that spirit. The activities of Apollonius of Tyana and of Alexander of Abonuteichus present impressive examples too, the first especially with respect to the advice he is supposed to have given to the cities of Asia Minor, the latter with respect to

Abonuteichus and the neighboring country. For us today the questions of an individual or personal nature and of personal choice dominate in the discussion of religion. In the ancient world, especially in the time of Hellenism, the collective and societal issues were the first considerations in most missionary activities. Having reviewed the primary evidence over and over again, it appears to me that the individualistic and privatistic character of the so-called missionary religions has been unjustifiably overemphasized. The Epistel of Aristeas, the Acts of the Apostles, and *The Golden Ass* by Apuleius, here especially the eleventh book, are only a few of many documents to demonstrate missionary interest in the well-being of all, where the propagated religion is proposed as the major instrument for bringing this about and for serving the best interests of the individual as well.

The practice and success of the propaganda of these foreign or new cults shows how they wanted to be "of help." As soon as it was possible for them, professional and especially "lay" missionaries established cult-related associations of their religious persuasion. These functioned as clubs for compatriots and fellow-believers in the same city. The Island of Delos, for instance, gives ample evidence for that.[8] As a foreign cult was introduced by a professional missionary or by a merchant, sailor, or traveler, the principal issue was not personal religious satisfaction. The foreign cult worked as protective and supportive agent for the migrant person or alien-resident and eventually for his or her compatriots. The respect for the new god or cult was good for the health of the host-city too, because it helped to avoid divine wrath and it made trade—and other religions—prosper. In many cases these foreign cults then attracted the attention of natives, and not only when full-time missionaries worked towards that goal but often also when "lay" people or part-time missionaries were the only ones responsible for the existence and appearance of their own religion in town. Again the Island of Delos provides evidence. Many cults which flourished in Rome, not the least of which was Christianity itself, seem to have been introduced there in this fashion. The exotic nature of the new or foreign religion, the peculiar traditions and customs, the extraordinary promises and experiences were the major means of stimulating curiosity and, finally, loyalty among the natives. Again the extraordinary offer from the outside was seen as something which made private and public life flourish.

The sixth satire of Juvenal gives us an idea of the diversity of these cults and of their attractiveness. The cults of Cybele, of Isis, and of the Jews are mentioned, along with those of magi and astrologers. The different means used were first and foremost customary to the cult. But Juvenal indicates that there was some extra effort displayed in order to attract attention, namely some more aggressive propaganda. Here extraordinary acts can be assumed, demonstrations of divine power. Juvenal criticizes the social phenomenon represented by these propagating cults. He castigates their upward mobility, their interest in gaining access to the social establishment. It is part of Juvenal's polemic to make it appear as a matter of an individualistic interest, wholly perverted. For example he attempts to make female curiosity paramountly responsible for this inroad of foreign cults into the Roman society. This gives him a chance for facetious ridicule of the development. The interest Caesar showed in Isis, for instance, proves Juvenal to be wrong. Caesar's interest was certainly not just a matter of individual and private religiosity. The concern of the Serapis-religion for the public is also well-known. In my study of Paul's opponents I have mentioned that even the mystery religions showed a tendency to relate to public life.[9] There is sufficient indication that other mystery religions imitated the Eleusis mysteries in order that they might promise at least as substantial a contribution to the vitality of the host-society as the prototype had given.

But there was also the possibility in these missionary movements of upsetting society. I am thinking of their

potential as expressions of the underground. The embodi-
ment of the divine power in human beings could be seen as
means of defying the given social structure. The structure
of the Dionysiac mysteries in Rome in 186[10] was sufficiently different from established Roman social values
and structures to make the Roman authorities fear the
growth of a state within a state, leading to sedition and
revolution. Women were not only emancipated in this cult
but they were in the leadership position. Slaves were fully
recognized also, and there was no outside control and
domestication, as there had been in Eleusis, through the
machinery of the state. The effect of allowing slaves into
the Eleusinian mysteries, for instance, was neutralized by
integrating the cult into Athenian society. Although many
more traces of an underground trend among religious
groups in the Hellenistic period could be mentioned, I shall
limit myself to two further examples.

In the Gnostic movement, especially in its Christian
form, women were fully liberated and all social distinctions were relinquished.[11] With the complete bedeviling of
procreation in the radical Gnostic groups and with sexual
abstinence as a powerful tool, population zero (in its most
literal sense) was the goal which promised the most drastic
and efficient liberation from the evils of this world.[12]
Being empowered by the divine was felt as the decisive
stage toward liberation, with deification as the end. It
promised a degree of world-defying ecstasy which made all
normal experiences of excitement meaningless and therefore nonexistent.[13]

Another example of religious underground propaganda
survives in popular literature, namely in Hellenistic ro-
mances. M. Braun in his *History and Romance in Graeco-
Oriental Literature*[14] has emphasized that properly. Braun
shows that in some of the romance-literature motifs of the
social and political establishment were ursurped and then
associated with traditional heroes of local lore. But traditional figures (and values) of the oppressed could be associated with established heroes of the ruling class too, thus

converting them into camouflaged spokesmen for the identity and liberation of the oppressed. In the Alexander-romance,[15] a collection of very different Alexander-traditions, the first part deals with the relationship of Alexander and Nectanebus, the pharaoh of the fourth century who mysteriously disappeared and whose reappearance was prophesied by some Egyptian prophets. The tradition which the Alexander-romance uses makes Alexander the natural son of Nectanebus and thus an Egyptian prince. Father and son possess supernatural powers, especially in the original tradition, somewhat belittled by Pseudo-Callisthenes. Alexander's first major activity is the conquest of the Mediterranean and the return to Egypt with the founding of Alexandria as climax. Here in the tradition Pseudo-Callisthenes used for the first part of his romance, Egyptians forcefully redid history, thus expressing the hope for a radical reversal of Hellenistic society.

Such eschatological elements in religious propaganda would not necessarily upset the established urban society, because the Hellenistic city itself in all its excessive and turbulent life was a utopia in stone, and therefore many forms of eschatological excitement were a rather natural accompaniment of the common way of urban life. But the reversal of all societal conditions, as can be seen in the examples described, could be a threat. Alexander was welcome as long as he appeared in propaganda and lore as successor to Heracles and imitator of Dionysus, as a divine warrior and even as a son of God, a divine man in the superlative. But as an Egyptian prince he reversed history, and that was not permissible. If the oppressed and ridiculed, the common people, saw in him not only the reservoir but also the representation of the heroic and divine—that smelled of revolution. The present text of the Alexander-romance has tried its best to correct these dangerous trends in order to make the lore readable to Hellenistic readers at large.[16] But the strands of undergound opposition and reversal were present under the surface of a large segment of popular religion. Still—the Hellenistic ghettos never broke out—and Chrisianity missed its chance too. Constantine meant the end to any serious attempt at radically correcting the urban society. Instead the urban society became increasingly pushed aside. Christianity as state-religion became a rural religion.

NOTES

1. The question of whether Alexander had already deified himself, or how much so, is of no importance to our subject. What the sources show is how easy such a deification could happen and how it found belief among educated and uneducated alike. The book by E. Mederer, *Die Alexanderlegende bei den ältesten Alexanderhistorikern* (Würzburger Studien, 8; Würzburg, 1936) demonstrates that even the oldest sources, including contemporary ones, must have spoken of miraculous events and circumstances in Alexander's life. The issue of Alexander's deification is discussed in all major biographies of Alexander (e.g., W. W. Tarn, U. Wilcken). For Alexander and Heracles, see A. R. Anderson, *Heracles and His Successors* (Harvard Studies in Classical Philology, 39; Cambridge: Harvard University Press, 1928). Regarding the enduring admiration that Alexander received, which often lead to imitation, see M. Bieber, *The Portraits of Alexander the Great* (Proceedings Am. Philos. Soc., 93; 1949), pp. 373–427; A. Heuss, *Alexander der Grosse und die politische Ideologie des Altertums* (Antike und Abendland, 4; Hamburg: Schröder, 1954); F. Pfister, "Alexander der Grosse. Die Geschichte seines Ruhms im Lichte seiner Beinamen," *Historia* 13 (1964), 37–79.

2. The transparency between the divine and the human makes it impossible to look for lingusitic demarcations or other distinctions. Where the extraordinary is experienced, the divine is felt, see below note 6.

3. Documentation in Ch. Habicht, *Gottmenschentum und griechische Städte,* 2nd ed. (Zetemata, 14; Munich: Beck, 1970); S.C. Mott, *The Greek Benefactor and Deliverance from Moral Distress* (Ph.D. diss., Harvard, 1971).

4. Habicht and Mott have specifically noted it.

5. See R. Bultmann, *History of the Synoptic Tradition* (New

York: Harper & Row, 1963), pp. 225f. In reacting to these miracles people do not confer divine titles upon Jesus. But this does not mean that they do not acclaim divine visitation in and through Jesus (divine beneficial acts).

6. Examples of the phenomenon are found in the works of Ch. Habicht and S.C. Mott, already cited, as well as in my book *Die Gegner des Paulus im 2. Korintherbrief* (WMANT, 11; Neukirchen: Neukirchener Verlag, 1964). Here also the discussion of the theological background and superstructure of the phenomenon. In the article "*υἱός κτλ*" in *Theologisches Wörterbuch zum Neuen Testament,* VIII (Stuttgart: W. Kohlhammer, 1969), 334–340 and 355–357, W. V. Martitz and E. Schweizer are methodologically insufficient because they limit the question of the existence or nonexistence of the religious and cultural phenomenon to the occurrence of the *terms* "divine man" and "son of God."

7. See the discussion of the problem of Jewish "apologetic" missionaries and their Christian (and pagan) counterparts in D. Georgi, *Die Gegner des Paulus.* Paul and the majority of Gnostic missionaries represented quite different options of missionary philosophy. One could say that they were less eudaimonistic. However, Paul showed strong concern for the human race, and even the Gnostics often retained a curious interest in a sane world—in the beyond.

8. See the material collected on Delos by Ph. Bruneau, *Recherches sur les cultes de Délos a l'epoque Hellénistique et a l'epoque impériale* (Bibl. des Ec. Franc. d'Athens et de Rome, 217; Paris: Editions E.D. Boccard).

9. D.Georgi, p. 190.

10. Livy 39.8–18; *CIL* 1.196; *ILS* 18.

11. Cf. for instance the hierarchical, anti-women and pro-establishment orientation of the polemics of the Pastoral Epistles against the Gnostics.

12. See the description of Gnostic attitudes in H. Jonas, *Gnosis und spätantiker Geist,* 2nd. ed. (Göttingen: Vandenhoeck & Ruprecht, 1954), pp. 140–251, esp. pp. 214ff; idem, *The Gnostic Religion* (Boston: Beacon, 1958), pp. 241–289. The paradigm which the Acts of Thomas offer for this revolutionary attitude has been all too frequently overlooked. The original documents discovered in Nag Hamadi have not altered our view of Gnostic ethics as expressed in Jonas's description.

13. But even Gnostic movements as much as other underground

religions were ready to compromise when a chance of becoming established religion or even state-religion occurred. The example of Mani at the court of Shapur I is the most striking one besides the Christian religion.

14. M. Braun, *History and Romance in Graeco-Oriental Literature* (Oxford: Blackwell, 1938).

15. Oldest extant version by Pseudo-Callisthenes. Text: W. Kroll, *Historia Alexandri Magni,* 2nd. ed. (Berlin: Weidman, 1958). Translation of Kroll's text into English by E. H. Haight, *The Life of Alexander of Macedon* (New York: Longmans, Green, 1955). The most comprehensive study by R. Merkelbach, *Die Quellen des griechischen Alexanderromans* (Zetemata, 9; Munich: Beck, 1954).

16. A good example for this rather superficial compromise is the present version of chap. 34 of the first book of Pseudo-Callisthenes, which tries to rationalize why the Egyptians with all their skills were overcome by the Macedonians. This is done in the face of the oracle of the return of the pharaoh and the presentation of Alexander as Sesonchosis redivivus. (The names of Sesonchosis and Nectanebus are becoming confused.)

3: The Divine Agent and His Counterfeit in Philo and the Fourth Gospel

Wayne A. Meeks

IT HAS BECOME FASHIONABLE TO SPEAK OF A "DIVINE MAN christology" in early Christian literature, and in some sense this paper may be regarded as a contribution to that topic. The expression is not a completely satisfactory one, but it can serve as a shorthand way of saying that the apologetic literature produced by various religious, ethnic, and philosophical groups in Roman Hellenism often depicts important figures as somehow intermediary between the divine and human. These figures play various roles, including the founders of the groups as well as mythical prototypes that, by clever allegories, could be shown to embody the group's ideals. On the other hand, writers could sometimes use similar motifs to pillory an opponent for counterfeiting the marks of deity. If there was no higher calling than to imitate the labors of the divine Heracles in certainty of divine reward, there was nothing more ridiculous than the attempt to wrest divinity for oneself by imitating Heracles' apotheosis. There was no nobler reward for the man of virtue than to be granted by the gods a share of their status; there was no more repugnant an act of *hybris* than, being man, to make oneself a god.

Recent discussions of the "divine man" motifs in John have focused almost exclusively upon the miracle stories and the ideology which they are presumed to convey. I shall not attempt to carry that discussion forward. But the suprahuman character of Jesus is the central issue also in

the speech and dialogue material of this Gospel. Particularly in the controversies with the Jews which are dramatized in John both the positive and the pejorative aspects
of the "divine man" play a role, which will be the object
of our analysis here. Space does not permit a comprehensive survey of the divers uses of such motifs in Jewish and
other Hellenistic literature contemporary with the New
Testament, although this alone might succeed in placing
the Johannine dialogues securely in a historical setting.
The alternative so often resorted to, construction of an
artificial stereotype of *the* divine man as a foil for New
Testament exegesis, is inevitably misleading. The proce-
dure adopted here presumes less but promises more limited
results.

This essay will not attempt to trace the influences upon
the Johannine community which produced its singular
portrait of Jesus, but only to suggest a perspective by
which some of the apologetic and polemic functions of
that portrait may be better understood. For that purpose
some of the uses to which Philo of Alexandria put the
"divine man" motifs are helpful in providing a grid against
which the Johannine usage may be compared. I do not, of
course, pretend that Philo has had any direct influence
upon the author of the Fourth Gospel, nor do I consider it
likely that the milieu of the Johannine Christians was very
much like the wealthy and sophisticated circles of Alexandrian Judaism to which Philo belonged. On the contrary,
while there are some striking parallels in the language and
symbolism of John which led many scholars of the nine-
teenth century and even some in the twentieth to posit a
direct relationship, it is just the remarkable differences in
their use of similar motifs that may be most valuable in
trying to come closer to a social location for Johannine
Christianity. Philo constitutes a fixed point of inestimable
value in every study of first century Judaism and Christianity, not only because of the volume of his extant
writings, but because he can be located precisely in place,
time, and social class. Our starting point is a comparison of

the image of the ideal emissary of God, the divine king Moses in Philo's *Life of Moses,* with his parody of divine kingship in his philippic against Gaius Caligula.

The Divine King

It is apparent from the extant literature that Moses was the most important figure in all Hellenistic Jewish apologetic. Certainly that is the case in Philo, who in several passages ascribes to Moses a dignity which surpasses the limits of the human. Already when Moses was a youth growing up in Pharaoh's palace, Philo says, his self-control was so amazing that observers wondered whether "the mind which dwelt in his body like an image in its shrine" was "human or divine or a mixture of both," because it "had nothing in common with *hoi polloi.*"[1] The focal passage for us comes later in the same book, where Philo describes the reasons for Moses' appointment as the king of Israel. First, he gave up the kingship of Egypt because of Israel's superiority (*Mos.* 1.149); second, he showed his *philanthropia* by not promoting his own sons (1.150).[2] Further, he practiced an austere life but was royal in the expenditure of virtue (1.153). For all these virtues God rewarded him by making him his friend and therefore heir, and by naming him both king and god of the world (1.157–158). Philo goes on to interpret Exod. 20:21, "Moses entered the darkness where God was," to mean that he entered "into the formless and invisible and incorporeal *paradigmatic essence* of existing things, perceiving things invisible to mortal nature. And, exhibiting himself and his life like a well-executed painting, a beautiful and godlike work, he established a *paradigm* for those willing to imitate it. . . . "[3] The notion of imitation is then stated again in less rhapsodic terms ("meaner men emulate men of distinction," 1.160–161), and finally in terms of another *topos* of the Hellenistic idealization of kingship, that the king should be a "rational and living law" (1.162).[4]

The notion that a ruler set forth a paradigm of virtue or vice to be imitated by his subjects was a commonplace, and Philo uses it in several places. For example, Philo applies it to Joseph in prison, who, in contrast with the jailer who had been corrupted by association with his criminal charges, was so awe-inspiring an athlete of virtue that he turned them to repentance.[5] But the Moses passage seems to go farther than that. Moses, having entered the divine realm, having seen what is "invisible to mortal nature," returns bearing the name and image of God; he manifests the divine to his subjects.

Even that conception is not unknown in Hellenistic idealizations of monarchy, as Goodenough and others have shown.[6] It is probably implicit in the frequent appelative of the Diadochoi and of some of the Roman emperors, *epiphanēs*.[7] And in Philo's own writings it is not only Moses who is depicted at times as having an intermediary status between the human and the divine. Thus the divine attribute of "standing," that is, immutability and stability, is "shared" by God with "chosen natures," Noah and Abraham as well as Moses (*Som.* 2.226–228).[8] Though Moses remains the primary example here, because God said to him, "Stand here with me" (Deut. 5:5), Philo can substitute for Moses' name the generalizing terms "the sage" (*sophos: Som.* 2.229) or "the good man" (*asteios anthrōpos:* 230). Further, both in this section and in an earlier passage in the same treatise, Philo interprets Lev. 16:17, "And no man is in the Tent of Witness when he [the High Priest] goes in . . . " to mean that the priest ceases to be a man when he enters, yet does not become God either. Instead, "he retains the intermediary order (*mesēn taxin*) until he comes out again into the home of body and flesh."[9] Aaron in the former passage may represent the Logos, as frequently.[10] Some confusion enters because, while Moses and Aaron seem to be used interchangeably in *Som.* 2.226–236 as symbols for the virtuous sage who transcends the human and becomes a *tertium quid,* yet in *Som.* 2.189 Philo directly contrasts them, in

the context of a similar exegesis of the same passage Lev.
16:17. The reason the High Priest cannot be God, he says
here, is because that prerogative (*klēros*) belongs to Moses!
(Exod. 7:1). Thus, while Philo can use Moses, like Aaron,
as a mere cipher for the philosopher's ultimate goal of
perfection, he remains fascinated by the scriptural and
traditional account of the Sinai ascent and of Moses'
having received the title *theos,* so that the legendary figure
of Moses himself keeps breaking through the allegories.

This peculiar fascination with Moses is confirmed by a
passage where Philo compares Moses with those heroes of
whom Scripture says that they were "added" (*Sac.* 1–10).
Abraham was "added to the people of God," i.e., he
became "equal to the angels" (*isos angelois gegonōs*), and
similarly Jacob (*Sac.* 5). Isaac was not added merely to a
"people," however, but to a *genos* (Gen. 35:29), a status
apparently higher than angels (*Sac.* 6). But, he goes on,
"there are still others, whom God has advanced even
higher, and has trained them to soar above species and
genus alike and stationed them beside himself. Such is
Moses to whom He says, 'Stand here with me' (Deut.
5:31)" (*Sac.* 8).[11] That is why the term "adding" is not
used of Moses' departure from this life, for he was called
"God," and "God is not susceptible of addition or diminu-
tion, being fully and unchangeably himself" (*Sac.* 10).[12] It
is obvious, then, that Moses is for Philo the intermediary
par excellence between the divine and the human. I have
tried to show elsewhere that this is the case because Philo
has blended the *topoi* of Hellenistic "divine" kingship with
Jewish traditions that elaborated the Sinai theophany and
exalted Moses. In those traditions Moses is seen as the
divine viceroy, the envoy of God, who not only brings the
heavenly secrets to men but recovers the image of God
which Adam lost.[13]

A similar blend of traditions appears in Philo's treatment of Moses' prophecy, which occupies the last section
of the *Life* (2.187–291). Prophecy properly so-called, for
Philo, means ecstasy, when Moses is "possessed by God

and carried away out of himself" (2.188).[14] This is important for our overall purpose because it emphasizes that the
words which Moses speaks are not his own; he is merely
the mouthpiece of God. However, space will not permit
further discussion of this aspect of the portrait of Moses.

Our immediate concern is to ask just what apologetic
function these stories and these curious allegories served.
That this question is inescapable becomes apparent on a
moment's reflection about the situation of the Jewish
community in Alexandria. The story of a hero who first
mastered the lore and rule of Egypt and then led the Jews
in successful rebellion against the Egyptians and escape
from their oppressive rule can hardly be told as casual
history. When we read of the pogroms which took place a
bit later, in the time of Flaccus, and of the desperate
legation which Philo was elected to lead to the emperor
Gaius Caligula, we are at once aware that the stakes are
extremely high. The story of the Exodus affords a fertile
but risky field for Philo's considerable powers of innuendo.
For example his description of Moses' childhood leads to
an aside in which he castigates people whose acquisition of
wealth dulls their sense of ethnic loyalty. When the opportunity for personal advancement arises, unlike Moses (but
very like Philo's famous nephew Alexander), they become
apostate (*Mos.* 1.30–31). Then Philo goes on (1.34–37) to
tell of the Egyptians' oppression of the Israelites in terms
which universalize and are immediately applicable to the
situation of his Alexandrian compatriots:

> For strangers (*xenoi*), in my judgement, must be re-
> garded as suppliants (*hiketai*) of those who receive
> them, and not only suppliants but settlers and friends
> (*metoikoi kai philoi*) who are anxious to obtain equal
> rights with the burgesses (*eis astōn isotimian*) and are
> near to being citizens (*geitniōntes ēdē politais*) because
> they differ little from the original inhabitants (*autoch-
> thonōn*). (*Mos.* 1.35, trans. Colson)

By rejecting that and "making serfs of men who were not
only free but *xenoi, hiketai,* and *metoikoi,*" the Pharaoh

(king: *basileus*) disdained "the God of liberty and hospitality and justice."[15] Similarly Philo's allegorical homily on the burning bush (*Mos.* 1.67–68), while obviously apposite to the situation of the Israelites described in Exodus chapters 1–3, would also be singularly appropriate to a community that might at any time face the kind of persecution described in his *Flaccus* and his *On the Embassy to Gaius*. The bush that is not consumed is a sign "that the sufferers would not be destroyed by their aggressors" (*Mos.* 1.67). It is a *thorn* bush, which looks weak but is prickly (1.68);[16] the nation's weakness is its strength (1.69), for the angel if the flame represents the providence of God.[17] And, to give just one further example, the perennial problem of the Diaspora Jew is described succinctly in Philo's expansion of Balaam's oracle: The "people will dwell alone" (Num. 23:9 LXX), not literally, "but because in virtue of the distinction of their peculiar customs they do not mix with others to depart from the ways of their fathers" (*Mos.* 1.278, Colson).

As we search for the apologetic context of the portrait of Moses, then, we must recognize that our author is an extremely sophisticated practitioner of the art. Philo was a member of what was perhaps the wealthiest and most influential Jewish family in Alexandria, and he was directly involved in political affairs. He knew at first hand the workings of local and imperial diplomacy.[18] In the portions of his two political writings that survive, the *Flaccus* and the *Embassy to Gaius*, we see an example of his apologetic and polemic method which may be compared immediately with the portrait of Moses. We shall confine ourselves to the *Legatio*.

The Counterfeit God

Two observations concerning the *Legatio* are important for our purposes. The first is that one of the principal rhetorical threads that hold it together is a parody of the divine kingship *topoi* which we have seen used in Philo's description of Moses. The second is that the introduction to the philippic contains an odd excursus on Israel as "the nation that sees God" and as the "suppliant nation" (*hiketon genos*), which seems to have little to do with the subject at hand but which has many connections with elements of Philo's allegory.

First, the parody. The Cynic-Stoic hero-king is an "athlete of virtue."[19] In Moses' early training for the kingship into which God was to initiate him, consequently, he "was carrying out the contests of virtue (*tous aretēs athlous*) with an excellent trainer, the reason within him" (*Mos.* 1.48). With harsh irony Philo, after describing the despicable plots by which Gaius had arranged the murders of Macro and Silanus and the forced suicide of his younger cousin, says "Gaius had thus won the three contests (*athlous*) described above in three vitally important departments" (*Leg.* 74, Colson).[20] That accomplished, says Philo, Gaius "no longer considered it worthy of him to abide within the bounds of nature but overstepped them in his eagerness to be thought a god" (*Leg.* 75, Colson). This astonishing *hybris* obviously parodies the achievement of the true *sophos*, like Moses, who, having mastered his passions in the contest of virtue, is rewarded by the vision of God which makes him, as a *teleios anthrōpos*, "god" in the earthly realm, an image of God to be imitated by his subjects. In *Moses* 1.60–62, Philo takes advantage of the biblical report of Moses' tending Jethro's sheep to introduce the familiar *topos* that the king is shepherd of his people, for "the only perfect king . . . is one who is skilled in the knowledge of shepherding . . . " (*Mos.* 1.62, Colson). In the *Legatio* he has Gaius use the same *topos* as a basis for his deduction that the emperor is a god, since the shepherd is a superiour being to the creatures he herds (*Leg.* 76). One of the principal themes of the *Life of Moses* is that Moses is the instrument of God's providence; one of the major themes of the *Legatio* is that Gaius flouted the providence of God by attacking the people who were under God's special protection. Finally, the notion of the king as "living law" (*nomos empsychos*), which is so important in Philo's descriptions of Moses and the patriarchs, is parodied in *Legatio* 119: "For considering that he himself was a law, he [Gaius] abrogated those laid down by legislators in the several states, treating them as empty talk."[21]

The second observation is that the rhetorical introduction to the *Legatio* introduces a description of Israel which seems to have nothing to do with the matter at hand. Through want of perception, says Philo (*Leg.* 1), men childishly look to fortune (*tychē*) rather than nature,[22] since the eyes of the body can only see what is immediately at hand, while the reason (*logismos*) is required to see the unseen and future, *physis*, which endures (2). Yet even the "present time," that is, the recent events he will describe, would be sufficient to prove God's providence (3)—especially the providence he exercises toward Israel, the "race of suppliants" (*to hiketikon genos*) which he elected. For this is the race "that sees God" (4). *That* vision requires even more than *logos*, though *logos* may apprehend the powers of God (5–7). Then Philo breaks off abruptly and turns to the story of Gaius (8).

Leaving aside the question of the awkward transition,[23] let us see if we can guess why Philo has included in the introduction to his most political tract an allusion to his allegory of "Israel" as "the nation that sees God." Very often he uses this etymological play to describe the mind or soul, or sometimes the whole "guild of wise souls" (*psychōn sophōn thiasos*),[24] but here he speaks of the nation as such.[25] That the nation can be the symbol for all who "see the one who truly is"[26] reminds us that the same is said of Moses.[27] Whatever this "vision" may mean, Philo frequently suggests that it becomes accessible for those who will follow Moses' lead, as in the fascinating passage in his book on *The Confusion of Tongues*:

> But the work proper to those who serve Being is not
> that of cupbearers or bakers or cooks, or any other

earthly work, nor to shape or assemble bodily things like brick, but to ascend in mind to the aethereal height, setting before them Moses, the God-loved type, as leader on the road. For then they will behold the "place" which is really the Logos, where God, the immovable and immutable, stands, 'and that which is under his feet, like brickwork of sapphire and like a kind of firmament of heaven,' the perceptible world, which he thus enigmatically portrays. For it behooves those who have joined the association with knowledge to long to see Being, but if they should not be able to, then to see its image, the most holy Logos, and, next to that, the most perfect work in the perceptible realm, the world. For to philosophize is nothing other than to strive to see these things accurately. (*Conf.* 95–97)[28]

The very name of Israel therefore implies a special relation to God because of a special *knowledge* of God. And that is precisely why, says Philo, Gaius singled out the Jews for persecution: "They alone opposed him on principle," because they were trained in monotheism from the cradle (*Leg.* 114–115). When all other groups outdid themselves in flattering the emperor, the Jews stood apart (*Leg.* 117) because in their eyes this "deification"[29] of corruptible human nature was "of all impieties the worst" (*Leg.* 118). What Philo seems to be suggesting is that the Jews, since they have the true "image" of God always set before them in the ideal king-prophet-lawgiver, the perfect *sophos* and best human symbol of God's own Logos, they cannot be taken in by a counterfeit image of deity. They see through the ludicrous masquerades of Gaius.

The major apologetic points which Philo makes in his philippic, then, are these: (1) Gaius by refusing to recognize the *limits* of kingship, as Augustus, for example, had done, becomes a caricature of divine kingship. (2) Israel, the God-seeing nation, was uniquely endowed to see through his pretense. (3) Israel, as the "suppliant race," is under God's special protection, as both Flaccus and Gaius found out to their destruction.

There is one further step which we must take before

turning to the Fourth Gospel. Concretely, what could
"seeing God" and "imitating Moses" have meant to the
ordinary Jew of Alexandria? They had neither king nor
prophet. There is no hint of any political office or leader
in the Jewish community that could be identified with the
idealized portrait of Moses. Philo nowhere suggests that
ecstatic prophecy of the type he attributes to Moses is
practiced by any "charismatic" figures in the synagogue.
To be sure, one of the apologetic functions of Moses and
the patriarchs is as great ethnic heroes, to instill pride in
the Jewish heritage on the part of its members and respect,
if possible, on the part of the Gentiles. Yet some of the
language we have been examining would seem excessive, if
that were the only role. E. R. Goodenough, as is well
known, posited a great "Jewish Mystery," in two parts, the
one symbolized by Aaron, the higher one by Moses,
though he was unable finally to be very specific about the
extent to which such a mystery could be understood as
existing in actual organization and rituals of initiation, to
what extent merely as metaphor for a peculiar intellectual
discipline.[30] Certainly Philo uses the language of mysticism and of mysteries a great deal, but much of it may
already have become stereotyped expressions in the philosophical schools. Still, we cannot exclude the possibility
that genuine contemplative mysticism, or even ritual ecstasy, was practiced by a few, perhaps even Philo himself.[31]

Mainly, however, the average Jew must have met Moses
in just one place: the Torah. Even Philo's extravagantly
rhetorical description of Moses' ascent into the invisible
realm to return as a model of the unseen forms, which the
followers should stamp upon their souls, is paralleled in a
description of his legislation. For the books of Moses were
composed and handed on "for the use of those who are
worthy to use them, to be their fairest possession, like-
nesses and copies of the patterns enshrined in the
soul . . . " (*Mos.* 2.11, Colson).[32] Philo has combined the
Hellenistic theory of kingship with the scriptural tradition

of the apostolic prophet in order to emphasize the uniquely divine quality of Moses' *politeia.* That is very important
for the Alexandrian Jews, because they are not *citizens*
(*astoi, politai*), but *metoikoi,* yet they strove to gain rights
if possible equivalent to citizenship or, if not, at least
recognition of their "ancestral laws."[33] Thus, while being
a disciple of Moses included, for those who could attain it,
a knowledge of the allegorical interpretations as well as the
positive laws, and not only a modelling of one's life after
Moses' virtues, but an intellectual and mystical "soaring"
after Moses in the attempt to see God, it also carried a very
immediate political and social obligation. That was the
defense of the autonomy of the Jewish *politeia* in the
Hellenistic city.

All Philo's writings are intended to facilitate his fellow
Jews' maintaining a delicate balancing act. On the one
hand, by his allegorical interpretation of the Torah, made
possible by his sophisticated philosophical eclecticism, he
showed that one could accept as the Jews' own the highest
values of the "Greek" civilization which were aspired to by
the urbane classes of Alexandria (in contrast to the native
Egyptians, whom he treats with disdain, or the city "rab-
ble"). On the other hand, he insists upon absolute loyalty
to the Jewish *ethnos* and to its scriptures, laws, and traditions. The story of the embassy to Gaius, from which Philo
tells us quite credibly that he did not expect to return
alive, is testimony that he himself kept that balance with
remarkable devotion and skill.

The Johannine Controversies

The scale of the struggle which we can glimpse behind
the apologetic sections of the Fourth Gospel is much
smaller. While in Philo's writings we see the Moses traditions being used in a broad *Kulturkampf,* here in John
they are employed in a sectarian controversy. And both
sides in this controversy have used the same scripture and

similar traditions. What the Jews say about Jesus is rather
like what Philo says about Gaius: that he, a man, makes
himself God. They may have added that such a divine-man
is not only blasphemous but superfluous, since they have
Moses and the Patriarchs. ("Are you greater than our
father Jacob?" [4:12] "Are you greater than Abraham?"
[8:53].) The Christians reply by using the traditions of
Moses and the Patriarchs to describe Jesus, but by exag-
gerating those traditions to a point at which, in Jewish
ears, they become absurd. Let us examine some of the
more important passages.

In John 5:18 the accusation is first put forth that Jesus
"made himself equal to God." The story of Sabbath healing has furnished the occasion, linked to the discourse by
the statement, "The Father is working still, and I am
working." To call God "father" in this way is for the Jews
tantamount to claiming equality with God, that is, *huios
tou theou* = *theos* here, as in 10:33, 36. But the other side
of the statement is what is emphasized by the Christian
writer, not "sonship," but imitation: "The Son cannot do
anything *aph heautou,* except what he sees the Father
doing" (v. 19). This statement, repeated in verse 30, forms
an *inclusio* that frames this part of the discourse.[34] The
dependence of the messenger on the sender is a leading
motif in the Jewish conception of the apostolic prophet, as
we saw even in Philo.[35] Further, the notion that some
messengers of God could be commissioned to perform
tasks that are ordinarily God's unique works (raising the
dead; executing judgment, vv. 21–22) appears in a number
of aggadic traditions[36] and is at least implicit in Philo's
account of Moses' miracles.[37] In verses 23 and 24 something like the "standard rule of agency"[38] is invoked:
"that all who honor the Father should honor the Son. He
who does not honor the Son does not honor the Father
who sent him." Yet there is nothing specifically Jewish or
religious about the rule. It is universally understood that
the treatment of a king's ambassador, for example, will be
taken to imply the subjects' attitude to the king. Of course

the continuation in verse 24 is specifically Christian: "He who hears my word and believes the Sender has life eternal and does not enter judgment but has been translated from death to life."

The same motifs are developed further in John 10:22–39. Here the stage is set by Jews who "surround" Jesus and ask the question which in the synoptic tradition (Luke 22:67//Matt. 26:63) is at the center of the trial before the High Priest. Since the further question of Jesus' "blasphemy" in calling himself "Son of God" is also raised in the dialogue (v. 36, cf.//Mark 14:62), there is reason to believe that the evangelist has worked up this dispute from material that originally stood in the trial tradition.[39] A "judgment" is taking place here. The major leitmotif is the testimony of the "works" (*erga*) of Jesus (cf. 5:36; 8:17–20), but the central issue is the (Christian) redefinition of *Christos* as Son of God in a way that is impossible for Jews to accept.[40] This is implicit in the statement "I give them eternal life" (v. 28; cf. 5:24), and explicit in the statement "I and the Father are One" (v. 30), and "The Father is in me and I in the Father" (v. 38). In both instances the offense of the remark is underscored by the action of the Jews: they want to stone Jesus (v. 31), to seize him (v. 39).

In this context then a curious midrashic argument is inserted. Its form is *qal ve-ḥomer* (*a fortiori*): if those "to whom the Word of God came" (at Sinai)[41] were called "gods," how much more he "whom God sanctified and sent into the world"? From what we have seen in Philo (and could find multiplied in other Jewish and Samaritan sources), we see that the Christians are using an argument which could readily have been applied to Moses—as indeed the Syrian church father Aphrahat later says explicitly. [42] But of course the Johannine Christians want to *deny* this exalted role to Moses, as they deny that he ever ascended to heaven (3:13). Note further that the one "consecrated and sent into the world" is authenticated by the *erga* which he is given to do. If they are the "works of God," then they should be believed.[43] Since "works" and "signs" are interchangeable for the evangelist, we may perhaps here recall the *sēmeia* (*kai terata*) given to Moses that the Israelites might believe that God sent him (Exod. 4:19, 30–31; Deut. 34:11).

In the two passages we have examined so far the mediatorial or apostolic mission of Jesus shows striking parallels to the Moses traditions, but the notion of the messenger as an "image" or "paradigm" to be seen and imitated plays no role. That motif as well is present, however, in other passages in John, for example, in the dramatic pronouncement 12:44–50. The pronouncement, introduced by the solemn formula "Jesus cried aloud and said,"[44] has no audience save the readers of the Gospel, for the final confrontation with "the Jews" has taken place, and after a warning that "now" comes the judgment of the *kosmos* (12:30) for the light is "only a little while" among them (v. 35), Jesus has withdrawn and hidden himself from them. The evangelist inserts the familiar early Christian proof-text for the Jews' rejection of Jesus, from Isa. 6:9–10, and a remark that even though some of the "rulers" believed in Jesus, they would not confess him for fear of the Pharisees, "because they preferred the *doxa* of men to the *doxa* of God" (v. 43). Then comes the pronouncement: not only "he who believes in me does not believe in me but in the one who sent me," but also "he who sees me sees the one who sent me." From the prologue on it has been made clear that "seeing God" is impossible except through the Son (1:18; 6:46). This Christian claim is set in sharp contrast to traditional Jewish (and Samaritan) interpretations of the Sinai theophany. *Ḥesed we-'emeth* did *not* come through Moses, but only through Jesus (1:17). [45] Moses did *not* ascend to heaven (3:13). Israel at Sinai not only did not see God's "form" (*eidos*), they did not even hear his "voice" (*phōnē*) (5:37)—in contradiction to Deut. 4:12 and to Philo's standard allegory of "Israel" as "the nation that sees God." Indeed, they do not even have his "word" abiding in them (5:38), contradicting Deut.

30:11–14. And the proof which is offered for this cavalier denial of a central Jewish belief is that, since the Scriptures of Moses point to Jesus, if the Jews do not accept him then they are exposed as not believing Moses (5:38–47). That is, here again we have a thorough Christian reinterpretation of Jewish traditions, in which the Johannine christology is made the touchstone for all use of Scripture.

Thus it is already apparent that a radical choice, a *krisis*, is demanded. For Jesus not only "testifies" what he has seen and heard (3:11, 12; 8:38), he also manifests the *doxa* of God (note especially 11:40).[46] The *krisis* is stated in 12:45 (see above) and most graphically in 15:24: "But now you have both seen and hated both me and my father."[47] The agency—or, more precisely, vice-regency—motif reaches its climax in the final trial narrative in which the Jews, determined not to have Jesus as their king, are reduced to admitting that they have *no* king but Caesar (19:15).[48] That is, by rejecting the envoy of God, they have rejected God's rule over them (in vain: 19:19–22). On the other hand, the "farewell discourses," which deal primarily with the status of the Christian community after Jesus' "departure to the Father," emphasize the positive side of the same motifs,[49] for "he who has seen me has seen the Father" (14:7–9). The farewell discourses present the disciples as the group to whom the Messenger has delivered the Name of God and his Word, his "commandments," but, more, has shown them God's *doxa* through himself enabling them to "see the Father." His return to the Father leaves them in the world as, like himself, aliens from the world, to continue with the aid of the "other Advocate" his work of revelation and judgment. The allusions to the Sinai revelation and to Moses' mission are obvious and probably not accidental. It is perhaps not too farfetched, even, to compare this little group's vision of themselves with Philo's description of Israel as "the race that sees God."

That audacious claim was advanced, almost certainly, in the context of the mission of the Johannine Christians within a Jewish community. The special metaphors which describe Jesus as the messenger from God, the metaphors we have been concerned with here, certainly owe a great deal to Jewish apologetic language about Moses and the Patriarchs and Prophets, and they took on the sharp polemic twist which they now have in the Fourth Gospel in the context of the kind of controversy which we can still glimpse in chapters 5 and 9, for example. There we see the issue drawn for Jews who "believe" in Jesus in some not insignificant sense—believe that he is God's messenger, believe that he is a prophet, perhaps even *the* Prophet, a new Moses—but who are still attached to the synagogue community. The choice, at a certain stage of the development of the Johannine groups, has been forced: in or out. It has, moreover, been forced from both sides. From the Jewish side, the Christian development of the "envoy of God" notion has reached the point of blasphemy, and anyone who makes that kind of claim about Jesus has to be expelled. From the Christian side, to remain in the synagogue now means to remain "in the world," in its hostility toward God and his messenger.

That stage, the stage of the wrenching separation between the Christians and the Jews, lies already in the past at the time of the composition of the Fourth Gospel. The attempt to distinguish strata in the Johannine developments of the motifs we are interested in, however, is complicated by the fact that the earlier struggle so massively shaped the Christian's sense of who they were, including their sense of who Jesus was, that these same motifs become central parts of their religious vocabulary and therefore become major themes for that unknown master of irony and drama who drew the traditions together into a gospel. Certainly some progress has been made in the last few years in the attempts to distinguish the sources of John and the editorial stages through which the gospel apparently went. There have even been some attempts to suggest the social, intergroup context of each of the stages,[50] but these are far from real clarity. The

history of the Johannine mission and apologetics must
have been far more complex than I have hinted here, for
certainly a peculiar relationship with the Samaritans played
a role which I have not even mentioned and which is even
more difficult to approach historically than the relationship with the Jews. If only we knew with comparable
certainty one-tenth as much about the Gospel's author and
the setting of his community as we know about Philo and
the Alexandrian Jews, then our task would be much sim-
pler. Even so the comparison between the two, now that
we have rid ourselves of the extravagant claims for direct
influence or exclusive connections that were regularly
made two or three generations ago, can suggest many
fruitful lines of inquiry about the way in which Jews and
Christians established their identities and worked out their
various pictures of "the world" and their place in it.

NOTES

1. *Mos.* 1.27–29, trans. Colson in the Loeb Classical Library (I
use the abbreviations employed by the Loeb editors throughout).

2. This *topos* is developed more extensively in *Virt.* 51–79.

3. *Mos.* 1.158, my translation.

4. νόμος ἔμψυχος τε καὶ λογικός E. R. Goodenough, extending
suggestions by E. Bréhier, has shown that this notion as well as the
imitation of the ruler by his subjects were common *topoi* in Hellenistic kingship theory, particularly as it appears in fragments of neo-
Pythagorean writings. See his "The Political Philosophy of Hellenistic Kingship," *Yale Classical Studies* 1 (1928), 55–102, and his
disucssion of "Law in the Subjective Realm" in *By Light, Light*
(New Haven: Yale University Press, 1935), pp. 370–413.

5. *Jos.* 80–87. Philo uses the same phrase here as in *Mos.* 1.158:
οἷα γραφὴν ἀρχέτυπον εὖ δεδημιουργημένην ἐν μέσῳ θείς. . . (*Jos.*
87). On this passage see Goodenough, *The Politics of Philo Judaeus*
(New Haven: Yale University Press, 1938), pp. 53–55. Goodenough
makes a very plausible case that Philo uses the story of Joseph to
portray an ideal Roman prefect of Egypt.

6. "Hellenistic Kingship." Arnold Ehrhardt, starting from a remark by Plutarch (*Moralia* 330d) tries to reconstruct a Stoic *topos* describing Hellenistic monarchs and, later, Roman emperors as "descending saviors," ἰσόθεοι, imitators of Heracles ("Ein antikes Herrscherideal," *Evangelische Theologie* 9 [1948—49], 101—110; "Jesus Christ and Alexander the Great," in *The Framework of the New Testament Stories* [Cambridge: Harvard University Press, 1964], pp. 37—43). One would immediately think of Philo's remark about God's "lending him [Moses] to sojourn among the earthly" (*Sac.* 9). But A.D. Nock warns against understanding such statements as implying "pre-existence" in the Christian sense and thinks them a mere "conventional expression" (review of H. J. Schoeps, *Paulus, Gnomon* 33 [1961], 587, n.5).

7. See the references in E. Schürer, *The History of the Jewish People in the Age of Jesus Christ (175 B.C.—A.D.135)*, rev. & ed. by G. Vermes and F. Millar, vol. I (Edinburgh: T. & T. Clark, 1973), 147, n. 23.

8. Cf. *Gig.* 45—54, where "stability" is the ability to be "bodiless" and thus to behold Being (τὸ ὄν), the prerogative granted Moses as representing the λόγος ἐνδιάθετος contrasted with the λόγος of speech (=Aaron).

9. *Som.* 2.232, cf. 2.189 and *Quis her.* 84, where the High Priest is taken as a symbol of the mind (νοῦς) which when "ministering to God in purity" is "not human but divine" (οὐκ ἔστιν ἄνθρωπος ἀλλὰ θεῖος).

10. So Colson, p. 529, n.C.

11. Trans. Colson. On the three degrees of immortality or three "places" for the departed souls this seems to imply, see H. A. Wolfson, *Philo* (Cambridge: Harvard University Press, 1947), I, 402—403.

12. Elsewhere Philo is more careful, pointing out that the term θεός is not used "properly" of Moses as of "Him who is," but only by analogy (*Det.* 161—62). See Goodenough, *Light,* pp. 223—229.

13. See "Moses as God and King," in *Religions in Antiquity,* ed. J. Neusner (Studies in the History of Religion, 14; Leiden: Brill, 1968), pp. 354—371.

14. For the "three kinds of prophecy" see *Mos.* 2.188—191. The ecstatic type is discussed in 246—291; see also 1.57, 175, 201; 2.67, etc. See my *The Prophet-King* (NovTSup 14; Leiden: Brill, 1967), pp. 127—129.

15. The gentile reader would recognize these as common attri-

butes of Zeus; in 1.72 Philo explicitly attaches them to the God of Israel. It was H. A. Wolfson ("Philo on Jewish Citizenship in Alexandria," *Journal of Biblical Literature* 63 [1944], 165–168) who first observed that Philo here gives a precise definition of the Jews' legal and political status in Alexandria in his own time. Cf. E. Mary Smallwood, *Philonis Alexandrini Legatio ad Gaium* (Leiden: Brill, 1961), pp. 3–14, and below, n.33.

16. Compare his innuendoes in *Leg.* 214–217 and *Flac.* 45–48 about the power of the Jews if all of them throughout the empire were to be mobilized by an attack on their basic institutions. Cf. Goodenough, *Politics*, pp. 16, 20.

17. Which brings δίκη against an oppressor: a major theme in both *Flac.* and *Leg.*

18. This has been stressed and illustrated abundantly by Goodenough, *Politics.*

19. See, for example, Ragnar Höistad, *Cynic Hero and Cynic King* (Lund: Carl Bloms, 1948), pp. 41–43, 51–52, 61–63, 199–200; V. C. Pfitzner, *Paul and the Agon-Motif* (NovTSup 16; Leiden: Brill, 1967), pp. 16–37; on Philo: 38–48.

20. At the same time Philo here cleverly exploits the resentment of the emperor that was felt by the equestrians and senators by emphasizing that these "victories" were at the expense of those groups, as well as of the ties of family which had been so sacrosanct in the traditions of republican Rome. Cf. Goodenough, *Politics*, pp. 13–14.

21. Goodenough, *Politics,* pp. 107–110.

22. G. Delling argues that φύσις almost always means "God" for Philo ("Wunder - Allegorie - Mythus bei Philon von Alexandreia," in *Studien zum Neuen Testament und zum hellenistischen Judentum* [Göttingen: Vandenhoeck & Ruprecht, 1970], pp. 72–129).

23. Goodenough (*Politics,* p. 12), following Cohn, Massebieau, and Reiter, thinks there is a lacuna between *Leg.* 7 and 8. These brief paragraphs were the beginning of a description of "the Mystery." "Philo must have continued with the claim that the great rule of God was the first fact of nature, and that, a second fact of nature, humanity was joined to God by the Jews, who were the link between man and God because of their mystic powers of vision, and hence were the 'race of suppliants' who alone could bring to men God's favor" (p.13). But this "must have" is sheer conjecture. Further, while it is true that Philo can ascribe a mediating function to Israel as a whole (e.g., *Mos.* 1.149, evidently alluding to Exod.

19:6), that is not the way he uses the term ἱκετικός and cognates. See, e.g., *Mos.* 1.36, 72: the Israelites are called "suppliants" because they depend on God for protection. Colson, on the other hand, questions the existence of a lacuna and, because he regards *Leg.* 4–7 as merely a "parenthesis," a "thoroughly Philonic ramble," he finds no reason to propose any connection with the themes of the treatise. He has not, however, persuaded many; see Smallwood, *Philonis . . . Legatio,* pp. 157–158.

24. *Plant.* 58.

25. For the frequency and variety of Philo's use of the allegory, see the collection of passages in the Index to the Loeb edition by J. W. Earp (vol. X, 334–335).

26. *Congr.* 51. On the apparent contradiction, since for Philo the essence of God cannot be seen or known, see Wolfson, *Philo* II, 82–93. Wolfson thinks what is meant is "direct" knowledge of God through revelation. But see also Goodenough, *Light,* pp. 136, 170, 211–215.

27. Beside *Mos.* 1.158, discussed above, see, e.g., *L.A.* 3.100–102.

28. Note the contrast implied in *Mos.* 1.263–299 between this conception of Israel (and of the prophetic sage) and the false pose of Balaam, who "claimed to see not only the world but the world's maker," yet cannot even see the angel whom his donkey sees so clearly! The allegory is based, of course, on Num.24:3–4, 15–16 LXX Βαλααμ . . . ὁ ἄνθρωπος ὁ ἀληθινὸς ὁρῶν.

29. It is impossible to render in English the parody implied in θεοπλαστῆσαι. As Philo remarks in *Leg.* 110, Gaius' divinity is an obvious counterfeit of the real coin.

30. Goodenough, *Light*; A.D. Nock's critical review in *Gnomon* 13 (1937), 156–165, reprinted in *Essays on Religion and the Ancient World* (Cambridge: Harvard University Press, 1972), I, 459–468; Goodenough, "Literal Mystery in Hellenistic Judaism," in *Quantalacumque: Studies Presented to Kirsopp Lake . . .,* ed. R.P. Casey et al. (London: Christophers, 1937), pp. 227–241.

31. Note, for example his enthusiastic description of the Therapeutae, itself in an apologetic work (*Vit. Cont.*)

32. A little farther on he can speak of the laws as "stamped with the seals of nature itself" (σφραγίδι φύσεως αὐτῆς σεσημασμένα).

33. See the passage quoted above, *Mos.* 1.34–37. The publication by H. I. Bell of a papyrus copy of Claudius' letter to the Alexandrians of A.D. 41 (*Jews and Christians in Egypt* [Oxford: Clarendon

Press, 1924], pp. 1–37) effectively settled the long controversy over the question whether the Jews were citizens of the Greek *polis* of Alexandria. It is now clear that they were not, but were organized as a πολίτευμα which had substantial rights usually upheld by the Romans and resented by the Alexandrians. The Jewish πολίτευμα was often called, loosely, a πολιτεία and the Jews, as members of it, πολῖται, but their legal status was that of resident aliens, κάτοικοι or μέτοικοι. They sought periodically to elevate their status to parity with the ἀστοί, while the latter attempted to reduce them to ξένοι. See S. Tracy, *Philo Judaeus and the Roman Principate* (Williamsport, Pa.: Bayard Press, 1933); Goodenough, *Politics*; Wolfson, "Philo on Jewish Citizenship"; V. Tcherikover, *Hellenistic Civilization and the Jews* (Philadelphia: Jewish Publication Society, 1961), pp. 296–328; Smallwood, *Philonis . . . Legatio*, pp. 3–14.

34. V. 19 emphasizes "seeing," v. 30, "hearing," so that vv. 19–20 introduce the theme of the ἔργα done by Jesus (vv. 20–26, cf. v. 17), while v. 30 sums up the theme of κρίσις (vv. 22, 27–30) and thus also provides the transition to the following theme of μαρτυρία (vv. 31–40).

35. See Meeks, *Prophet-King*, pp. 45–46, 57, 137–138, 301–302, 304.

36. A rabbinic aggadah says that God never gives to a šalîah the key to three things: the rain, the womb, and the grave—yet to Elijah, Elisha, and Ezekiel respectively he did give them. (bTa'anit 2a; bSanhedrin 113a; Midrash on Psalms 78:5).

37. On which see Delling, "Wunder," p. 76.

38. See P. Borgen, "God's Agent in the Fourth Gospel," in *Religions in Antiquity*, ed. J. Neusner (Studies in the History of Religion, 14; Leiden: Brill, 1968), pp. 137–148; Meeks, *Prophet-King*, pp. 140, 226–227, 301–305.

39. On this see R. E. Brown, *The Gospel According to John* (Anchor Bible, 29; Garden City, N.Y.: Doubleday, 1966), pp. 408–409; cf. Meeks, *Prophet-King*, p. 60.

40. See M. de Jonge, "Jewish Expectations about the 'Messiah' according to the Fourth Gospel," *New Testament Studies* 19 (1972-73), 246–270. Note the way these motifs are picked up in the dialogues of the next chapter, 11:25–27.

41. C. K. Barrett, *The Gospel According to St. John* (London: SPCK, 1955), pp. 319–320; N. A. Dahl, "The Johannine Church and History," in *Current Issues in New Testament Interpretation*, ed. W. Klassen and G. Snyder (New York: Harper, 1962), p. 133; J. Jervell,

Imago Dei (FRLANT n.s. 58; Göttingen: Vandenhoeck & Ruprecht, 1960), p. 103. The application of the psalm to Israel at Sinai appears often in rabbinic midrash, e.g., b*Aboda Zara* 5a; *Pesikta Rabbati* 1:2; 14:10; *Mekilta, Baḥodesh* 9 (ed. Lauterbach, II, 272). Brown (Anchor Bible 29, p. 409) prefers the identification of *'elohîm* as "judges," as in Midrash on Psalms 82:6. A. T. Hanson ("John's Citation of Psalm LXXXII," *New Testament Studies* 21 [1964–65], 158–162) takes the argument to work at a theological rather than verbal level, and the whole of Ps. 82 to be in the evangelist's mind as an eschatological prophecy, which is possible but not supported by anything in the text (see de Jonge and van der Woude below). The suggestion by J. A. Emerton ("Some New Testament Notes: I. The Interpretation of Psalm lxxxii in John x," *Journal of Theological Studies* n.s. 11 [1960], 329–332) that the psalm is understood as addressed to angels, receives some support from further discoveries at Qumran (M. de Jonge and A. S. van der Woude, "11Q Melchizedek and the New Testament," *New Testament Studies* 12 [1965–66], 312–313) but does not suit the Johannine context (v. 23: ἄνθρωπος / θεός).

42. *Demonstration* 17.3; see translation by J. Neusner, *Aphrahat and Judaism* (SPB 19; Leiden: Brill, 1971), pp. 68–70. Aphrahat also cites Ps. 82:6 and, for Moses' being called god, Exod. 7:1.

43. Ἔργα τοῦ θεοῦ is used differently here than in 6:28, where the question, What *are* the works of God? is answered, "to believe in the one whom he sent," though of course the two uses are related: the works given by God to the Messenger to perform ought to lead to belief, which is the proper "work" of the believer. The "works" are on one level the "signs," but more importantly the whole mission which, like the signs, is a self-testimony, a μαρτυρία that Jesus *is* the Messenger and the manifestation of the Light. The latter is the "work" which he "perfects" at the crucifixion (19:30; cf. 4:34; 5:36; 9:4; 17:4).

44. For rabbinic parallels to this formula see A. Schlatter, "Die Sprache und Heimat des vierten Evangeliums," reprinted in *Johannes und sein Evangelium,* ed. K. Rengstorff (Darmstadt: Wissenschaftliche Buchgesellschaft, 1973), pp. 43–44.

45. Dahl, "Johannine Church," pp. 132–133.

46. There are perhaps three different but interconnected senses in which the word group δόξα, δοξάζω is used in John (they are not used at all in the Johannine letters): (1) Jesus, through the "signs," can "manifest" the δόξα of God (2:11; 11:4, 40; cf. 17:22). (2)

Δόξα can mean honor, credit, fame, or approval, which may be
sought either from men or from God. But to seek "glory" from men
is the same as seeking one's "own glory"; its opposite is to seek
God's glory, and the corollary of that is that the messenger who does
so will be "glorified" by God (5:41–44; 7:18; 8:50–58; 11:4; 12:28;
43; 17:1, 4, 5, 10, 22, 24; cf. 14:13; 15:8; 16:14). (3) The very
special Johannine usage in which Jesus' δοξασθῆναι is his crucifixion
(7:39; 12:16, 23; 13:31–32). This meaning so encroaches upon the
more ordinary ones that for the informed reader it is an overtone in
all the above passages, and 1:14; 12:41; and probably 8:56 must also
be understood in terms of a vision of the crucifixion-exaltation of
the Son of Man.

47. Cf. 9:39–41.

48. For the possible ironic allusion to the Passover hymn Nišmat
kol ḥay see Meeks, Prophet-King, p. 77.

49. The theme is announced in 13:31: "Now the Son of Man is
glorified, and God is glorified in him. . . . " Chap. 14:1 "Believe in
God, and believe in me"; v. 6b "No one comes to the Father but by
me"; vv. 7–12 knit together several aspects of the theme: "knowing"
Son and Father; "seeing" the Father by seeing the Son; the Son "in
the Father" and the Father in him; Jesus' words not his own; the
Father dwelling (μένων) in him works his ἔργα; believe Jesus or
believe the works. Cf. vv. 14, 20, 21, 24. The chapter ends on the
less sublime statement of the relationship in terms of orders and
obedience (v. 31). Chap. 15 emphasizes more the analogous relation
between Jesus and the disciples: "bearing fruit" (v. 8); mutual love
of Son for disciples as Father for Son (vv. 9–10) extends to mutual
love of disciples for one another (vv. 12–17). The hatred and
persecution by the world, by contrast, is analogous to and the result
of the hatred of the world for Jesus (15:18–16:4). That is because
he exposed the world's sin (15:22–25), just as now the Paraclete
through the disciples will go on "testifying" against the world
(15:26–16:2). The "agent" motif reappears in 15:23: "He who
hates me also hates my Father." The Paraclete will have a similar
"prophetic" or apostolic function, for "He will not speak ἀφ' ἑαυτοῦ
but what he hears he will speak" (16:13). Chap. 16:28 is a summary
of the "mission," to which the disciples respond, "See, now you are
speaking openly, not in riddles." Yet the limits of the relationship
between Jesus and the disciples, in contrast to the relationship
between Jesus and the Father, is underscored in the following verses.

The "prayer" of chap. 17 is a remarkable summation of the "apostolic" mission: see my "The Man from Heaven in Johannine Sectarianism," *Journal of Biblical Literature* 91 (1972), 66.

50. J. L. Martyn, "Source Criticism and Religionsgeschichte in the Fourth Gospel," in *Jesus and Man's Hope* (Pittsburgh: Pittsburgh Theological Seminary, 1970), I, 247–273.

4: Josephus as an Apologist to the Greco-Roman World: His Portrait of Solomon*

Louis H. Feldman

IN THE LATE SECOND CENTURY B.C.E., THE GREAT RHETORI-
cian Apollonius Molon, perhaps to be distinguished from
the teacher of Cicero and Caesar,[1] said of the Jews that
they are "the most witless of all barbarians, and are consequently the only people who have contributed no useful
invention to civilization" (*ap.* Josephus, *Contra Apionem*
2.148). In the following century Apion repeats the charge,
asserting that the Jews had failed to produce any geniuses,
inventors in arts or crafts or eminent sages (*ap. CA* 2.135–
136). Perhaps, to paraphrase Nietzsche, the Jews might
have produced saints, but it was for the Greeks to produce
sages.

To refute this charge, Josephus refers in his *Contra
Apionem* to his *Antiquities,* where, he says, the reader will
be able to discover for himself that the famous men
produced by the Jews "are entitled to rank with the
highest" (2.136). The *Antiquities* is, indeed, as we read in
the proem, directed not merely toward Greek-speaking
Jews but toward the entire Greek-speaking world (1.5).
That it is a non-Jewish audience he has in mind is apparent
from the fact that Josephus at the beginning seeks to
establish that there is a precedent for communicating information about Jewish history to non-Jews (1.9), and
that the Greeks had, indeed, been curious to learn about

Jewish history, as seen in the fact that Ptolemy Philadelphus had commissioned the translation of the Torah into Greek in the third century B.C.E. There are still today, asserts Josephus, many lovers of learning (φιλομαθεῖς) like the king (1.12). He notes that only the first five books of the Scriptures were translated for the king, whereas Josephus proclaims it his intention to make available to his audience all the scriptural books.

At first sight Josephus' portrayal of Solomon appears to have fewer divergences from the biblical text[2] than is the case with his depiction of other biblical characters, such as Abraham, Joseph, Moses, Samson, or Esther.[3] But here too he has hardly adhered to his promise to set forth the precise details of the biblical records, "neither adding nor omitting anything" (*AJ* 1.17).[4] Perhaps Josephus is taking for himself the same liberty that was assumed by the translators of the Torah into Greek, who, despite the injunction in Deut. 12:32, did make certain deliberate changes, which are approved of by the rabbis (Talmud, *Megillah* 9a), while Philo says that the Greek is a precise, indeed divinely inspired, translation of the original (*De Vita Mosis* 2.38).[5] And perhaps, when he says that he has translated (or interpreted, μεθηρμηνευμένην) his work from the Hebrew records, he means that his source is Jewish tradition generally and not merely the Bible. Some of this tradition had been committed to writing by Josephus' time, as we see from the Dead Sea *Genesis Apocryphon* and Pseudo-Philo's *Biblical Antiquities*, both dating probably from the first century C.E.

If we examine the portrait of Solomon that emerges in Josephus, we find that it is distinctly Hellenized, and that it is intended to appeal to the Hellenized Jew and educated Greek in his audience. He uses his paraphrase of Solomon to present certain apologetic motifs such as are found elsewhere in the *Antiquities* and especially in the *Contra Apionem*.[6]

In particular, there are indications that Josephus may have had the character of Oedipus in mind in adapting the biblical character of Solomon. Thackeray has contended, on the basis of a close study of Josephus' vocabulary and style, that books 15 and 16 of the *Antiquities* are the work of one of Josephus' Greek assistants who was especially steeped in Sophocles.[7] While most critics since then have for good reasons declined to accept this hypothesis,[8] there are many marks of Sophoclean style in these books, as well as in the other books of the *Antiquities.* We here suggest that it is not merely in vocabulary and style that the influence of Sophocles is to be felt, but also in the coloring of the character. Furthermore, Josephus consciously colors his narrative with Stoic phraseology to make it more intelligible and attractive to his readers.

Overall, Josephus heightens the importance of Solomon and endeavors to defend him and to raise his stature.[9] In Josephus, the place of Solomon is highlighted by G-d's prediction that after David's death the Temple would be brought into being "by his son, and successor to the kingdom, whose name would be Solomon" (*AJ* 7.93), although neither 2 Sam. 7:12 nor 1 Chron. 17:11 names Solomon there.

In 1 Chron. 22:11 it is David who prays that G—d may send his prosperity, while in Josephus the statement has greater force since David tells Solomon that G—d Himself has promised to bring prosperity to the country of the Hebrews during his reign (*AJ* 7.337).

In *AJ* 7.338, David's statement to Solomon that G—d chose Solomon to be king even before his birth, raises the stature of Solomon. 1 Chron. 22:9 reads merely that a son is to be born to David. Likewise the omission by Josephus of the name of David in his version of Solomon's prayer to G—d (cp. 1 Kings 3:6–7) serves to keep attention focused on Solomon (*AJ* 8.23). Similarly, the anointing of Solomon is more vividly colored in Josephus than in 1 Kings.[10]

Solomon's greatness is increased in Josephus' version by his stress on the fact, not mentioned in 1 Kings 2:12, that he was a mere youth upon ascending the throne (*AJ* 8.2; according to *AJ* 5.8, 211, he was fourteen upon accession

to the throne).[11] Josephus adds that despite this handicap
of youth, Solomon performed all his tasks with as great
scrupulousness (ἀκριβείας) as those of advanced age and
mature wisdom (AJ 8.21). The youth of Solomon is likewise stressed in Josephus' account of Solomon's judgment
in the case of the two women; in addition to what is said
in Scripture, after he orders the two children cut in half,
all the people secretly make fun of Solomon as a mere lad
(AJ 8.32).

Josephus makes effective use of G—d's prediction, even
before Solomon's birth, that David would have a son by
that name who would build the Temple (2 Sam. 7:12; 1
Chron. 17:11; AJ 7.93), repeating it at the time of the
dedication of the Temple (AJ 8.110). Solomon's stature is
further magnified by G—d's promise, after the completion
of the Temple, that He will, in Josephus' words, raise
Solomon "to a height and greatness of happiness beyond
measure" (AJ 8.126)—a promise that has no parallel in 1
Kings 9:4—5 or 1 Chron. 7:17—18.

The focus in Josephus' narrative is to an even greater
degree on Solomon than in the Bible. Thus, in G—d's
appearance to Solomon after the completion of the Temple, He warns him in 1 Kings 9:6 that "if ye [i.e., the
Jews] should turn away from following Me," He will cut
off Israel from the land which He has given them. In
Josephus' account, it is Solomon himself who is warned
that if he should prove to be faithless G—d will cut him off
root and branch (AJ 8.127).

The fact that Josephus assigns to Solomon a reign twice
as long as that given to him in both of the accounts of the
Bible (AJ 8.211; cp. 1 Kings 11:42 and 2 Chron. 9:30) and
in the Septuagint, adds to the stature of the king. He is
depicted as having reigned for eighty years, a period ex-
ceeded by no Greek, Roman, or Oriental sovereign,[12] and
as having lived to the age of ninety-four.[13]

Josephus praises the character of Solomon by a number
of touches not found in the biblical narrative. Thus,
whereas 1 Kings 1:52 does not mention Solomon's quali-

ties of mildness and moderation, Josephus does so, knowing that this was one of the four cardinal virtues of the Greeks and that *singularis moderatio* was particularly prominent in the emperor Tiberius, according to Velleius Paterculus (2.122.1). This mildness, shown in granting an amnesty to Adonijah, is stressed in Josephus' version of 1 Kings 1:53, for whereas the Bible reports that Solomon told Adonijah to go to his house, Josephus' version has Solomon bidding him to go to his own without any fear or suspicion (*AJ* 7.362).[14]

Solomon is portrayed by Josephus as distinguished particularly for his piety toward his parents.[15] 1 Kings 2:10 states merely that David was buried in the city of David, whereas Josephus adds that it was Solomon who arranged a splendid funeral and buried him with great abundance of wealth (*AJ* 7.392). Similarly, when his mother Bathsheba comes to him with Adonijah's request for Abishag, he is quoted in 1 Kings 2:20 as saying: "Ask on, my mother, for I will not deny thee." In *AJ* 8.8, however, he dilates on "the sacred duty to do everything for a mother," and chides her for not speaking in complete confidence of obtaining her request. In the list of virtues which David exhorts Solomon to cultivate in *AJ* 7.338, we find in fact, that he is urged to be pious, just, and brave. It is, in fact, the same virtues of piety, justice, and fortitude which, together with obedience, are set forth by G—d Himself to Samuel as the virtues which comprise beauty of soul and which He seeks in a king (*AJ* 6.160). In contrast, 1 Chron. 22:13 is more diffuse and hardly reduces to three such adjectives: "Then shalt thou prosper, if thou observe to do the statutes and the judgments which the L—rd charged Moses with, concerning Israel; be strong and of good courage; fear not, neither be dismayed." The first two of these epithets are repeated in a passage in Josephus which has no biblical parallel in 1 Kings 1:35, which it paraphrases. David, according to Josephus, gives instructions to Solomon that he rule with piety and justice over the Hebrew nation (*AJ* 7.356). Again, in an extra-biblical

extension of David's exhortation to Solomon in 1 Chron.
28:9, Solomon is urged to be pious and just (*AJ* 7.374).
And whereas David, in his dying charge to Solomon in 1
Kings 2:3 stresses piety alone, in Josephus' version there is
equal stress that he be just toward his subjects and pious
toward G—d (*AJ* 7.384). The attribute of piety is stressed
throughout Josephus' treatment of Solomon.[16]

Another quality of Solomon stressed by Josephus is his
sense of gratitude. 1 Kings 5:25 reports that in return for
Hiram of Tyre's gifts, Solomon gave Hiram 20,000 measures of wheat for food. Josephus prefaces this gift with
the statement that Solomon commended Hiram's zeal and
good will (*AJ* 8.57). Solomon's gratefulness is likewise
stressed in Josephus' paraphrase of Solomon's prayer at
the dedication of the Temple in 1 Kings 8:23—24, cp. *AJ*
8.112—113. In the Bible, Solomon says that there is no
G—d comparable to the G—d who has kept his promise to
David. In Josephus, Solomon renders thanks to G—d "first
for my father's sake whom Thou didst raise from obscurity
to such great glory, and next on my own behalf, for whom
unto the present day Thou hast done all that Thou didst
foretell."

Solomon is depicted as a man of faith in G—d. Whereas 1
Kings 8:15 speaks sweepingly of the fulfillment of G—d's
promises to David, Josephus has Solomon assert that some
of the prophecies had been fulfilled and that others would
likewise come to pass (*AJ* 8.109). He thus proceeds to
exhort the people not to despair of anything that G—d had
promised but, on the contrary, to have faith because of
what they had already seen (*AJ* 8.110).

Solomon's modesty is stressed in a passage cited by
Josephus from Menander's Greek translation of Tyrian
records stating that a certain young lad named Abdemonos
was always able to solve the problems submitted to him by
Solomon (*AJ* 8.146). Josephus even quotes the statement
of Dios, the historian of Phoenicia, that this Abdemon(os)
not only solved Solomon's riddles but himself proposed
riddles which Solomon was unable to solve and that on

account of this failure Solomon had to pay large sums to Hiram (*AJ* 8.149).[17]

1 Kings 10:13 notes that Solomon gave the Queen of Sheba all that she asked for in addition to gifts of his own, but in Josephus' account, Solomon's generosity is stressed still more by the statement that he showed his magnanimity by giving what she desired far more rapidly than he gave her the gifts of his own choice (*AJ* 8.175).[18]

In summarizing Solomon's character, Josephus remarks that he was the most illustrious of all kings, the most beloved by G–d, and more outstanding in wisdom and wealth than any of those who had ruled the Hebrews before him (*AJ* 8.190).

Still, Josephus realized that Solomon's vengeful slaying of Joab required apology. The only reason David himself did not do so, according to Josephus' addition to 1 Kings 2:5, was that Joab had hitherto been stronger and more powerful than David (*AJ* 7.386). It was out of envy, says Josephus in another addition to 1 Kings 2:5, that Joab killed Abner and Amasa, and this again helps to justify Solomon's action (*AJ* 7.386). It was Solomon's piety toward G–d, according to Josephus' addition, that led Joab to flee for refuge to an altar (1 Kings 2:28, cp. *AJ* 8.13). Lest Solomon be thought to have killed him in cold blood, Josephus remarks that he sent Beniah "with orders to remove him and bring him to the judgment hall to make his defense,"[19] contrary to 1 Kings 2:29 where Solomon gives orders to Beniah to "go fall upon him."

Similarly, Solomon's seemingly harsh action in punishing Shimei is more clearly justified in Josephus' version, for whereas 1 Kings 2:8 says merely that Shimei cursed David, Josephus reports that he did so repeatedly (*AJ* 7.388). Again, whereas 1 Kings 2:43 has Solomon ask simply why Shimei had not kept "the oath of the L–rd, and the commandment that I have charged thee with," Josephus builds up Solomon's defense by stressing that Shimei "had made light of his commands and—what was worse—had shown no regard for the oaths sworn to G–d"

(*AJ* 8.19). Further, Josephus has Solomon emphasize to
Shimei that he is punishing him so that he may know that
transgressors gain nothing through a postponement of their
punishments (*AJ* 8.20).

Although Solomon had earlier, in a Josephan addition
(*AJ* 7.362), shown mildness and moderation toward Adonijah, we later find him arranging to have him slain in an
apparently ruthless fashion. Josephus consequently feels
the need for an apology (*AJ* 8.3), though 1 Kings 2:13
does not, and this he does with his reminder that Adonijah
had even in David's lifetime attempted to seize the royal
power. In 1 Kings 2:15 Adonijah merely notes that the
kingdom had been taken from him and given to Solomon.
Josephus adds Adonijah's reaction, namely, that he was
"willing and happy to serve under him and was satisfied
with the present state of affairs" (*AJ* 8.4). Hence the
reader has less sympathy for Adonijah's request to change
the *status quo* by marrying David's widow Abishag. The
request would indeed appear to be outrageous were it not
for Josephus' addition to 1 Kings 2:17 which makes it
clear that David, by reason of his age, had not had intercourse with her and that she still remained a virgin (*AJ*
8.5). Josephus builds up to Solomon's seemingly harsh
action toward Adonijah by having Solomon note (a fact
not found in 1 Kings 2:22) that Adonijah had powerful
friends in Joab and Abiathar and implying therefore that
his marriage to David's widow could make him a real
threat to Solomon's rule (*AJ* 8.9).

The worst charge that could be made against Solomon
was that he worshipped foreign gods (*AJ* 8.192). Josephus
seeks, wherever possible to omit data on Solomon's contributions to such worship or to other direct violations of
Jewish law (Halachah). Although Theophilus, a first century B.C.E. Hellenistic Jewish historian,[20] mentions that
Solomon sent some gold to the Tyrian king out of which
the latter constructed the pedestal for a life-sized statue of
his daughter (*ap.* Eusebius, *Praeparatio Evangelica* 9.34),[21]
Josephus tones the story down. Mindful of the prohibition

against making images of human beings in Exod. 20:4, Josephus did not want to present Solomon as contributing to such a violation, and so, though he does mention a golden column[22] in the temple of Zeus (*AJ* 8.145) he does not indicate that it was Solomon who sent it.[23]

The rabbis are divided in their opinions as to Solomon's marriages;[24] but on the whole they berate him. For example, they record that after his wedding to Pharaoh's daughter he overslept the morning sacrifice the following day,[25] and that to please another of his foreign wives, he crushed five locusts in his hands in the name of Molech, whereupon he was deprived of the Divine Spirit and of his wisdom and strength.[26] Josephus, however, omits the reference in 1 Kings 11:7 to Solomon's building of high places for Chemosh the Moabite god, and for Molech, the Ammonite god, Solomon's grossest misdeeds in the worship of foreign deities. In place of these incidents, Josephus refers to a much slighter sin,[27] namely, of setting up images of bronze bulls in the Temple and lions in his palace (*AJ* 8.195).

Josephus is sympathetic to Solomon even after he has sinned in building altars to alien gods, for when G–d rebukes him for doing so, he shows contrition by feeling pain, in Josephus' report, and by being especially confounded at the thought "that almost all the good things for which he was envied were changing for the worse" (*AJ* 8.199).

Solomon's virtues appear all the greater when they are praised by others, particularly non-Jews. Hiram praises Solomon's wisdom in 1 Kings 5:21; in Josephus he praises him as a wise man endowed with every virtue (*AJ* 8.53).[28] The friendship of Hiram for Solomon is an important part of Josephus' defense of the Jewish people against anti-Semites such as Apion, who charged that the Jews lacked fame in antiquity. Indeed, in the *Contra Apionem* 1.109, Josephus is careful to record the fact that the Temple is mentioned in a source external to the Bible, namely, the records of the Tyrians. These chronicles likewise show, according to Josephus, that Hiram was a friend of Solomon and that he contributed a great deal toward the construction of the Temple (*CA* 2.19). To supply still further evidence for Hiram's relations with Solomon, Josephus twice cites Menander, who had translated the Tyrian records into Greek (*AJ* 8.114 and *CA* 1.116), as well as Dios, the author of a history of Phoenicia (*AJ* 8.147–149).[29]

The fact that the Queen of Sheba bestows even higher praise on Solomon in Josephus' account than she does in 1 Kings 10:7 adds to the picture of Solomon's magnificence (*AJ* 8.170). Josephus tells us that she admired beyond measure what she saw "and was not able to contain her amazement." Furthermore, Josephus' account exaggerates Solomon's prosperity, for the Queen remarks that the reports about Solomon failed to convey the dignity of his state to its full extent (*AJ* 8.172; cp. 1 Kings 10:7). She says that she could not believe what she had heard because of its multitude and greatness, but that now she has witnessed things far greater than these. In an effort to present Solomon and the Queen as rulers of equal importance, Josephus reduces the gift of gold that the Queen gives Solomon from 120 talents (1 Kings 10:10; 2 Chron. 9:9) to 20 talents (*AJ* 8.174) in order that it not seem a tribute.

Since the Jews in antiquity[30] were often accused of hatred of humanity, *odium generis humani,* as Tacitus puts it (*Histories* 5.4), Josephus is constantly concerned to answer this charge (e.g., *CA* 2.209–210). In connection with Apion's statement that the Jews "swear by the G–d who made heaven and earth and sea to show no goodwill to a single alien, above all to Greeks" (*ap. CA* 2.121), Josephus not only repeats Solomon's prayer to G–d that He listen to non-Jews when they come to pray in His temple, but he adds his hope that G–d will do so in order to prove that Jews are "not inhumane by nature nor unfriendly to those who are not of our country but wish that all men equally should receive aid from Thee and enjoy Thy blessings" (*AJ* 8.117).

Inasmuch as Apollonius Molo (*ap. CA* 2.148) and Apion (*ap. CA* 2.135) had accused the Jews of failing to make any useful contribution in the arts and sciences, Josephus stresses the greatness of the Temple, which had been acknowledged even by Polybius (*ap. AJ* 12.136) and which was Solomon's supreme achievement. Whereas 1 Chron. 22:14 ff. enumerates what David had prepared for Solomon, Josephus leads up to Solomon's great achievement by having David reassure Solomon: "Do not be dismayed at the magnitude of the labor, nor shrink from it" (*AJ* 7.339). According to both the Hebrew text and the Septuagint of 1 Chron. 22:14, David had already prepared no less than a hundred thousand talents of gold and a million talents of silver. These are huge sums, and would have made David a wealthier king than Solomon, for the latter, according to 1 Kings 10:14, received in one year only 666 talents of gold and would have required 150 years to accumulate an equivalent sum. Josephus modifies the mention of this apparently fantastic sum, and in the process accomplishes his purpose of diminishing David's role and magnifying Solomon's in the building of the Temple by changing the figures to ten thousand talents of gold and one hundred thousand talents of silver (*AJ* 7.340). Similarly, whereas 1 Chron. 29:3–4 reports that David gave an additional gift of three thousand talents of gold and seven thousand talents of refined silver, Josephus omits the mention of the silver (*AJ* 7.378).

Josephus adds to the elaborate description of the Temple in the Bible a number of details calculated to enhance Solomon's prestige. Whereas 1 Kings 6:2 ff. contents itself with giving the dimensions of the Temple, Josephus adds that the foundations of the Temple consisted of strong stones capable of resisting the wear of time, and he refers to its massive height, graceful beauty, and magnificence (*AJ* 8.63). Relying perhaps on his recollections of the

Temple that Herod built, he adds that it was built up to
the roof of white marble; he doubles the height of the
lower story, and states that it had a second story, details
not found in 2 Chron. 3:4 (cp. *AJ* 8.64). Again, whereas
Kings 6:5 says that Solomon made side chambers round
about, Josephus gives the actual number, and exact dimensions of each chamber (*AJ* 8.65–66), perhaps on the basis
of the passage in Ezek. 40:17, which speaks of thirty
chambers in Ezekiel's version of the Temple. In general,
Josephus emphasizes the sheer size of items in the Temple;
thus he explains that the bronze sea in 1 Kings 7:23 was so
called because of its size (*AJ* 8.79). He likewise exaggerates
numbers by remarking that Solomon set up a great number
of tables in the Temple, whereas 1 Kings 7:48 mentions
only one table, and even 2 Chron. 4:8 mentions only ten
(*AJ* 8.89). Again, whereas the Bible leaves the number of
vessels in the Temple unclear and simply asserts that they
were exceedingly many, (so 1 Kings 7:47), Josephus records precise numbers, stating that there were 20,000 of
gold and 40,000 of silver (*AJ* 8.89). Both the Hebrew text
and the Septuagint of 1 Kings 7:49 state that there were
ten candlesticks in the Sanctuary; Josephus has expanded
this to no less than 10,000 lampstands (*AJ* 8.90). Similarly, in other places, Josephus' precise numbers for items,
such as the 80,000 pitchers, 100,000 golden bowls,
200,000 silver bowls (*AJ* 8.91 ff.) are his own invention,
not paralleled in 1 Kings 7:50, but based perhaps on
traditions available to him as one of the leading priests.[31]

Josephus likewise adds to 1 Kings 6:22 in describing the
dazzling effect of the Temple created by the radiance of
gold which met the visitor on every side (*AJ* 8.68). He also
praises the workmanship of the Temple by remarking that
one would marvel to see how cunningly the drums of the
wheels of the lavers were fitted into the rims (*AJ* 8.83). In
an unscriptural summary of his description of the vessels in
the Temple, Josephus states that Solomon made all these
things at much expense and with great magnificence to the
honor of G–d, sparing no cost and acting with utmost

munificence (*AJ* 8.95). In describing the Temple courts, Josephus adds to 1 Kings 7:51 the statement that the third court was so wonderful as to be beyond all words and even, so to speak, beyond all sight, since he filled up with earth great valleys into which one could not look without difficulty since they were of such great depth (*AJ* 8.97). He likewise adds details concerning the arrangement of the furniture in the Temple (*AJ* 8.104–105). Josephus particularly praises the naturalism in the art work of the Temple. Thus he adds to the account in 1 Kings 7:36 the statement that the animals on which the laver rested were so well fitted together "that to one looking at them they seemed to be one natural growth" (*AJ* 8.84).

Josephus emphasizes the fact that the Temple, despite its magnitude, was completed in a very short time (*AJ* 8.99), whereas 1 Kings 7:38 merely notes that it took Solomon seven years to build it. Josephus remarks, in addition, that Solomon made such a display both of wealth and of zeal that any viewer would have thought that the work could not have been completed in the whole course of time.

The ceremony at the dedication of the Temple is considerably enhanced by Josephus' additions, and thus reflects still greater glory on Solomon. Whereas 1 Kings 8:5 speaks of the sacrifices performed then, Josephus also adds that the ground was drenched with libations and that so vast a quantity of incense was burned that its sweetness penetrated even to people who were at a great distance (*AJ* 8.101–102). Not only was there singing, as described in 2 Chron. 5:12–13, but Josephus adds dancing as well, and notes that the people did not weary of this singing or dancing until they had reached the Temple (*AJ* 8.102).[32]

Although rabbinic agada tells of help from spirits and angel servants,[33] Josephus does not mention this aspect, as is his custom with reference to the supernatural. He does, however, remark that G–d approved of and assisted in the work, as a way of adding to the stature of Solomon's achievement (*AJ* 8.130).

By deferring the account of the building of Solomon's palace until after the completion of his description of the dedication of the Temple,[34] Josephus tends to stress the importance of the Temple and to diminish that of the palace.[35] Indeed, seeking to emphasize Solomon's piety in devoting greater attention to G–d's house than to his own, Josephus says explicitly that the palace was much inferior in dignity to the Temple and took longer to complete[36] because the materials had not been prepared so long in advance nor at the same expense and because it was intended as a dwelling place for a king and not for G–d (*AJ* 8.131). Yet, adds Josephus, it was worthy of note and was in accordance with the prosperity of the land and of its king (*AJ* 8.132). Although 1 Kings 7:2–5 simply gives the dimensions of the palace, Josephus describes the great and beautiful judgment hall (*AJ* 8.134), the chambers for eating and resting (*AJ* 8.134), the hall for feasts. He describes the materials used for building, and the painting and decorations, as well as as their variety. Josephus likewise notes the admiration of the Queen of Sheba for the palace (*AJ* 8.168).

Josephus also adds to Solomon's stature by noting that in addition to those cities mentioned in 1 Kings 9:17–19, Solomon built still others for enjoyment and pleasure, which enjoyed a mild climate and produced fruits in irrigated lands (*AJ* 8.153).

It is interesting that, aside from a brief mention—in accordance with the Bible—of Solomon's conquest of those Canaanites who were still unsubmissive (*AJ* 8.160), Josephus has nothing to say of Solomon the conqueror except in the treatise *Contra Apionem,* where he is answering Apion's argument that proof of the injustice of the Jewish laws is to be seen in the fact that they are not masters of an empire (*CA* 2.125). In his reply Josephus contrasts the Egyptian kings, who suffered many disasters, with David and Solomon, who subjugated many nations (*CA* 2.132). He further proudly states that Solomon governed his kingdom in perfect peace (*AJ* 8.21).

As was mentioned earlier, Josephus appears to have

modeled Solomon's character on Oedipus. Support for the
equation of Solomon and Oedipus appears at the very
beginning of Josephus' account of Solomon. In 2 Sam.
7:14, G–d warns Nathan that if Solomon should sin, He
will punish him "with the rod of men and with the stripes
of the children of men." In Josephus' narrative G–d says
that He will punish Solomon with sickness and barrenness
of the soil if he should sin (*AJ* 7.93). It is true that the
nature of the threatened punishment may have come to
Josephus through the Bible itself, notably the curses enu-
merated in Deut. 28:15–68, but when viewed in conjunc-
tion with other Sophoclean elements in Josephus' narrative, the analogy with the opening scene of Sophocles'
Oedipus Tyrannus is more striking. In *AJ* 2.191, another
passage reminiscent of Thucydides (2.61), he notes the
effect of famine in the days of Joseph on the minds of the
Egyptians in that it drove them to degrading means of
subsistence. Again, in Solomon's prayer at the dedication
of the Temple, he speaks in 1 Kings 8:33 of the time when
"Thy people Israel are smitten down before the enemy,
when they do sin against Thee." Josephus specifies, as the
evils by which the Jews will be smitten "unfruitfulness of
the soil or a destructive pestilence" (*AJ* 8.115; cf. 7.93
cited above). This picture is reminiscent of the plague from
which Thebes is wasting away at the beginning of Sophocles' *Oedipus Tyrannus* (25–29). The plague has afflicted
the blossom of the land and its herds, and it is manifest in
the barren pangs of women. The word νόσος used by
Josephus in *AJ* 7.93, is a leitmotif throughout the play.
Apollo is appealed to as a deliverer from the sickness
which has afflicted the city (*O.T.*, 150). The word likewise
occurs in lines 217 and 303 with reference to the plague.
Its central place in the play is shown by the fact that when
the messenger comes to Oedipus with the news of the
death of King Polybus, his first reaction (960) is to ask
whether he died through treachery or disease. Two lines
later he repeats: "Ah, he died, it seems of disease?" (962).
A major theme of the play, as Knox remarks,[37] is Oedipus' περιπέτεια from fame and honor to utter uncleanli-

ness, so that we find him at last a pollution that must be
covered up (1426). And at the end of the play the thought
of disease (by implication, the plague) recurs, when Oedipus, blind and miserable though he is, asserts that neither
disease nor anything else can destroy him (1455). One is
reminded likewise of the picture drawn by Hesiod in
Works and Days of nature responding to man's sins, where
the guilt of a single man can bring failure of harvests,
pestilence, and miscarriages (213ff.).

When Josephus summarizes Solomon's character, he
singles out his good fortune, wealth, and wisdom as the
respects in which he surpassed all other kings (*AJ* 8.211).
Hiram congratulates Solomon on his present good fortune
(*AJ* 8.50) when Solomon is anointed as king. The theme of
good and bad fortune is, of course, a commonplace in
literature generally, but it is perhaps more distinctive of
Sophocles' Oedipus because of the ironic element than it is
of any other ancient literary character. Thus, when Oedipus is one step from knowing the terrible truth about his
identity, he reaches the highest point of hope and confidence and proclaims (most ironically from the point of
view of the audience), "I hold myself the son of Fortune,
that gives good" (*O.T.* 1080–1081). The chorus exclaims
after Oedipus discovers his identity, "Where, where is the
mortal who wins more of good fortune than just the
seeming?" (*O.T.* 1189–1191).

Josephus exaggerates Solomon's wealth in a number of
places. Thus, while 1 Kings 5:3 declares that his provisions
for a single day were a hundred sheep, *AJ* 8.40 states this
as a hundred fatted lambs. Similarly, Oedipus is presented
as a wealthy king, and part of the effectiveness of the play
is the great irony in Tiresias' statement that the man whom
Oedipus is seeking (namely, Oedipus himself, as it turns
out) as the murderer of Laius is in reality a blind man,
though he now has sight, and a beggar, though he now has
riches (*O.T.* 455).[38] Of course, wealth is hardly a trait
restricted to Solomon and Oedipus, but in the context of
all other parallels, it acquires added significance.

In Josephus' account of 1 Chron. 29:19, David's prayer is that Solomon may be given a sound (ὑγιῆ) and just *mind* (διάνοιαν, *AJ* 7.381; cp. Hebrew *levav*, Greek καρδίαν: heart). And again, in contrast to Solomon's own request in 1 Kings 3:9 for an understanding heart (*lev*), Josephus' Solomon requests a sound mind (νοῦν ὑγιῆ) and good practical wisdom (φρόνησιν ἀγαθήν, *AJ* 8.23). One of the outstanding characteristics of Oedipus, as Knox has so well illustrated, is the use of intelligence.[39] Just as Solomon gains a great reputation through the ingenuity he shows in solving riddles, so Oedipus gained his through solving the riddle of the Sphinx by his intelligence (γνώμη, *O.T.* 398). Oedipus remarks in 396–398 that he used only his intelligence, unlike Tiresias, who might have used the birds to find his information. Again, the intellectual rivalry between Oedipus and Tiresias culminates in Oedipus' taunting Tiresias with failure of his νοῦς: "You are blind in ears and mind and eyes" (*O.T.* 371). As Knox, following a suggestion of Jebb, has remarked in a pregnant note,[40] the first part of the very name of Oedipus is close in sound to, and thus reminiscent of, οἶδα, "to know," a word that is constantly on Oedipus' lips. Indeed, as Knox continues, it is his knowledge that makes Oedipus the decisive and confident τύραννος.[41] Similarly, Josephus remarks of Solomon, "It was not gold or silver or other form of wealth that he asked to be bestowed upon him, as a man and a young one might have done—such are considered by most men as almost the only things worthy of regard and as gifts of G–d," but wisdom that he chose (*AJ* 8.23; cf. 1 Kings 3:6, 11).

The primary example of Solomon's wisdom, cited in 1 Kings 3:16–28, is his adjudication of the case of the two harlots. In an addition to 1 Kings 3:16, Josephus stresses the difficulty of the case and notes that it was troublesome to find a solution, adding "I have thought it necessary to explain the matter about which the suit happened to be, in order that my readers may have an idea of how difficult the case was"(*AJ* 8.26). He is presenting the case, con-

tinues Josephus, as a lesson in sagacity for his readers, so
that if a similar situation occurs, his readers may be able to
give a ready solution (*AJ* 8.26).[42]

To magnify Solomon's wisdom by increasing the difficulty of the problem, Josephus, unlike 1 Kings 3:18,
asserts that it was in the same room, on the same day, and
at the very same hour[43] that the two women gave birth to
their respective sons, whereas 1 Kings states the second
woman gave birth in the same house to her child on the
third day after the first. The tale is dramatized further by
Josephus, for whereas 1 Kings 3:18 states in a factual way
that there was no one but the two women in the house at
the time, in Josephus' version one of the women bitterly
complains that the other "contemptuously relying on the
fact that we were alone and that she had no one to fear
who can convict her . . . stubbornly persists in her denial"
(*AJ* 8.29). Likewise, 1 Kings gives no indication that
Solomon waited for others to resolve the case, but Josephus exaggerates Solomon's wisdom by asserting that
when all others had failed to give a judgment but were
mentally blinded as by a riddle, Solomon alone was able to
devise a plan to determine the true mother (*AJ* 8.30). Now
it is true that wisdom is a common trait for heroes to
possess, but it is this striking addition which makes the
story parallel to that of Oedipus, who likewise succeeded
after all others had failed to solve the Sphinx's riddle and
who, though mentally alert at that time, is blind to his own
identity and at the end of the play puts out his own eyes.

Again, there is added drama when, after Solomon orders
the children cut in half,[44] all the people secretly make fun
of the king as a mere boy, an incident not recorded in 1
Kings 3:25 (cp. *AJ* 8.32). Finally, Josephus expands the
statement in 1 Kings 3:28 of the impression made by the
case upon Solomon's subjects; in Josephus' narrative they
regard the judgment as a great sign and proof of Solomon's
prudence and wisdom (*AJ* 8.34). It is interesting to note
that while the Midrash[45] elaborates on the wisdom shown
by Solomon in this judgment, it emphasizes G–d's role in

bringing on the case and the heavenly voice ratifying the verdict, whereas in Josephus the focus of attention is on Solomon and on his human wisdom. Moreover, in the Midrash the litigants are said to have been not women but spirits; in Josephus the women are more human than ever, and the drama is consequently heightened. Moreover, in the midrashic literature, Solomon emerges as a prototype of the talmudic sage, for he is able to analyze the laws revealed to Moses and to give reasons for the commandments. It is Solomon's great mastery of the Torah that is praised,[46] unlike Josephus, who shows Solomon's wisdom as a king and judge.

Solomon's wisdom is further exaggerated by Josephus' expansion of the 3,000 proverbs and the 1,005 songs that he composed to 3,000 *books* of parables and similitudes and 1,005[47] *books* of odes (*AJ* 8.44).

In particular, appealing to his educated Greek audience, trained in philosophy, Josephus stresses philosophical study of nature (*AJ* 8.44). According to Josephus' addition to 1 Kings 5:13, there was no form of nature with which Solomon was not acquainted or which he passed over without examination (*AJ* 8.44). It is this knowledge of the world of nature that had been stressed by Josephus' predecessor who had composed the Book of Wisdom and who had put into the mouth of his alleged author Solomon the statement that G—d had given him "an unerring knowledge of the things that be, to know the ordering of the world and the working of the elements," (presumably the four elements basic to Greek philosophy).

In view of the popularity of charms and amulets, as indicated in the magical papyri, it is not surprising that Josephus emphasizes this aspect of Solomon's wisdom (cf. *AJ* 8.45). Conybeare conjectures that the *Testament of the Twelve Patriarchs* in its original form may have been the very collection of incantations which, according to Josephus, was composed by Solomon.[48] But, on the whole, Josephus emphasizes the human wisdom of Solomon.

Josephus elaborates considerably on the account in 1

Kings 9–10 of Solomon's wisdom. He notes that Hiram,
the king of Tyre, sent Solomon tricky problems and enig-
matic sayings, requesting to be relieved of his difficulties.
Because Solomon was clever and keen-witted, he solved
them all through the force of reason, and discovering their
meaning, he brought them to light (*AJ* 8.143). Their
passion for learning is, indeed, said to have been the main
bond of friendship between Hiram and Solomon (*CA*
1.111).

Solomon's wisdom is considerably magnified in Josephus' retelling of Solomon's meeting with the Queen of
Sheba. Josephus avoids emphasizing the magical element,
such as the tale in the Midrash's account[49] of the hoopoe
who reported to King Solomon (who understood the lan-
guages of birds and beasts) that there existed a land ruled
by the Queen of Sheba which was not yet subject to him.
Instead we read in what Ullendorff calls Josephus' "smart-
ened up" version of the biblical story,[50] that the Queen of
Sheba, who ruled over Egypt and Ethiopia, and who was
thoroughly trained in wisdom and worthy of wonder in
other respects, conceived a strong desire to meet Solomon
because she had heard reports about his excellence and
understanding every day (*AJ* 8.165). Josephus expands the
account in 1 Kings 10:3 of how Solomon answered all her
questions (*AJ* 8.167) and wins her admiration by mentally
grasping with ease the ingenious problems which she set
before him and by solving them more quickly than anyone
could have expected. In a further build-up of Solomon's
wisdom, Josephus says that it was because kings everywhere could not believe that what was told about Solomon's virtue and wisdom was accurate because of its
extravagance, they desired to see him with their own eyes
(1 Kings 10:24, *AJ* 8.182).

The speed with which the wise man works is a commonplace, but it is particularly important to the effectiveness
of Sophocles' Oedipus. As Knox has noted, the characteristic action of Oedipus is the *fait accompli*;[51] the characteristic word used to describe him in the play is ταχύς,

"swift"; even after his identity is revealed it is still characteristic of Oedipus, as we see in such statements of his as "Take me away from this place as quickly as possible" (ὄτι τάχιστα, 1340); "hide me away as quickly as possible" (ὄπως τάχιστα, 1410), and "throw me out of this land as quickly as may be" (ὄσον τάχισϑ᾽, 1430).[52] Indeed, one of the themes of the play is the danger of speed; for those who, like Oedipus, are quick to think things out are not infallible (*O.T.* 617). Knox has rightly remarked that the swift action of Oedipus is founded on reflection, which, in turn, is the working of a great intelligence.[53] Again, as Knox has remarked, the bitterest word of condemnation which Oedipus can hurl at both Creon and Tiresias is "stupid" (540 and 933).[54]

Beyond the seeming parallels between Oedipus and Solomon, Josephus has Hellenized his portrait of Solomon in yet other ways. Thus, whereas in 1 Chron. 22:9, G–d promises David that He will give Solomon "rest from all his enemies round about," in Josephus this promise is put in terms familiar to the student of Thucydides (2.65, 4.7), Xenophon (*Mem.* 4.4.11, 4.6.14), and Lysias (25.26, 30.13), namely, peace and freedom from war and civil dissension (*AJ* 7.337). Adonijah's request in 1 Kings 1:51 that Solomon swear that he will not slay him is Hellenized by Josephus, so that Solomon is asked to pledge to bear him no malice (*AJ* 7.361). This phrase, meaning not to remember past injuries, to pass an act of amnesty, is used by Thucydides, one of Josephus' favorite authors,[55] in his description of the Megarians, who recall their exiles, first binding them by the most solemn oaths to bear no malice (4.74).

Thackeray[56] has noted the Homeric echo in Josephus' addition to the prayer in 1 Kings 2:12 for Solomon at the beginning of his reign (*AJ* 8.2). In Josephus' version, the people pray that his affairs end well (καλῶς) and that he may complete his reign at a sleek (λιπαρόν) and utterly happy (πανεύδαιμον) old age (γῆρας).[57] This is highly reminiscent of the famous scene in the Odyssey in which

Tiresias foretells to Odysseus that his death will come from
the sea, "a death so gentle that shall lay thee low when
thou art overcome with sleek old age" (γήραι ὕπο λιπαρῷ
ἀρημένον, 11.134–136). The same words are found when
Odysseus repeats Tiresias' prediction to Penelope: "And
death shall come to me myself from the sea, a death so
gentle that shall lay me low, when I am overcome with
sleek old age" (γήρ᾽ ὕπο λιπαρῷ ἀρημένον, Odyssey
23.283).

Since much of Josephus' projected audience was sympathetic to Stoicism, it is not surprising that there are a
number of Stoic touches in his narrative. The incense
which, according to Josephus' addition to the biblical
narrative, was burned at the dedication of the Temple, was
a sign of G–d's presence in His newly consecrated home
(AJ 8.102).[58] Norden remarks that the phrase used by
Josephus in Solomon's dedicatory prayer for the Temple,
that G–d was now present and not far removed (AJ
8.108), shows Stoic influence.[59] Similarly in Josephus'
version of Solomon's prayer at the dedication of the Temple, he asks that if the Jews should in the future gather in
the Temple praying to be saved, G–d should listen to them
as though He were within (AJ 8.115). Again, whereas 2
Chron. 7:3 reports that when the fire from heaven consumed the sacrifice at the dedication, the people bowed
down at the sight and gave thanks to G–d, Josephus adds
that the people interpreted the divine manifestation[60] as a
sign that G–d would thereafter dwell in His temple and
consequently fell to the ground and prayed (AJ 8.119).
Finally, in dedicating the sanctuary at Bethel, King Jero-
boam uses Stoic terminology in telling his people that
every place has G–d in it, that there is no place set apart
for Him, but He hears and watches over His worshippers
everywhere (AJ 8.227). Likewise, as Norden remarks, [61]
the phrase that G–d sees all things and hears all things
(πάντ᾽ ἐφορᾶν καὶ πάντ᾽ ἀκούειν, AJ 8.108) is reminiscent of
Homer, Iliad 3.277, ἠέλλος θ᾽, ὅς πάντ᾽ ἐφορᾷς καὶ πάντ᾽

ἐπακούεις, a verse cited and explained by the Stoic Heraclitus (*Quaest.Hom.* 23).[62]

The Stoics, who, as Norden remarks,[63] were so fond of calling their wise men in need of naught (ἀπροσδεή) and self-sufficient (αὐτάρκη),[64] predicated these qualities also for G—d (cf. Chrysippus, *ap.* Plutarch, *De Stoic. Rep.* 39.1052 D; Plutarch, *Comp. Arist. et Cat.* 4).[65] Josephus also uses the word as an attribute of G—d, for he has Solomon say in his prayer at the dedication that the Deity stands in need of nothing (ἀπροσδεὲς γὰρ τὸ θεῖον ἀπάντων) and hence does not require gratitude (*AJ* 8.111).

One finds Stoic overtones also in the non-biblical addition in Solomon's prayer when he says that there is no more fitting way to appease G—d than through the voice (φωνῇ) "which we have from the air (ἐξ ἀέρος) and know to ascend again through this element" (*AJ* 8.111–112). Zeno (*SVF* 1.21, the founder of Stoicism, and Chrysippus (*SVF* 243), his follower, define sound (φωνή) as smitten air or a smiting of the air (ἀὴρ πεπληγμένος, πληγὴ ἀέρος).[66]

The terminology which Josephus adopts, even in religious matters, is calculated to be intelligible to his pagan Greek readers. Thus in Solomon's prayer he says that he has built the Temple to G—d's name so that when sacrificing and seeking good omens the Jews may pray to Him (*AJ* 8.108). The word used for obtaining good omens (καλλιεροῦντες) is, as Schorr in his commentary has noted, completely strange to Judaism, since it is the pagan practice of obtaining favorable signs in a sacrifice.[67]

In general, Josephus attempts to tone down the miraculous and supernatural element in his narrative, since he apparently thought that such details might appear incredible to the Greek reader. Thus, whereas 1 Kings 8:10 states with emphatic simplicity that "the cloud filled the house of the L—rd," Josephus gives a more precise and rationalized description of the cloud in *AJ* 8.106. It was not, he says, like a swollen rain-cloud but diffused and temperate.

Josephus carefully avoids categorically equating the cloud with G—d but noted instead that it produced in the minds of the people an impression and belief that G—d had taken up residence in the Temple (*AJ* 8.106). The Midrash remarks that at the dedication of the Temple a heavenly voice was heard to proclaim: "You all shall have a share in the world to come,"[68] but Josephus avoids such an account of supernatural intervention.

N.G. Cohen, in a suggestive article, argues that Josephus takes considerably greater liberty with his biblical material in the part of the *Antiquities* which parallels the five books of Moses than he does in the later books.[69] Perhaps this is so because the midrashic traditions for these books were more highly developed, since these were the portions of the Bible that were constantly read and expounded in the synagogue from week to week. But the present study of Solomon shows that Josephus, here as elsewhere, in his eagerness to appeal to his Greek-speaking and Greek-educated audience, made very considerable changes in his version. These modifications are, in fact, generally paralleled by modifications found elsewhere in his Midrash-like paraphrase of the Bible.

NOTES

*Condensed from the lecture delivered by Dr. Louis H. Feldman as part of the *Apologetics and Mission in Early Christianity and Judaism* seminar at the University of Notre Dame, Indiana by Barbara Cullom Bondi.

1. See R.J.H. Shutt, *Studies in Josephus* (London: SPCK, 1961), p. 48.

2. A. Rahlfs, *Luzians Rezension des Königsbücher* (Septuaginta Studien 3; Göttingen: Vandenhoeck and Ruprecht, 1911), p. 92, notes that for the story of Solomon Josephus follows the Massoretic text even though it deviates strongly from the Septuagint.

3. On Josephus' reworking of the biblical narrative see my essays "Hellenizations in Josephus' Account of Man's Decline," in *Religions in Antiquity* ed. J. Neusner, (Studies in the History of Religions

14; Leiden: E. J. Brill, 1968), pp. 336–353; "Abraham the Greek Philosopher in Josephus," *Transactions of the American Philological Association* 99 (1968), 143–156; and "Hellenizations in Josephus' Version of Esther," *Transactions of the American Philological Association* 101 (1970), 143–170.

4. Dionysius of Halicarnassus, whose *Roman Antiquities* parallel Josephus' *Jewish Antiquities* in title and number of books, and often in motifs, similarly warns (*Thucy.* 5) that the historian should not add or subtract from his sources. But we should not suppose that Josephus derived his statement from Dionysius, since the Bible itself (Deut. 12:32) has a similar statement: "Everything that I command you you shall be careful to do; you shall not add to it or take from it." *The Letter of Aristeas* (311) notes that after the completion of the translation of the Torah into Greek, it was regarded as so perfect that a curse was pronounced upon anyone who would change the text by adding or omitting anything. In view of the many divergences in existing manuscripts of the Septuagint, this injunction was apparently not taken literally. For a further discussion of the meaning of Josephus' phrase "neither adding nor omitting anything" and for the rabbinic parallels to Josephus' omissions, see L. H. Feldman, "Hellenizations in Josephus' Account of Man's Decline" (above, n. 3), pp. 336–339.

5. Philo here says that the translation corresponds literally with the Chaldean (Χαλδαϊκοῖς), which usually means Aramaic, and if so, this would seem to indicate that the translation, as Azariah dei Rossi had already indicated in the sixteenth century, was made from an Aramaic Targum rather than from the Hebrew original.

6. While it is true that W. Sarowy, *Quellenkritische Untersuchungen zur Geschichte König Salmos* (Königsberg: Druck von K. Leupold, 1900), pp. 44–48, does summarize the high points of Josephus' account, noting where it differs from the Bible, he does not do so systematically and he makes no attempt to evaluate the Hellenizations in Josephus' portrait.

7. H. St. J. Thackeray, *Josephus the Man and the Historian* (New York: Ktav Publishing House, 1929, reprinted 1967), pp. 116–117.

8. Shutt, pp. 64–66; L. H. Feldman, *Scholarship on Philo and Josephus 1937–1962* (New York: Yeshiva University, 1963), pp. 53–54; and L. H. Feldman, review of the reprint of Thackeray's *Josephus the Man and the Historian* in the *Journal of the American Oriental Society* 90 (1970), 545–546.

9. In general, the rabbinic tradition offered sharply contradictory

opinions about the character of Solomon. So R. Faerber, *König Salmon in der Tradition* (Vienna: Schlessinger, 1901), p. 1.

10. See *AJ* 7.358, 359 for extra-biblical details.

11. Seder Olam Rabbah, cited by Faerber, pp. 42 ff., says that Solomon was twelve at the start of his reign.

12. Agathonius of Gades, according to Cicero, *De Senectute* 19, reigned for 80 years and lived for 120.

13. S. Rappaport, *Agada und Exegese bei Flavius Josephus* (Vienna: J. Kauffmann, 1930), p. 58, n. 239, suggests that Josephus based his figure on 1 Kings 11:4, which speaks merely of Solomon's old age, but no extant source gives a figure as high as that of Josephus.

14. Josephus also stresses the moderation of Gideon (*AJ* 5.230), the appeal to sobriety of Phineas (5.109), and Moses' attempt to teach sobriety (4.49 and 4.189). Josephus also introduces an extra-biblical remark about Moses' forgiving nature (4.188). Abigail likewise appeals to David's mildness and humanity (6.304). Josephus stresses the Jewish mercy in general towards enemies (6.290), David's mercy towards Saul (6.284), in particular, David's mildness and humanity (7.391), David's forgiving nature (7.235) and David's gentleness (7.43). Josephus stresses the humanity (ἀνθρώπινον) and compassion (ἐλεεινόν) of the Jewish kings Jehoram and Jehoshaphat toward the king of Moab when they beheld him sacrificing his eldest son. Josephus emphasizes the very mild disposition of the third messenger sent by King Ahiziah to fetch Elijah.

15. Josephus likewise introduces the theme of *pietas* toward a parent in Judah's appeal to Joseph (*AJ* 2.152). Of course, the emphasis on *pietas* is not restricted to Virgil's portrait of Aeneas, but it is most notable there, and Josephus, or his assistant, as Thackeray, *Josephus the Man*, has noted, has clear reminiscences of the *Aeneid*.

16. E.g. *AJ* 8.25

17. Josephus also introduces the theme of humility in noting that Moses dressed like an ordinary person (*AJ* 3.212). Just as Solomon is generous in acknowledging the wisdom of the Tyrian youth Abdemon, so Moses gives Balaam credit for his prophecies instead of appropriating them as his own (*AJ* 4.157–158). Josephus likewise expands on the modesty of Saul (*AJ* 6.51,63), and the humility of Samson (*AJ* 5.302) after he has been seized by a mighty thirst.

18. Josephus repeatedly deals with the themes of generosity and

thankfulness: in the Joseph story (*AJ* 2.140–142, 153, 157, 162, 191, 195, 197, etc.); Moses (*AJ* 3.59; 4.315 etc.); David (*AJ* 6.317, 323; 7.69, 111, 160, 235, 272, 273, 274) and Jewish opposition to selfishness (*AJ* 4.238) and generosity in the case of the vintagers (4.235–236) and numerous other cases.

19. So also in rabbinic tradition, Joab has a long trial before Solomon has him put to death. See L. Ginzberg, *Legends of the Jews*, IV (Philadelphia: Jewish Publication Society of America, 1913), 126.

20. Theophilus is probably identical with the historian mentioned in *Contra Apionem* 1.216.

21. See Sarowy, pp. 54–55.

22. Perhaps this is identical with the golden column in the temple of Hercules at Tyre mentioned by Herodotus 2.44.

23. So Eupolemus. See Sarowy, pp. 53–54.

24. See Ginzberg, VI, 281–282, n. 16, and 294–295, n. 59.

25. Ibid., IV, 128–129.

26. Ibid., 153–154.

27. Marcus notes, Loeb Classical Library, *ad. loc.,* that this was no sin according to either Scripture or rabbinic tradition. So Ginzberg, VI, 280, n. 12. Cf. however, Josephus' *Bellum Judaicum* 1.648–650, where a similar act committed by Herod, namely, the setting up of a golden eagle over the gate of the Temple is condemned by the rabbis.

28. With regard to Hiram, Josephus states clearly that he has given the correspondence of Hiram and Solomon in detail (*BJ* 1.9, 16) in faithfulness to critical inquiry (ἐξέτασιν). So close was the friendship between Solomon and Hiram, Josephus notes in an extrabiblical detail, that they swore it should continue forever (*AJ* 8.57–58).

29. On Menander and Dios see Sarowy pp. 48–53.

30. Cf. A. Schalit's commentary on Josephus in his Hebrew translation (Jerusalem, 1944) *ad AJ* 8.117, n. 173, who cites *AJ* 13.245, Hecataeus *ap.* Diodorum 40.3, Appolonius Molon *ap.* Josephum *CA* 2. 143, Quintilian 3.7.21, *AJ* 19.290; cf. J. Lewry in *Zion* 8 (1943), 7. Philo, we may note, wrote an essay *On the Lore of Mankind.* Furthermore, in connection with the cessation of sacrifices in the Temple for Rome, he presents a strong statement (*BJ* 2.412) by the chief priests recalling that their forefathers had always accepted the gifts of foreign nations and had never forbidden any non-Jew to offer sacrifice.

31. A Schorr, Hebrew translation of Josephus' *Antiquities* (Jerusalem, 1945), 2.199, n. 6, admits that there is no biblical source for Josephus' exaggerated numbers and concludes that they were taken from a lost Midrash. Cf., e.g., Rabba's remark to this effect in Babylonian Talmud, *Tamid* 29a.

32. Josephus likewise stresses the splendor of the celebration in his account of the feast. Cf. *AJ* 8.123–124.

33. Rappaport, p. 57 no. 237 and citations, p. 132, no. 243.

34. The Septuagint and Lucianic texts defer the descriptions of the palace until 1 Kings 7:38, but Josephus postpones it even further until after the account paralleling 1 Kings 8.

35. It may be noted that whereas Strabo, 16.37, speaks of the majesty (εὐπρέπεια) of the Temple, this term is applied in Josephus to Solomon's palace, not by Josephus but by the Queen of Sheba (*AJ* 8.169).

36. So also the Agada. Cf. Rappaport, p. 57, n. 236, and citations, p. 132, n. 242.

37. B.M. W. Knox, *Oedipus at Thebes* (New Haven: Yale University Press, 1957), p. 32.

38. Josephus emphasizes the importance of wealth in a leader in the case of Korah (*AJ* 4.14). In his summary of the good king Josiah's career, Josephus notes that he enjoyed wealth (πλούτῳ) and the good opinion (εὐδοξίᾳ) among all men (*AJ* 10.73).

39. Knox pp. 124–125.

40. Ibid., pp. 183–184.

41. Ibid.

42. Cf. Thucydides 1.22.

43. Rappaport, p. 56, n. 231, asserts that Josephus probably derived this view that the children were born simultaneously from the statement in 1 Kings 3:17 of one of the women that "I was delivered of a child *with her* in the house." But the very next verse explicitly states that the other woman was delivered on the third day thereafter.

44. J. A. Montgomery, in H. S. Gehman ed., *The Book of Kings* (ICC; New York: Charles Scribner's Sons, 1951), p. 109, cites a close parallel from Indian lore, and notes that Gressmann has assembled twenty-two such parallels. Cf. R. B. Y. Scott, "Solomon and the Beginnings of Wisdom in Israel," *Supplements to Vetus Testamentum* 3 (Leiden: E. J. Brill, 1955), 262–279, esp. 270–271.

45. Ginzberg, IV, 131 ff.

46. Ibid., VI, 282, n. 18.

47. For 1005 the Septuagint reads 5000. Josephus thus follows the Hebrew text as far as the number is concerned, but diverges from it by speaking of *books* of odes. The Agada, as Rappaport, p. 56, n. 232, notes, similarly exaggerates in its remark (*Erubin* 21 b) that Solomon had 3000 similitudes for every statement of the Torah and 1005 arguments for every statement of the Scribes. Cf. Ecclus. 47:15: "Thou didst gather parables like the sea."

48. F. C. Conybeare, "The Testament of Solomon," *Jewish Quarterly Review* 11 (1898–99), 11–12.

49. Ginzberg, IV, 142–144.

50. E. Ullendorff, "The Queen of Sheba," *Bulletin of the John Rylands Library* 45 (1962–63), 491–492.

51. Knox, pp. 15–17.

52. Cited ibid., p. 188.

53. Ibid., p. 18.

54. Ibid.

55. See H. Drüner, *Untersuchungen über Josephus* (Marburg: J. Hamel, 1896), pp. 1–34.

56. In Loeb Classical Library *ad AJ* 8.2.

57. For a number of other instances where Josephus uses γῆρας with Homeric overtones, see H. St. J. Thackeray and R. Marcus, *A Lexicon to Josephus* (Paris: Librairie orientaliste P. Geuthner, 1948).

58. This is in contrast with the view, as noted by Schorr, II, 210, n. 7, of some of the Zealots (*BJ* 5.458), who cry out to Titus that the world itself is a better temple for G–d than the structure in Jerusalem. Cf. also *AJ* 6.230 where, in an addition to the Bible, Josephus speaks of G–d as "everywhere extended," literally, "poured out" (πανταχοῦ κεχυμένον).

59. E. Norden, *Agnostos Theos* (Leipzig: B. G. Teubner, 1923), p. 19, n. 2.

60. Cf. Schalit, n. 175, who cites A. Schlatter, *Die Theologie, des Judentums nach dem Bericht des Josephus* (Gütersloh: Bertelsmann, 1932), pp. 53 ff., for instances where Josephus speaks of ἐπιφάνεια θεοῦ. Cf. also Dionysius of Halicarnassus 2.68, and Plutarch, *Them.* 30.

61. Norden, *Agnostos Theos.*

62. For G–d the all-seeing and all-hearing see Josephus 5.413: ὃς τά τε κρυπτά πάντα ἐφορᾷ καὶ τῶν σιγωμένων ἀκούει. Cf. also *CA* 2.294, where everything in the universe is said to be under the eye and direction of G–d. Xenophanes' (Diels-Kranz, B 24) remarks about G–d being all-seeing, all-perceiving, and all-hearing are likewise

reminiscent of Homer: οὖλος ὁρᾷ οὖλος δὲ νοεῖ οὖλος δὲ τ'ἀκούει. Cf. also Epicharimus' remark (Diels-Kranz, B 12) that "mind sees and mind hears": νοῦς ὁρῆι καὶ νοῦς ἀκούει.

63. Norden, p. 14.

64. In his summary of Jewish theology in *CA* 2.190, Josephus uses this Stoic term in calling G—d self-sufficient (αὐτάρκης).

65. Cf. R. Marcus, "Divine Names and Attributes in Hellenistic Jewish Literature," *Proceedings of the American Academy for Jewish Research* 3 (1931–32), 55, s.v. ἀπροσδεής also cites occurrences of this word as an attribute of G—d in Aristeas 211, 2 Macc. 14:35, 3 Macc. 2:9, Plutarch, *Tim.* 33 d, and Philo, *Deus Immut.* 56.

66. Cf. Homer, *Iliad* 15.686, where we read that the sound (φωνή) of Ajax's battle cry reached the air (αἰθέρ). Cf. also Philo, *De Decalogo* 33; *De Agric.* 53.

67. Schorr, II, 201, n. 9.

68. Ginzberg, IV, 156.

69. N. G. Cohen, "Josephus and Scripture: Is Josephus' Treatment of the Scriptural Narrative Similar throughout the Antiquities I–XI?" *Jewish Quarterly Review* 54 (1963–64), 311–332.

5: In Defense of the Spirit: Paul's Letter to the Galatians as a Document of Early Christian Apologetics

Hans Dieter Betz

THE PHENOMENON OF RELIGIOUS APOLOGETICS, AS WE know it primarily from the Jewish and Christian religions,[1] provokes disturbing questions. It is puzzling that apologetics should be found in association with those religions which make claims to absolute truth. That they use apologetics for the purpose of their expansion, of facing the competition of other religions, or of preventing violent or nonviolent persecution and suppression, seems understandable. Less understandable is the fact that apologetics was perfected by Judaism and Christianity, religions which claim that what they regard as the "truth" cannot, by definition, be demonstrated or defended. As far as Judaism and Christianity are concerned, there is in these religions a fundamental conflict between their self-understanding and their practice of apologetics. Let me illustrate this by some further considerations:

1. Apologetics is also the admission of certain "deficiencies." Apologetics admits that there is a basic conflict between the religious claims of truth—i.e., the absoluteness, and the exclusiveness of that truth—and the obvious need to explain the presumably correct "misunderstandings," "errors," "relativity," and "embarrassments." Not only do those claims produce counterclaims, but apologetics admits *nolens volens* that the "deficiencies" are real and evident.

2. Apologetics has the taste of the illegitimate. In Judaism, how can the worshipping of the invisible God be defended as reasonable? In Christianity, how can the belief in Jesus of Nazareth, the crucified and resurrected Lord, be defended as a reasonable type of religious belief? They cannot. Therefore, apologetics is the defense of the indefensible.

3. In terms of strategy, apologetics is a function of rhetoric. It belongs to the "art of persuasion." This "art of persuasion" has its place in the lawcourts, and it is, for that reason, beset with a number of unpleasant characteristics. As antiquity saw it, lawcourt rhetoric, like any rhetoric, has little in common with "truth." Rhetoric is the exercise of those skills that make people believe something to be true. For that reason it is interested in demonstration, in persuasion, in talking people into something, but it is not interested in finding out what the truth is. How can one be concerned with defending something as the truth and, at the same time, be disinterested in that truth? One cannot. It is, therefore, not a surprise that apologetics has never shown much respect for what one calls "the facts." It is only the defense strategy which determines what the facts are allowed to be. Quite understandably, apologetics was always associated with intellectual manipulation, dishonesty, and cynicism. It was always regarded as a handy tool of power-politics. Those who were sophisticated enough always knew that apologetic demonstrations depend primarily upon the believer's *naiveté*, rather than upon the soundness of the case. Rhetoric works only as long as one does not know *how* it works.

4. As a part of rhetoric, apologetics inadvertently turns the judgment over to incompetent judges. The defense is made before a forum of people who know nothing or have a distorted picture of the matter to be defended, before people who can only be "persuaded" but never fully "convinced." Yet, such people are made the judges. How can people without the qualifications for proper judgment be made judges? They obviously cannot.

5 6 5 5 7

Points such as these make apparent the irreconcilable conflict between apologetics and the self-understanding of religions like Judaism and Christianity. To a degree this problem was recognized already in antiquity. Nevertheless, it remains one of the great historical questions, why precisely those who recognized the problems also perfected the apologetics which caused these problems.

One of the fundamental assumptions of apologetics is its claim to "reason." The aim of Jewish and Christian apologetics, for example, is to show that Judaism or Christianity are, contrary to what is commonly believed, reasonable religions—"reasonable" understood as that which the general public agrees is reasonable. This means that, in the case of Christianity, apologetics claims that the Christian message, the "gospel," is also reasonable, even if *reasonable* is defined by the common standards. The Christian gospel is not simply the irrational, absurd faith of an exclusivistic sect, but while being irrational, absurd and esoteric, that gospel is also "reasonable." However, the Christian claim to reason is a deflected one. One cannot simply assume that like philosophy and the sciences the Christian faith is also built upon reason. To use scientific categories, the Christian faith, like other religions, must be regarded as irrational. In terms of scientific categories this is no doubt the case, but the question is, how far these scientific categories can adequately be applied. We have to realize that the Christian claim to reason is a far more complex issue than commonplace definitions want us to believe. The whole field of phenomena like the "rational," "rationalism," "the reasonable," and conversely, the "irrational," "irrationalism," and the "unreasonable" is far more complex than textbook truisms would like to have it.

II

When we speak of Paul's Letter to the Galatians, we must first explain why we regard this letter as a case of "apologetics." Usually, as everyone knows, this is not done. Instead, with the possible exception of the writer of Luke-Acts, apologetics is reserved for the period following the New Testament writers. However, this neat distinction must be given up. It does not really fit the data provided by the literature of the New Testament, where the phenomenon of apologetics is no doubt present, though of course in a form different from the second century A.D. The term *apologetics* must be defined within the limitations and possibilities of the historical context, not in the abstract.

In terms of its historical context, the Galatian letter functioned in the earliest period of primitive Christianity, in the beginning of the mission to the Gentiles. We cannot presuppose that there was already then a unified church structure and organization, as one would assume for the second century. There were instead clusters of Christian congregations, founded by different Christian missionaries.[2] These clusters were shaped theologically and organizationally by their founders, a fact that provided for a great diversity. More than that, the clusters were related to each other by a variety of relationships, ranging from close cooperation to competition and even hostility. Some of the clusters had broken with Judaism, while others considered themselves still part of the old religion. This implies that the borderlines between inner-Christian polemics and apologetics toward the outside were not yet clearly drawn. All of this must be applied to the Galatian situation.

Paul's letter contains a defense of his version of the gospel addressed to his churches in Galatia. To this degree it is an inner-Christian "apology," or an apology within the Pauline cluster of churches. However, since Paul's Jewish-Christian opponents have almost succeeded in winning the Galatians over to their side, which is also the side of Judaism, the apostle's defense amounts to a defense of his theology before the forum of Judaism. On the other hand, since the Galatians were pagans before becoming Christians, Paul's defense is at the same time a defense before the forum of paganism. In this sense, his letter is apologetic. He must show the Christian Galatians why they should remain within the Pauline form of Christianity. This means he must answer the two questions, why they should not become Jewish Christians (=Jews) and, by implication, why they should not revert to paganism. He must demonstrate that it is more reasonable to become and remain a Christian of the Pauline variety than to stay in paganism or to move into Jewish-Christianity. Such a situation necessitates apologetics.

III

In terms of its literary form,[3] the letter to the Galatians is an "apologetic" letter, one of the conventional letter forms used in the Hellenistic period. Galatians, however, is also more. The main body of the letter is composed as an apology of the type used by the philosophers of the time. Without entering into the complicated problem of the formal structure of the letter, let me state the major elements constituting the "body" of the letter.[4]

The beginning (1:6–10), although peculiar, conforms to the *prooemium.* Setting aside all forms of politeness, Paul at once introduces the cause of the letter: "I am astonished that you are so quickly deserting him who called you in the grace of Christ and turning to a different gospel—not that there is another gospel, but there are some who trouble you and want to pervert the gospel of Christ" (1:6–7).

Next comes Paul's reaction, a double-curse issued conditionally (1:8–9). Complemented by a conditional blessing at the end of the letter (6:16), this special feature turns the letter into a "magical letter." The passage 1:10 seems to mark the gradual transition from the *prooemium* to the next section, the *narratio.*

The *narratio* ("statement of facts") takes up the first major section of the letter, ending in 2:14. Here Paul gives

an account of the preceding history that led to the present
situation and caused him to write the letter. He starts with
the main thesis (1:11–12), then narrates his conversion, his
appointment as an apostle, his various relationships and
non-relationships with the Jerusalem church, all culminat-
ing with the conflict between himself and Peter at
Antioch.

Between the *narratio* and the next major section, the
argumentatio, stands what appears to be the *propositio*
(2:15–21). This is designed to sum up the points which
have been made in the *narratio,* to set forth the points of
agreement and disagreement, and to provide for a smooth
transition between the *narratio* and the *argumentatio.* The
propositio concludes with a sharp denial: "I do not nullify
the grace of God; for if justification were through the law,
then Christ died to no purpose" (2:21; cf. 1:10).

The central part of the defense is the *argumentatio* or
probatio which begins in 3:1 with the famous words: "O
foolish Galatians! Who has bewitched you. . . ." Covering
all of chapters 3 and 4, this section presents several *argu-
menta* which demonstrate that Paul's theology is legitimate
and that the claims of the opposition are illegitimate.

The last part of the "body" of the letter is the *parenesis*
(5:1–6:10). This composition reveals that the defense
which constitutes the "body" of the letter has the usual
structure of a defense speech: *prooemium, narratio, propositio, argumentatio,* and *parenesis.* The last part, the
parenesis, is frequent especially in philosophical speeches
of the "diatribe" tradition. This defense speech has been
cast in the form of a letter by giving it an epistolary
framework: the epistolary "prescript" (1:1–5) and the
handwritten "postscript" (6:11–18).

IV

When we move from the form of the letter to its
content, two basic questions have to be raised: What is it
that Paul is defending? How can it be defended?

The answer to the first question, "What is it that Paul is defending?" is far from obvious. Usually, commentators have argued that Paul is defending the gospel and his apostleship. This is certainly true, but the matter is much more complicated. Paul admits that there are at least two different concepts of the gospel, or even two gospels, so that defending the gospel means defending *his* gospel (cf. 1:6f,; 2:7). The question is, therefore, Why is Paul's gospel controversial and in need of a defense? Furthermore: How is the defense of the Pauline gospel related to the self-defense of Paul himself? Is the defense of his gospel identical with the defense of his apostolic office?[5]

The subject matter of Paul's defense is most clearly presented in the *propositio* (2:15–21). Together with all Jewish Christians Paul had received righteousness before God by becoming a believer in Jesus Christ, not "by works of the law." He had preached this Christian gospel to the gentile Galatians; they had heard the message and had accepted it; they had received the gift of the divine Spirit; they had been baptized and had come to regard themselves as "sons of God," partakers in the "body of Christ" and "heirs" to the salvation promised by God in the Scriptures, accomplished by Christ on the cross, and made available to them by the Spirit (cf., especially, 3:26–29; 4:1–7).

To us there seems nothing wrong with this. However, opinions were quite different in the early Church. Paul's defense was his reaction to severe criticism by other early Christian theologians who pointed out "deficiencies" in Paul's concept.

These "deficiencies" were provided by the situation of the Galatians themselves. We can see from a number of passages that they must have been concerned with problems of the "flesh" (*sarx*). Paul responds to these concerns in particular in the parenthetical section of the letter:

5:13 : "Only do not use your freedom as an opportunity for the flesh. . . . "
5:16 : " . . . walk by the Spirit, and do not gratify the desires of the flesh."

5:17 : "For the flesh produces desires directed against the
        Spirit, and the Spirit against the flesh."
5:19 : the "works of the flesh" are listed in a catalog.
6:12 : by demanding their circumcision the opponents of
        Paul want the Galatians to "make a good showing
        in the flesh."
6:13 : the opponents themselves want to satisfy their
        pride by making the Galatians succumb to their
        demands ("boast in your flesh").

All of these passages are ethical exhortations of one kind
or another. What is the issue behind them all?

Paul sees two dangers threatening to destroy the "freedom in Christ" that describes the salvation of the Galatians. They may lose this freedom by taking up the "yoke
of the Torah" (5:1–12). This is what they are presently
considering, for Jewish Christian missionaries[6] have persuaded them that entering into the Torah covenant is
necessary in order to assure their salvation in Christ. The
second threat to freedom comes from allowing the Christian community to be corrupted by the "works of the
flesh" (5:13–6:10). Both these dangers are very real and
by no means hypothetical. The Galatians are in fact considering taking up the yoke of the Torah, and in 6:1 Paul
admits that there are cases of "transgression." In that same
passage the apostle calls the Galatians by the name of οἱ
πνευματικοί ("the pneumatics," "the spiritual people"). In
antiquity, this name was an almost technical self-designa-
tion of people who regarded themselves as having more or
less reached the final goal of "salvation" already here on
earth.

When we put these elements together we gain a picture
that makes sense historically. The basic problem of the
Galatians must have been this: On the one hand, they had
claimed to be pneumatics, sons of God, heirs of the divine
salvation. They claimed to have risen, as the "people of the
Spirit," above the law, to have been liberated from "this
evil world" (1:4) and its corrupted ways. On the other

hand, "transgressions" had occurred in their midst. There was, in other words, failure, abuse, and exploitation of what they considered to be their Christian freedom. The Galatian Christians did not take all this lightly, as their willingness to listen to the Jewish-Christian missionaries opposed to Paul bears out. These anti-Paulinists must have convinced them that their problems arose from the fact that they had remained outside of the Torah covenant. Of course, from the Jewish point of view it is logical that people apart from the Torah become lawless. Immorality among those who reject the law cannot be a surprise! In fact, they must have pointed out that in their eyes Paul, with his "gospel," had made Christ a "servant of sin" (2:17; cf. 2:21). It is, therefore, also logical to accept Torah and circumcision, in order to become partakers of the Sinai covenant and the securities that this step would include.

Given this background, we can say that Paul defends primarily his "gospel without law," that is the inclusion of the Gentiles into God's salvation on the basis of their "faith in Jesus Christ" but without committing them to the Torah covenant. Such a defense must, of course, include Paul's self-defense, because he is the one who claims to have been appointed by Christ himself to preach this gospel and to convert these Gentiles. The defense must also assure the Galatians that, being Paulinists, they lack nothing, that they are full partakers of the divine salvation, and that their status outside of the Torah is sufficient. This assurance must be accompanied by the thorough demolition of the theological position of the anti-Paulinist opposition.

All of this leads up to a defense of the Spirit. As a result of Paul's missionary preaching the Galatians have received the Spirit (cf. 3:1–5). The founding of the Galatian churches was initiated by an ecstatic experience of the Spirit. Therefore, if anything needs a defense it is this experience of the Spirit.

Once we have identified the central issue of the letter,
we may raise some puzzling questions. It is not absurd to
try to defend the Spirit of God?

From a theological perspective, such a defense is absurd
indeed. The Spirit of God's self-manifestation among men
and, by this very fact, it is ungraspable, uncontrollable,
uncontradictable and of course undefendable. "The wind
blows where it wills, and you hear the sound of it, but you
do not know whence it comes and whither it goes; so it is
with everyone who is born of the Spirit" (John 3:8). In
terms of phenomenology of religion, a "defense" of an
ecstatic experience makes little sense. By definition, ecstasy
is an overwhelming experience which can neither be pre-
vented nor manufactured. It is the experience of the irrational *par excellence*. On the other hand, *irrational* in this
connection means neither rational nor irrational, neither
"reasonable" nor "unreasonable," so that irrational as the
experience is, it has a connection to rationality.

Perhaps it is for this reason that Paul does not consider
it impossible or inappropriate to present a defense of the
Spirit of God. He does not do this as an act of condescen-
sion, the expert explaining the inexplicable to the ig-
norant. On the contrary, he defends the Spirit before the
forum of those who regard themselves as the "people of
the Spirit" (οἱ πνευματικοί). Who could be better judges of
things concerning the Spirit than the "people of the
Spirit?"

V

The other question in regard to the content of the
defense is this: *How* can the Spirit be defended? Which
"method" could possibly be adequate for such a case?

The perplexing thing is that Paul's letter demonstrates
very clearly that he regards the conventional methods as
good enough. He uses "arguments" and thus appeals to
reason. In Paul's theology there is a strange and mostly

unexplained relationship between possessing the Spirit and being "reasonable."[7] We must, of course, immediately warn that for Paul *reasonable* is not the same as "moderate" or "mediocre," but rather describes a position which is endowed with reason and sound judgment.

What are Paul's arguments? Let me mention at least the most important ones:

1. The most important argument, which he introduces first as any good lawyer would do, is his reference to indisputable evidence. In 3:1–5 he poses some questions which the Galatians cannot but answer affirmatively: "Did you receive the Spirit by works of the law, or by hearing with faith" (3:2). There can be no discussion about the fact that they did receive the Spirit purely by listening to Paul's message and without doing any "works of the law." This experience makes them first-hand "witnesses" of the case, an advantage which Paul fully exploits. The question cannot be whether they had this experience of the Spirit, but whether or not they had it "in vain" (3:4).

2. The second most important argument is that of historical consistency. This argument is most forcefully presented in the *narratio* section (1:12–2:14) but also in the *argumentatio* (chapters 3 and 4). If the anti-Paulinists had argued, and they probably did argue this way, that the spiritual experience of the Galatians was "illegitimate" (cf. "in vain" 3:4), they have made a good observation. Because "illegitimacy" has been the trademark of the Christian faith all along! It should never have happened, but it did happen! Paul begins by explaining that his own conversion and appointment should not, by human standards, have happened. But brought about by God and Christ directly, it did happen (1:12ff.). Paul's law-free gospel should have never, by common Jewish standards, been officially recognized by the Church. But it was recognized officially, even by the "pillar" apostles of the Jerusalem church, Peter, James, and John (2:1–10). The Jewish Christians should have never taken up table-fellowship with the gentile Christians, because such an act would set

aside the Jewish law of purity and impurity. But it did
happen, initiated by the leader of the Jewish Christians,
Peter himself (2:11–14). Therefore, if Paul, in consistency
with the work of God in history, preached the Christian
faith to the Gentiles without subjecting them to the Torah,
this "illegitimacy" was identical with salvation itself. The
gift of the Spirit to the Galatians should have never happened, but through God's grace it did happen.

3. A third argument is the proof from Scripture presented in chapters 3 and 4. Paul shows that the gift of the
Spirit to the Gentiles did not happen by accident but in
accordance with the purpose of divine salvation, that is, by
the will of God. In 3:6ff. Paul shows by interpreting the
Abraham tradition that it was God's promise to Abraham
to bless as sons of Abraham those who "believe" as Abraham believed. Those "believers" are the "believers" in
Jesus Christ. The blessing and fulfillment of this promise is
the gift of the Spirit to those who have come to believe in
Jesus Christ.

These proofs from Scripture are, Paul shows, in agreement with christology. Christ's redemption occurred contrary to common religious standards but in accordance
with God's will (1:1–5). Christ was born as a man, "born
by a woman, done under the law" (4:4). He died on the
cross, like a condemned criminal (3:13). What looked like
a curse was, however, the act of self-sacrifice done by the
Son of God and resulting in the salvation of man (4:4–5).
God raised Christ from the dead (1:1) and sent Christ's
Spirit into the hearts of those who, like the Galatians, lived
in hopeless and inescapable imprisonment of "this evil
aeon" (cf. 1:4; 3:23; 4:1–10). Paul reminds them of the
moment when they first tasted their "freedom": this
moment had come when the Spirit cried in them: "Abba,
Father" (4:6).

4. We should also mention a whole series of negative
arguments by which Paul relentlessly demolishes the theological position of his opponents: lack of evidence, historical inconsistency, and again proofs from Scripture. There
is no evidence whatsoever that anyone has achieved salva-

tion by "works of the law" (cf. 2:16). All along, the anti-Paulinist opposition has tried to prevent or to sabotage Paul's mission to the Gentiles but without success, without a clear theological position, and without honesty. These accusations are, no doubt, stark; they show that the apostle does not hesitate to use all the arguments he has.

5. The final argument is found in the ethical exhortations in chapters 5 and 6. They are summed up in the paradoxical gnome of 5:25: "If we live by the Spirit, let us also follow the Spirit." Again, the argument is one of consistency: if the Galatians, like all gentile Christians, have received salvation through the Spirit, they will drop out of salvation (cf. 5:4) only if they fall away from the power which made salvation accessible to them.

However, Paul does not simply appeal to trust and loyalty. He develops in chapters 5 and 6 a whole concept of individual and communal ethics, based entirely upon the Spirit. We do not need to explain this concept here in detail, but it may be enough to say that this concept makes sense in terms of the ethical theories prevailing at that time. Thus Paul shows that also his ethics, based upon the Spirit, is "reasonable" and can solve the problems the Galatians are having with regard to the "flesh."

At this point the question must be raised, whether Paul has betrayed his own theological principles by employing the "art of persuasion" to convince the Galatians. How can this demonstration of the reasonableness of the Pauline gospel keep people from turning away from that gospel, whose problems have to do with the concrete life and not primarily with reason? Of course, we would have to say that reasonableness alone cannot achieve Paul's goal. What then does he still have in stock?

VI

The final defensive weapon which we have to mention has to do with the function of the letter. The letter represents the apostle, when he himself cannot be present.

It serves as a carrier of the defense from one place to
another, from author to addressee. In terms of forcefulness
the letter can only be a substitute for the apostle's personal appearance. He can trust that the Galatians will be
able to follow his arguments and come to logical conclu-
sions, to be honest with themselves, to be "reasonable"
people. The ground for such confidence is that they possess the Spirit and do not simply depend upon common
sense.

However, the letter carries also another item. At the
beginning it has the conditional curse, very carefully form-
ulated and thought through, cursing every Christian who
would dare to propagate a "gospel" different from that
Paul had preached and still preaches, different from that
which the Galatians have accepted (1:8–9). At the end, the
letter pronounces a blessing (6:16), but this blessing is
limited to those who remain loyal to the Pauline gospel.
This means that the Galatians are once again confronted
with the choice between salvation and condemnation.
When they have finished reading the letter Paul wrote to
them, they will inescapably make that choice, and, thereby,
activate either the curse or the blessing. If they decide to
remain loyal to the Pauline gospel of "grace," the blessing
of 6:16 will become effective for them, but if they decide
to follow Paul's opponents, they will bring upon themselves the curse of 1:8–9.

As the carrier of curse and blessing the letter becomes a
"magical letter," a category of letters in antiquity. Paul
does not simply rely on arguments put down on paper and
left to the decisions and opinions of the addressees. He
introduces the dimension of magic, the curse and the
blessing, as instruments of the Spirit, in order to confront
the Galatians with the choice between salvation and loss of
salvation. Reading the letter will automatically produce
the "judgment." The readers will either go free and be
acquitted, or they will be sent to the cosmic "prison"
constituted by the "evil elements of this world" and their
demonic and tyrannical regime (cf. 4:1–10). By including

the dimension of "magic" Paul repeats the Galatians' initial confrontation with the gospel. Having read the letter they see themselves transferred back into the moment when they first encountered the gospel, so that suddenly Paul's defense of the Spirit coincides with the proclamation of the gospel of Jesus Christ.

NOTES

1. For a survey, see E. Kamlah et al., "Apologetik," in *Die Religion in Geschichte und Gegenwart,* 6 vols., 3rd ed. (Tübingen: Mohr, 1957), I, 477–495. For Jewish apologetics, see especially the older works by M. Friedländer. *Geschichte der jüdischen Apologetik als Vorgeschichte des Christentums* (Zurich: C. Schmidt, 1903); P. Krüger, *Philo und Josephus als Apologeten des Judentums* (Leipzig: Dürr, 1906); J.Bergmann, *Jüdische Apologetik im neutestamentlichen Zeitalter* (Berlin: Reimer, 1908).

2. See J.M. Robinson and H. Koester, *Trajectories through Early Christianity* (Philadelphia: Fortress Press, 1971).

3. For an introduction to early Christian epistolography, see W.G. Doty, *Letters in Primitive Christianity* (Philadelphia: Fortress Press, 1973); also H.D. Betz, *Der Apostel Paulus und die sokratische Tradition* (Beiträge z. historischen Theologie, 45; Tübingen: Mohr, 1972).

4. For a literary analysis of Galatians, see H.D. Betz, "The Literary Composition and Function of Paul's Letter to the Galatians," *New Testament Studies* 21 (1975), 353–379. For the technical meaning of concepts, see the respective sections in H. Lausberg, *Handbuch der literarischen Rhetorik,* 2 vols. (Munich: Hueber, 1960); G. Kennedy, *The Art of Persuasion in Greece* (Princeton: Princeton University Press, 1963); G. Kennedy, *The Art of Rhetoric in the Roman World* (Princeton: Princeton University Press, 1972).

5. Cf. also my paper "Spirit, Freedom and Law: Paul's Message to the Galatian Churches," *Svensk Exegetisk Arsbok* 39 (1974), 145–160; the German version has appeared in *Zeitschrift für Theologie und Kirche* 71 (1974), 78–93.

6. For an attempt to reconstruct the theology of Paul's Galatian

opponents, see H.D. Betz, "2 Cor.6:14–7:1: An Anti-Pauline Fragment?" *Journal of Biblical Literature* 92 (1973), 88–108.

7. Cf. G.Bornkamm, "Glaube und Vernunft bei Paulus," in *Studien zu Antike und Urchristentum* (Munich: C. Kaiser, 1959), pp. 119–137.

6: The Magic
of Magic and Superstition

In profound admiration, to Jacob Lewittes

Judah Goldin

BY THE MAGIC OF MAGIC AND SUPERSTITION I MEAN
their astonishing persistence, and universal diffusion, and
success.[1] A thirteenth floor between the twelfth and four-
teenth in fashionable twentieth-century American high-rise
apartment houses would be a refreshing discovery. That
magic is everywhere, the anthropologists and scholars of
comparative cultures and civilizations have documented.
That it succeeds does not mean that every time a spell is
whispered the wished-for result is obtained, despite the
promise by the magus. But then, neither is the outcome of
every surgical operation successful. By the success of magic
is meant simply that very many insist on believing in it,[2]
and that even those who may have some doubts about it
wonder periodically: "Maybe, maybe." There are so many
examples, it is impossible to do justice to the subject; let
us take two that are fairly well known.

The younger Pliny is in many ways a sensible person and
a cultivated one. He writes a letter (VII, xvii, Loeb Classics
2.67–77) to his friend Sura for advice about spectres,
"whether you believe they actually exist and have their
own proper shapes and a measure of divinity, or are only
the false impressions of a terrified imagination?"

The letter, Pliny goes on to say, is prompted by three
circumstances: (1) by the story he heard of what overtook

one Curtius Rufus as the figure of a woman had foretold; (2) by what was related to him about Athenodorous the philosopher in an ill-reputed house in Athens; and (3) finally, by what he can himself affirm of one of his own freed-men and slave boys who had their hair cut off by apparitions.

Nothing in the letter is hysterical or panicky. Pliny simply wants to know. "And though," Pliny ends his letter, "you should after your manner, argue on both sides"—this by the way is itself instructive: it's possible to argue on both sides of the question—"yet," Pliny says, "I hope you will throw your weightiest reasons into one scale, lest you should dismiss me in suspense and uncertainty, whereas I consult you on purpose to determine my doubts."

Remove my doubts, says Pliny, for he is ready to believe, one way or the other; but does not dismiss the possibility that there are spectres. That's the whole point of the letter.

Let us look at another example, a different kind of puzzled belief: After Pentecost of 164 B.C. (so it seems), Judah Maccabee's forces engaged Gorgias, the governor of Jamnia, in battle and ran into difficulties: "and it came to pass that a few of the Jews fell" (2 Macc. 12:34). When subsequently the Jews rested and went to recover the corpses of the slain to bury them properly, "they discovered under the shirts of every one of the dead men amulets of the idols of Jamnia—a practice," adds the author of 2 Maccabees (12:39; or is he quoting Jason of Cyrene?), "forbidden Jews by law. All saw at once that this was why they had perished," and so forth. Who were these Jews wearing amulets of the idols of Jamnia? The Hellenizers, as fifth columnists? The author of 2 Maccabees would not have suppressed this fact. On the contrary, these were loyal Partisans of Judah's army, Zealots of the Law, risking their lives for the Torah and Temple of the God of Israel! Yet under their shirts are idolatrous amulets.[3] They too very likely belong to the Maybe Maybe tribe, a numerous tribe historically.

Belief, or wonder about the plausibility of belief as in magic, is pervasive because fear and desire, and fantasy which is the product of these, are permanent: fear of sickness, of an enemy, possibly of a business competitor,[4] of bureaucracy, of the dangers of childbirth, of the day of death, or death in battle, or uncertainties of the harvest, of removal of your crops by neighbors,[5] of wild beasts and floods, of the effects of the evil eye;[6] desire to win at the horse races, to know the future, to win the favor of officials or the favor of a woman (prominent, rich or beautiful), to gain admission to kings and judges, to consult the stars or ghosts (as did Saul) or spirits, or to know the meaning of your dreams, to disturb your enemy's sleep, to heat up a stove in the cold, to overcome magical spells against you, to assist your friend, to put down fire in the bath-house, to behold Helios "who informs you whether the man lying sick will live or die."[7] And there are "initiatives" (*katarchai*) like, Will a son about to be born have a big nose?[8]

This list of fears and desires can be multiplied and diversified,[9] and for all of them there are concrete prescriptions. These prescriptions, in fact, add to the sense of mystery which surrounds the whole business of magic. Far from making the belief grotesque, the mystery encourages it. And no one is altogether unaffected by it.

For self-protection, and to reduce the amounts of confusion and disorderly conduct within society, the authorities do well to draw up lists of the forbidden and the not-forbidden. In talmudic literature there is a list like that. Items: *mi-darke ha-Emori,* of the Ways of the Amorites; Items: not *mi-darke ha-Emori,* not regarded as superstitious Amorite acts. Already the author of Jubilees (29:11) speaks of Amorites as "wicked and sinful, and there is no people today which has wrought to the full all their sins."[10] Why one should speak of the ways of the Amorites rather than of the ways of the Canaanites, for example, I still do not understand, despite Jubilees. Or is *Emori* (Amorite) a deliberate "metathesis" for *Romai* (Roman)? At all events, in the Tosefta an (incomplete) list of forbidden superstitions and magical practices called "Of the Ways of the Amorites" is conveniently drawn up.[11]

To begin with, these are not really Jewish magic at all, that is to say, there is hardly anything ethnic about the practices (though ethnic touches may be added) any more than you could attach their invention to any particular nationality.[12] They are practices, however, current among Jews; and if you will consult Heinrich Lewy's translation and comments in the *Zeitschrift des Vereins für Volkskunde* for 1893, Ludwig Blau's *Das Altjüdische Zauberwesen* (Strassburg, 1898), Saul Lieberman's *Greek in Jewish Palestine* (New York, 1942), pages 97 and following, and above all his Commentary on the Tosefta (*Tosefta Ki-Fshutah, Shabbat* [New York, 1962], where he supplies our first two and still other references), you will immediately be brought into contact with identical and virtually identical data from the Hellenistic and Roman worlds and even the world of the Middle Ages. To exclaim "Gesundheit" when someone sneezes is apparently dangerous in several cultures.[13] A cock crowing in the evening or at the wrong time is a bad sign for Trimalchio no less than for superstitious Jews.[14] And so it goes, and there is nothing unexpected or striking about this.

What does call attention to itself and may create perplexity is the seemingly utter arbitrariness of the *reaction* to the practices. For example:

Tie a red string around your finger—that's Amorite behavior. (Lewy has already shown that this was widespread in the ancient world.) But later authorities, on the sensible principle that one is not to add to the original list of the *Darke ha-Emori* practices, do not forbid a red string around any other part of the body.[15] It is forbidden to say, "Leave a light on the ground to the discomfiture of the dead," but some post-talmudic teachers apparently have no objection to leaving a light on the floor at the entrance of the house so that the soul of the dead person might find its way back.[16] To throw an iron object into the cemetery and call "Hada" (possibly like the hic, hoc pagan spell to which the elder Pliny refers)[17] is the way of the Amorites; on the other hand, to throw it there in order to nullify the actions of sorcerers is permitted—because you may defeat sorcery by sorcery (Satan cast out Satan?). Sympathetic magic is everywhere appealing. If a bone gets stuck in your throat, the Babylonian Talmud[18] tells us, put on top of your head a bone of similar kind and recite (with the bone in your throat?), "One (to?) one, down, swallow; swallow, down, on (to?) one." And this is *not* classified as Amorite practice. Fortunately, both Talmuds, the Palestinian and the Babylonian,[19] declare that whatever heals is not to be regarded as of *Darke ha-Emori*. But what heals, and how can you ever be sure? Professor Lieberman quotes a wise and beautiful observation by one of my favorite talmudic commentators, the Meiri of Perpignan[20] (thirteenth century, died 1315), that since in those times people had confidence in such practices (e.g., spells, incantations, popular remedies), they really would get better by resorting to these nostrums, and because they were accustomed to them, they truly helped them. Hence, allowable. The law permits you to wear outdoors on the Sabbath a tried and tested amulet—whose healing powers have been demonstrated once, twice, and thrice—even if you do not fear to be overtaken by serious illness.[21]

That we have difficulty arriving at the principle that divides the magical from the non-magical, the forbidden from the permitted or at least tolerated, is to be expected because frankly there are such wide gaps between the pieces of our knowledge of antiquity, and the vagaries of the human spirit are unpredictable. We must attempt at least a temporary suspension of disbelief and the ancients must be allowed their tastes. My point is, however, that many types of ambiguity are inherent in the response to magic, be the response cautious, or negative, or for that matter positive, and these ambiguities are in the minds of the ancients themselves. It is this I wish to underline.

For even in pieties insulated (possibly) from magic and superstition, ambiguities may persist, and the most austere halakists can put up with the contradictory and the puzzling and the irrational ceremony with humble affirmation. Life itself being filled with ambiguities, how can pieties or impieties escape them?

Magic, however, pretends that it is more clear-minded and efficient; hence its demands for absolute precision of operations and accuracy in recitation, even if what is recited is unintelligible, and confident promises of fulfillment. Do this and that *will* follow, say the following and the outcome *will* be—so the magician declares with authority.[22]

Many obviously believe him—the rhetoric of confidence produces persuasion. Nevertheless, in response to magic shades and traces of ambiguity continue to hang on. For example:

According to the Palestinian Talmud,[23] Rabbi Yohanan is the authority for the rule that whatever (*kol she-hu*) heals does not fall under the heading of an "Amorite Way." Yet in the Mishnah it is stated that one who whispers charms over a wound and recites the verse (Exod. 15:26), "I will not bring upon you any of the diseases that I brought upon the Egyptians, for I the Lord am your healer," will have no share in the World to Come.[24] That's meant to convey quite a stiff penalty, as is obvious from the context of that whole Mishnah; and if Rabbi Aqiba, to whom the statement is attributed, is prepared to go to such lengths, it seems to me fair to say that (1) despite the great risk involved, this practice is noticeably widespread and perhaps out of control, and (2) that he must feel that such recitation is downright sacrilegious and blasphemous. I hasten to add that this particular bit of sorcery is *not* included in the list of *Darke ha-Emori,* maybe because the Amorites don't know Scripture![25] But apparently a current Jewish superstitious practice is reported and condemned strongly, though there must have been those who wondered why. In the Talmud[26] we are informed that you lose your share in the World to Come only if you spit as you recite the verse, for[27] the offensive part is in the spitting. This must refer to imitation of the practice of heathen magi.[28] Other sages add indeed that the objection extends to the recitation of thoroughly innocuous verses. Not bibliomancy disturbs them therefore, but the act of spitting which accompanies it. But the distinction and prohibition do not put a halt to the practice, and rabbinic ingenuity is compelled to continue in later centuries to find some ways of coming to terms with the practice.[29] People don't want to lose their share in the Future World, but they want to get well in this one.

Nowhere, it seems to me, is the internal perplexity over the phenomenon of magic more candidly—and hence movingly—displayed than in the following Midrash[30] which is reproduced in several midrashic compilations. Here we are not dealing at all with *Darke ha-Emori* but with the ritual of an explicit biblical command.

> A heathen once asked Rabban Yohanan ben Zakkai: These things you do (cf. Num. 19) appear like acts of witchcraft. You bring a (red) heifer, slaughter it, burn it, beat it down to a powder, then take the ashes; and if one of you is defiled by a dead body, you sprinkle two or three drops and say to him, You've been cleansed.
>
> Said Yohanan to the heathen, Has a demonic spirit [31] ever taken possession of you?
>
> The heathen replied, No.[32]
>
> Yohanan said to him, Have you ever seen anyone possessed by a demonic spirit?
>
> Indeed, the heathen replied.
>
> What do you do in such a case, Yohanan asked him.
>
> The heathen said: We bring (certain) roots, (kindle them,) let the smoke rise under him; then we spray water on the (demonic) spirit and it flees.
>
> Said Rabban Yohanan to him: Why don't your ears listen to what your own mouth is saying? That (demonic) spirit is a *spirit of uncleanness,* as it is written (Zech. 13:2), "And also I will remove from the land the prophets and the *unclean spirit,*" etc. (Sprinkle water of lustration on the unclean person and the unclean spirit runs away.)[33]

When the heathen took off, Yohanan's disciples said
to him: Master, him you could put off with a straw
argument;[34] what have you to say to us, however?
   Yohanan said to them: By your life![35] It is not the
corpse that makes unclean, and it is not the waters that
make clean. But this all is a decree of the Holy One,
blessed be He. The Holy One, blessed be He, declared, I
have proclaimed a statute,[36] I have decreed a decree,
and you are not permitted to transgress what I have
decreed. "This is the ritual law that the Lord has commanded" (Num. 19:1).

What honesty and pathos in this story. The heathen is of
course right: the goings-on do resemble witchcraft, and
when Yohanan compares the rite of cleansing one defiled
by a corpse to the practice of expelling a demonic spirit
familiar to the heathen, he, Yohanan, has only confirmed
what the heathen said. If one is magic, why is the other
not? Yohanan's disciples are right to be puzzled: Is this
how one is to interpret a biblical ritual? Yohanan has given
an answer in the end which does not make the ceremony
intelligible. But it is an honest answer: what is the meaning
of what we do, I do not know; but it's what God commanded.
   Put in less awesome terms, what is magic and what is
not, the authorities determine,[37] and what they declare as
legitimate is what has come down as commanded or approved from the past and has thus been purged of possibly
compromising ingredients. And if now something new-
fangled appears, or something that was disapproved of (or
resembles something that was disapproved of) in the past,
the Establishment is likely to regard it with suspicion. But
ambiguousness does not disappear. One is simply to obey
and trust the authorities.
   It is as A.D. Nock observed, that for the ancients there
was not, "as with us, a sphere of magic in contrast to the
sphere of religion,"[38] and we may go on with Pfister
whom Nock quotes with approval, "dass kein prinzipieller
Unterschied zwischen Zauberspruch und Gebet so wenig

wie zwischen Zauberei und Religion besteht." All the more reason, I would say, why the Establishment resents the magician. He is fundamentally a threat, because he boasts that he has recourse to powers and influences superior to and independent of the order and limitations which regulate society. He says he can produce desired results promptly.[39] Like respectable healers he demonstrates that he too can unite high and low. And not only the simple folk but the Establishment believes him, it believes he can do what he says he can. It believes because there are practices and beliefs it endorses which are indistinguishable, sometimes even to the opponents of the magician, from the magician's actions. Because of its own belief, therefore, the Establishment declares the magician's exercises illegitimate. It sees in him both competition and caricature of itself. Sometimes perhaps it may believe him more even than he believes himself.

The rabbis too forbid, but apparently when they find that they are helpless to destroy the whole complex of magic, they try to outwit it.[40] Needless to say, there were practices and notions they themselves accepted as legitimate, as did their contemporaries in the Greco-Roman and Babylonian worlds, for these were the science of the day.[41] Some embarrassing practices they left alone, doubtless out of prudence, despite their affinity to pagan practices, because there was something like precedence for them in ancient Jewish custom.[42] And I can't resist guessing that there must have been practices which surely irritated them, but they simply shut their eyes to them and must have muttered under their breath the equivalent of, Oh, to hell with it. Or they cleverly converted what may have been magical spells to begin with into religious prayers, and thus removed the sting of superstition from them.[43] Or it might be that they would sanction a superstition which they themselves accepted, by endowing it with a religious value.[44]

A case in point is a form of bibliomancy, which is of course universal: among Jews, Christians, Muslims, anyone with sacred scriptures. There are at least 180 Old Testament verses that have been used for omens and spells at one time or another.[45] Some of this so-called misuse may have annoyed the rabbis; on the other hand, this also gave them an opportunity to drive home a lesson they were delighted to inculcate. For instance:

> For an inflammatory fever take an all-iron knife (that is, whose handle is also of iron) and go where there is a thorn-bush and tie to it a white twisted string. On the first day make a small notch and recite (Exod. 3:2), "An angel of the Lord appeared to him in a blazing fire out of a bush." On the morrow make (another) notch and recite (Exod. 3:3), "Moses said, I must turn aside to look at this marvellous sight; why is the bush not burnt?" On the following day make (still another) small notch and recite (Exod. 3:4), "When the Lord saw that he had turned aside to look, God called to him out of the bush: Moses, Moses! He answered, Here I am." . . .
>
> And when cutting (the bush) down, bend down low and recite as follows: "Thorn-bush, O thorn-bush, not because you are the tallest of all trees did the Holy One, blessed be He, cause His Shekinah to rest upon you; rather because you were the smallest of all trees did the Holy One, blessed be He, cause His Shekinah to rest upon you. And even as the fire beheld Hananiah, Mishael, and Azariah and fled from them, so may the fire (of fever) behold So-and-so son of that woman[46] and flee from him."[47]

The ingenious manipulation of the biblical verses associates the burning bush that would not be consumed at God's self-revelation with a high fever. But note how an actual Midrash and moral lesson have unexpectedly been incorporated in the mumbo jumbo. The Midrash is none other than Rabbi Eliezer's, who is *not* discussing fevers: "Rabbi Eliezer says:[48] Why did the Holy One, blessed be He, reveal Himself from the high heavens and speak to him (i.e., Moses) out of the midst of the bush? Only because the bush is the lowliest of all the trees in the world. So Israel descended to the very lowest level and the Holy One,

blessed be He, came down to be with them and redeemed
them, as it is said (Exod. 3:8), 'And I came down to save
them from the power of Egypt.' "

That is the Midrash. And who knows? Maybe it was not
the spell that drew upon a Midrash but Rabbi Eliezer who
drew upon an old incantation for his own midrashic purposes. Rabbi Eliezer was not entirely a stranger to magic.
He was able to teach three hundred—perhaps three thousand—*halakot* in connection with the verse (Exod. 22:17),
"Thou shalt not suffer a sorceress to live."[49]

In post-talmudic times we come upon a ceremony
whose background and subsequent course have been described in detail by J.Z. Lauterbach.[50] The ceremony is
called "Tashlik." On the afternoon of the first day of Rosh
ha-Shanah, the Jewish new year, if it does not come on the
Sabbath Day (otherwise the ceremony takes place on the
second day of Rosh ha-Shanah), you go to a seashore or a
river or some body of water, empty into the water what
crumbs you may have brought along, and recite a number
of biblical verses and passages. They are beautiful verses,
and from one of them, Micah 7:19, comes the Hebrew
word *tashlik* (which may be rendered in this context as
"the casting-off," or "away-with-you!"), from which the
ceremony gets its name: "He will again have compassion
upon us; He will subdue (or, suppress)[51] our iniquities:
And Thou wilt cast (*we-tashlik*) all their (=our) sins in the
depths of the sea." The elements which seem to have
united behind the practice, sometimes far behind, sometimes close, include the feeling that the deity prefers an
abode by water, that other supernatural beings also favor
such a location, that it was a favorite spot for synagogues
(Tertullian also mentions "the prayers at the seashore")[52]
and so on, along with ideas about angels and evil spirits.
Compounded with these is naturally the expectation of
good-riddance to one's sins, the notion of atonement by
means of surrogate (a ceremonial development once part
of the Tashlik conceptions), and of course the warding off
of those powers who block forgiveness from arriving.

Down through the ages there has been considerable opposition to the ceremony itself or to parts of it. Some protests are strong and some are mild.[53] But clearly the folk won't give it up. The rabbis who let it go on offer reinterpretation and this in turn is seized upon as justification. Again, therefore, what we have is an aspect of the relationship between magical or superstitious behavior and the rabbinic authorities. It's a sort of "If you can't beat them, join them"—that is, the practice can't be eliminated, hence it is diverted to the approved avenues of piety. In the end you may even discern several sophisticated symbolic lessons in the people's conduct.[54]

It is certainly correct to see in such a development the successful deliverance of a folk from the dangers of superstition. On the other hand, it is not incorrect to see here another instance of the magic of magic, that is, it simply refuses to disappear, and because it has few scruples it is even prepared to adopt the alibis and masks of piety in order to survive. A small price to pay.

Ambiguity in magic, which is partly created by the offensive of the authorities, persists despite the simultaneous insistence on precision in recitation of the formulas and in the actions demanded by the prescriptions; and that is not fatal to it any more than it is to the legally prescribed forms of piety. This may be an additional reason why the Establishment is uncomfortable with the magus: for the ambiguity makes it possible for him to adapt to all requirements, and that which remains inexplicable may fascinate even more than what is intelligible. Haggadic Midrash is no stranger to this. Let me illustrate:

One of the Amorite practices, the Tosefta tells us,[55] is to cast stones, pebbles, into the sea and count as one does so. The counting is the objectionable feature and the reference is to a form of hydromancy. Nevertheless, counting pebbles or not counting, the depths of waters as such are not an innocuous region;[56] demons may lurk or abide there.[57] Strange scenes may be seen at the sea.[58] What, therefore, are we to make of the following?

When the children of Israel left Egypt, the Mekilta reports,[59] Moses recalled Joseph's adjuration that his bones were to be taken out of Egypt along with the redeemed Israelites. Where, however, was Joseph buried? According to one view, actually presented as the first by our source, Serah, the daughter of Asher, informed Moses that Joseph was in a metal casket which the Egyptians had sunk in the Nile.[60] Thereupon Moses went to the shore of the Nile and—I now quote the reading of the Munich manuscript which Lauterbach (not Horovitz-Rabin)[61] adopted in his edition—"took a gold tablet, engraved on it the Ineffable Name, cast it into the Nile and cried out: Joseph ben Jacob, the time has come for the oath to be fulfilled which the Holy One, blessed be He, promised to Father Abraham, that He would redeem his children. If you rise to the surface, fine; otherwise we're scot-free of the oath you placed us under! Forthwith Joseph's coffin rose to the surface," and so forth. And the Mekilta reassures us that the iron casket rising to the surface is no more astonishing than what is reported in 2 Kings 6:1–6. Moses was more than a match for Elisha.

This is embarrassing, to say the least. Moses engraving the Ineffable Name of God on a golden tablet[62] and casting it into the Nile (itself, by the way, something of a deity), then calling on Joseph and only thereafter does the casket rise. Clearly we have here a remarkable survival of a belief—if not more—once regarded by Judaism as inoffensive. Once, but not for long. For if you consult the parallel passages you will look in vain for the golden tablet. Mekilta de-Rabbi Simeon (ed. Epstein-Melamed, 46) supplies only, "Moses went and stood at the shore of the Nile and called, Joseph, Joseph," and so forth: thoroughly impeccable behavior. No tablet, no Ineffable Name, no casting.[63] No sign of these either in the Tosefta (Sotah 4:7). The Babylonian Talmud (Sotah 13a) is like the Tosefta. The Midrash, Exodus Rabba (20:19) in the regular editions refers to magical golden dogs[64] guarding the royal burial place where Joseph's tomb had been deposited. But this belongs to an alternative view of where Joseph was buried, and has nothing to do with our passage, in connection with which Exodus Rabba says, "What did Moses do, etc.(!)[65] ... He began to cry, Joseph, Joseph, the time has come. . . . Forthwith the coffin bestirred itself and Moses took it. . . . "

The reading in Pesikta de-Rav Kahana (ed. Mandelbaum, 187) is illuminating on two counts. First, as in the other sources above, not a word is said about tablets, engravings, Divine Name, casting into the Nile. But once that comment is done with, we read: "And some say, Moses took a *shard* and wrote the Ineffable Name on it, and cast it into the Nile:[66] forthwith the coffin rose to the surface." Everything Moses did in the Mekilta de-Rabbi Ishmael, he did in the Pesikta—with the one exception that he used a shard, a fragment of cheap everyday pottery, rather than a gold tablet. As though this could eliminate the toxic ingredient from the story.

The Midrash Tanhuma[67] also deserves to be looked at. "Moses stood by the Nile, took a small stone (a pebble), engraved on it 'Rise, O Ox,'[68] and cried out, Joseph, Joseph, the time has come" and the rest of it. The tablet has now become a valueless pebble thrown in the sea which serves no purpose.[69] The inscription "Rise, O Ox," which may indeed be a spell anyway, takes the place of the Ineffable Name. (Our text probably has a lacuna and should include the clause, "Moses cast the pebble into the Nile," after the words "Rise, O Ox.") Finally, for our purpose, Lekah Tob, Exodus, 40b, has cleaned it all up with the reading, "Moses came and stood by the Nile, took a pebble and threw it into (the Nile),[70] and said, Joseph . . . " and the rest.

This brief excursion into variations on a textual reading need not suggest that *all* versions other than that of the Munich MS of the Mekilta have been doctored and been made respectable: in any event, some still retain traces of attempts at modification. It may be that there were once different traditions about the way Moses recovered Joseph's remains, some so-called "rationalistic," explaining that Moses simply summoned Joseph to rise, others frankly magical in outlook. The Mekilta belongs to the latter and unblushingly describes Moses as engaged in a rite which at the least excites surprise. In time, later texts apparently prefer to present the story in more restrained terms. And displacement of the golden tablet by shard and pebble reflects in my opinion just that ambiguity and bewilderment of the Establishment to which we referred.

There may be one more aspect to this bewilderment which deserves consideration—and by bewilderment I do not mean that the talmudic sages are reluctant to take a stand. They certainly condemn, for example,[71] a cult in which there were libations of wine and offerings of myrrh and frankincense and sacrifice of whole white cocks to angels, spirits, constellations. But what is condemned does not for that reason go out of existence; the condemnation, in fact, may add impetus. This requires neither underscoring nor documentation.

Nor is it at all necessary to assume that the populace in general, by responding to the whispered invitations and performances of magi intended rebellion against rabbinic authority, though some very likely did. Some forms of magic fascinate by their very strangeness,[72] as we have already suggested. But there is also such a thing as the very appetite for piety which sometimes seems to know no bounds. It craves to do more and more, more than what the by-now habitual orthodoxy provides, and therefore it reaches out to, and takes hold of, suggestions, prescriptions, acts beyond the pale. Here, you might say, superstition outwits the rabbis. The Tashlik ceremony we mentioned earlier becomes an example of this in the course of time. There are other examples. In getting dressed, put on your right shoe first, but lace the left one first.[73] I see a young Jewish girl going off to a party, and as she leaves her house she lifts her right hand to the *mezuzah* on the doorpost and kisses it. By what right may I tell her that I saw the identical behavior on the part of a Greek girl with an icon in a Christian chapel? And who knows, perhaps these gestures and acts reminded both of them at their respective parties of how not to behave as the evening grew merry? Call such, if you wish, the mnemonic aids of piety.

On the other hand, there is also the browbeating which may be called strong-arm piety, which is of course interdenominational and pan-sectarian and is not far removed from the lesser forms of brainwashing so appealing to religious no less than to political bigots. The element of superstition in these should never be minimized, for the fears of omission of the apotropaic act can assume a lunatic fixation in the mind of the believer, whose self-righteousness is perhaps less susceptible to doubts and hesitations than is the self-confidence of any other kind of magician or legal authority.

One should not underestimate the margin of elasticity, patchwork, downright inconsistency and contrariness admitted resignedly, sometimes even gladly, by prescribed religious practice and doctrine whose approved forms may themselves have been, to begin with, reconciliations between conflicting interests inside a pattern of indoctrination. And there is never a loss for a prooftext to validate what desire can't resist.

In a religion like Judaism this inconsistency is especially likely to happen, I think, for the religion is so severely and imperatively monotheistic, and monotheism[74] is the hardest system on earth to live by *day by day,* crisis after crisis. Even intellectuals stumble. Summarizing the talmudic views regarding idolatry, Maimonides writes:

> In the days of Enosh, the people fell into gross error, and the counsel of the wise men of the generation became foolish. Enosh himself was among those who erred. Their error was as follows: "Since God," they said, "created these stars and spheres to guide the world, set them on high and allotted unto them honour, and since they are ministers who minister before Him, they deserve to be praised and glorified, and honour should be rendered them; and it is the will of God, blessed be He,

that men should aggrandise and honour those whom He aggrandised and honoured—just as a king desires that respect should be shown to the officers who stand before him, and thus honour is shown to the king." When this idea arose in their minds, they began to erect temples to the stars, offered up sacrifices to them, praised and glorified them in speech, and prostrated themselves before them—their purpose, according to their perverse notions, being to obtain the Creator's favour. This was the root of idolatry. . . . [75]

The intellectuals arrive by analogy at the realization that though there is one God, He must have many ministers who are to be treated with religious courtesy. The simple man, driven by his impulses and instructed by his authoritative Scriptures and by the tradition that angels exist—after all, they too were created by God—need not speculate interminably. He turns to these angels and spirits for assistance. He has been reassured many times that the Lord is nigh; but angels and ministers of grace, and demons, are nigher. Soon the universe gets congested with beings, some of whom the rabbis themselves believe in (why not?) and address. It has been observed[76] that one of the reasons for the influence of Jewish magicians in the Hellenistic-Roman world of magic was Judaism's angelology. How many angels that Jewess in Juvenal (*Satires* VI, 542–547) who predicted the future and interpreted dreams for elegant Roman matrons, was familiar with, the satirist fails to tell us, doubtless because he was too outraged to investigate. But if she had needed any, there was no lack of them. To give an idea of what this could be like, let me say that in the *Sefer ha-Razim* (a word about this book in a moment) discovered several years ago, the index lists 704 angels, and while a few names may be doublets, the reality of a number in the several hundreds in that small treatise remains unaffected. The empty space between God and man is filled, the world grows a little cozier, but at the same time a little less private and therefore calls for more precaution and secretiveness. But then again there's someone close by to talk to, and is there anyone who doesn't need a confidant?

Now that someone is near, what do you say and what do you do? Inevitably you draw on the forms and vocabulary from the worship you're familiar with in the established institution,[77] or on an imitation of what's familiar (like everyone else, the magician is seldom original). Familiar are some of the names of deity[78] and angels, slogans that are repeated in prayers and psalms, verses that are used as refrains and that read nicely also as they are read backwards. There are also, however, varieties or a new prescription that has been recommended as having been successful elsewhere. This last-named is at first a departure from the familiar, but in an emergency one must hazard because there seems to be no alternative. Besides, if some words and names sound odd, that's all the more mysterious and thrilling. Above all, one has professional assistance and guidance.[79] He is our magus.

A Jewish magician of either the third or fourth century A.D.[80] has left us a beautifully written booklet in Hebrew, *Sefer ha-Razim,* the Book of Secrets or Mysteries, which was discovered and pieced together by the late Mordecai Margalioth. It contains a description of the seven heavens and the names of their guardian (officer) angels under whom serve troops or "camps"[81] of angels, as well as of the services they perform if they are approached the right way. A number of the angelic names are intelligible; some can be deciphered as Greek terms or names in a kind of Jewish disguise;[82] many remain incomprehensible. Following the names, the author furnishes the prescriptions: If you want this or that, do and recite the following. There is no need to go into detail for the requests and recipes are similar to what we find in Greek (and other) magical papyri and in amulets, and Professor Margalioth has already called attention to quite a number of similarities, often of phraseology and of objects employed. One example should be enough to convey the flavor; it is connected with the fifth camp of the first heaven:

Now if you wish to consult a ghost (*'ob!* cf. Deut. 18:9–14), stand over against a grave and name the angels of the fifth camp while in your hand is a new glass phial in which is a mixture of oil and honey, and recite the following: "I adjure you, spirit of Kriophoros (=Hermes) who dwells in cemeteries by the bones of the dead, that you receive this offering from my hand and do my will, and bring back to me So-and-so son of So-and-so[83] who is dead. Set him up so that he may speak with me without fear; and let him tell me the truth, (speak to me) without deception; and let me not be afraid of him; and let him answer me as I require of him." (The dead person) will then rise at once. But if he doesn't, adjure still another time, up to three times. And when (the dead person) has come forth, place the phial before him and then say what you have to say. A myrtle-rod should be in your hand. And if you wish to release (dismiss) him, strike him three times with the myrtle (-rod) and pour out the oil and the honey, and break the glass, and throw away the myrtle (-rod) and go home another way.[84]

The work is plainly a textbook or book of magical recipes whose purpose is utilitarian, but it is a genuine literary composition with an introduction,[85] peroration, and the principal substance in well-organized order.

Who is the author? Of course he won't tell us. Doubtless he is as vain as the most modest of us, and if in his time there had been such a thing as royalties, he would not have scorned them. But what he wants above all is to be read in all seriousness. He knows that no one will take the trouble to consult a book of *his.* Who or what is he, after all? But a book given to Noah, or possibly to Adam, and handed down very carefully from one generation to another until it finally got to that master of wizards and the wise, Solomon, and which the magus has a copy of—that may command acceptance.[86]

There is a possibility that the work in our hands is not by one author but by several, and only the modern editor has made of it a single unified treatise. But nothing I can see in it reveals breaks or inconsistency between parts or forced cohesion of disparate, mutually antagonistic views or teachings. Doubtless the possibility remains that several hands, not one, are responsible for the work. But nothing compels us to adopt such a view. That the magus drew on various sources, compiled and organized them into a unitary composition, does not deprive him of the right to be called author.[87]

For whom did he prepare the work? I suspect for apprentices, come to learn his trade. Perhaps they studied it with him so he could teach them how to do what the book prescribed, and especially the lore about the numerous angels. However, one ought not to rule out the possibility that it is also meant as a do-it-yourself manual; though this is not decisive, note that the idiom throughout (as in kindred compositions) is, "If thou seekest" this or that or the other, recite the following and do as follows—second person singular, addressed directly. Yet I don't think he meant to be only an author and to give up practice. Further, I don't think that the book was intended for women—not because the second person singular is in the masculine (that is simply conventional style), but because there is a level of culture to the writing which probably was not common among women with or without an appetite for sorcery, although we do know of some women in talmudic times with noteworthy culture. Even if women could handle the work on their own, men were certainly the chief audience. *Razim* will tell you several times how a man will win a woman, but never how a woman can make a man want to win her.[88]

The modern editor, who was a devout talmudist as well as a fine scholar, confesses in his preface that the composition shocked him profoundly. Prayers to Helios, offerings to angels, making stone images, appeals to Aphrodite,[89] consulting ghosts explicitly forbidden by the Scriptures, petitions to win at horse races: what place, he asked, have such within talmudic Judaism? Maybe halakists can answer his question.

But one may turn the question around in a discussion like this and ask, What place has Judaism in magic like this? This, I think, has some significance for historians of culture no less than religion.

As among all peoples, all along there have been practitioners of magic among the Jews, as biblical and talmudic and post-talmudic protest reflects, and in the pagan world too there are references to Jews as expert magicians.[90] Along with their magic, by the way, these practitioners, when they moved in gentile circles, may even have been purveyors of certain Jewish ideas and tabus. *Sefer ha-Razim,* as we shall see in a moment, expresses not only (what we might call) the crude but some fairly fundamental Jewish emphases about God. Maybe those Roman fathers who abstained from pork (Juvenal, *Satires,* XIV, 96–106) did so because some mendicant Jewish magician advised the abstinence,[91] even as he urged not working one day in seven, to the exasperation of Seneca.

Wherever magic has been practiced, as the footnotes by Margalioth themselves demonstrate, it's been more or less along the lines described by the author of *Sefer ha-Razim.* (We are not discussing black magic.) It is questionable whether he introduced anything new into the world—neither his prescriptions for healing, nor the way to capture a woman's heart,[92] nor the methods for destroying an enemy, nor even for winning at the races and praying in behalf of the jockey.[93] Margalioth, however, points to something which may be significant, namely, that though the suppliant prays to the angels and spirits and demons and the moon, and even brings offerings to them, he does not regard them as autonomous or as deities. For him they are all not divinities but angels, in other words, ministers and emissaries of the Supreme God. The magician is very careful not to slip. Even Helios, as Margalioth points out, is not the Greek sun god for the magus but only the "angel Helios."[94]

Margalioth's observation of the fact is fair enough, but I would like to press this just a bit further, because while an individual is busy with his strenuous magical operations, how much room remains in his mind to remember the God who alone is God? Yet, as we noted earlier, it is from his tradition that a person inherits his vocabulary for religious discourse and even for the formulae of many of his spells. This is not to deny that he also learns new words and new ideas, some, like Abraxas for example,[95] apparently being irresistible. But if he does not completely abandon (does one ever?) association with his basic vocabulary, though he may fill those words with different meanings, the original momentum of those words continues. Even as he behaves in less than monotheistic ways, the solemnity of his monotheism weighs upon him. The monotheistic vocabulary of the magician affects him too, the magician.

We have here, I think, once again ambiguity, that is, the ambiguity of a monotheist. The author of the *Sefer ha-Razim* is a magician; he teaches and practices his craft with all the reverence due it. But the language he uses he borrows heavily from the language of his religion. This is true all along and may even be of some comfort to his clients who recognize the words from other contexts familiar to them. Finally, we might say, he is overcome: when he pauses to contemplate not the heavenly crowd with whom he must maintain contact, but the heavenly sovereign, his reverence shifts, as it were, from the pragmatic practitioner to the awe-struck visionary. Toward his angels and spheres he is most respectful; but when he finally gets to his description of the seventh heaven with its sevenfold light, he is spectacularly uplifted. Our author writes a beautiful, lucid Hebrew: his clichés are no more numerous than in other texts of his time. He knows the Scriptures and helps himself freely to the biblical expressions, and not necessarily in a stereotyped or mechanical way. The regions he describes, and the roles he reports, he conveys with vivid directness; I do not know whom specifically he has in mind when he says that those on the sixth station of the second heaven are "awe-inspiring like the sages of the academy (?)," or perhaps, "like the sages in session," [96] but the whole description there would do no justice to certain traditional statements about the talmudic savants, the *hakamim.* Like others, our author is fully conscious of the effects of rhetoric: [97] "I adjure you angels cloaked in fire by Him who is wholly fire and whose seat is on a throne of fire and whose ministers are a flaming fire, and camps of fire minister before Him. . . ."[98] He uses post-biblical Hebrew expressions in a natural way: "by Him who Spake and the World Came to Be";[99] on one occasion he falls into the standard way of introducing a prooftext, *she-neemar* ("as it is said.")[100] Margalioth has also called attention to forms hitherto familiar to us only in *piyyut.*

Our magus is a cultivated man who unquestionably drew on magicians' handbooks for the necessary *materia magica.* But he knew his Bible too and drew on it as well. And when he reaches the seventh heaven where the Throne of Glory is, all hocus pocus is ended. Here is description of Glory, and the One in His holy habitation seeks justice and righteousness and none can see Him, not even His entourage, and there is enormous luminosity, and heavenly hosts proclaim the trisagion [101] out loud but with humility too—all is splendor and doxology. The whole is a kind of Merkabah and Hekalot exaltation, and the Jewishness runs through not only the words and imagery, [102] and four-teen-fold repetition of *Baruk shemo . . . u-mevorak* ("Blessed be His Name . . . and be it blessed") in the different parts of the universe, [103] but through the thorough monotheistic commitment. Now there is no client to help out, no petition to present or formula to follow. Like the traditional Jew (= the Jew submitting to talmudic authority) our magus declares that only God is the King over kings of kings and besides Him there is no El and other than He is no Elohim. But the tension between serving Him alone and serving His agents too remains. After all, in addition to the seventh heaven there are the other six. For these likewise biblical language is apt. Ambiguity is still with us therefore. As in other respects, the holy and profane accompany each other uneasily, but, in all fairness let it be added, they reenforce each other as well.

NOTES

B.	Babylonian Talmud
BhM	*Bet ha-Midrasch,* ed. A. Jellinek (Jerusalem, 1938)
LC	Loeb Classics
M.	Mishnah.
Mekilta	*Mekilta de-R. Ishmael,* ed. Lauterbach (Philadelphia, 1933–35)
MhG	Midrash ha-Gadol
MRS	*Mekilta de-R. Simeon,* ed. Epstein-Melamed (Jerusalem, 1955)
P.	Palestinian Talmud
PA	Pirqe Abot
PGM	K. Preisendanz (et. al.), *Papyri Graecae Magicae,* I (Leipzig-Berlin, 1928)
PK	*Pesikta de Rav Kahana,* ed. Mandelbaum (New York, 1962)
R.	Rabbi.
Razim	M. Margalioth, *Sepher ha-Razim,* (Jerusalem, 1966)
T.	Tosefta
TK	S. Lieberman, *Tosefta Ki-Fshutah,* III, (New York, 1962)

1. For the purposes of this paper, I think little is to be gained by distinguishing and classifying the different forms of magic and superstition, such as oaths, divination, astrology charms, amulets, etc. They all share a belief in the efficacy of the object or act or the recital in compelling supernatural forces to perform in some desired way if the act or recitation is carried out properly.

2. Philostratus, *Life of Appollonius* 7.39 (LC, II, 259): "Nor does any amount of failure in their [i.e., the athletes', the simple-minded

people's] enterprises shake their faith in it, they merely say such things as this: 'If I had only offered this sacrifice or that, if I had only burnt that perfume in place of another, I should not have failed to win.' And they really believe what they say." But see also M. Nilsson, *Greek Piety* (Oxford: Clarendon Press, 1948), pp. 169f.

3. Cf. W.O.E. Oesterley in R.H. Charles, *Apocrypha and Pseudepigrapha,* I (Oxford: Clarendon Press, 1913), 1 Macc. 5:67 and J. Moffatt in 2 Macc. *ad loc.* Did they wear amulets of the idols of Jamnia because such would prevail over the hosts of the governor of Jamnia? Or were there hucksters in the neighborhood selling Jamnia amulets? On the conjuction, by the way, of Temple and Torah, cf. the charge against Stephen in Acts 6:13.

4. Cf. Razim, 93, n. 16, and this may well be the intent behind "capsize a ship," 69.

5. A. D. Nock, *Essays on Religion and the Ancient World,* ed. Z. Stewart (Cambridge, Mass.: Harvard University Press, 1972), I. 316.

6. See Fragment 17, verso, *Fragmenta Hebraica Cairensia Talmudica,* II, Westminster College (Cambridge): "To overcome fear of the evil eye, take the eye of a wolf, let it dry, put it in a garment or inside a skin (pouch) and wear it around your (neck?). Then so long as you wear it, you'll have no fear of the evil eye or sorcery. In whatever you turn to you'll succeed. Your enemies also will fall under (=be defeated by) you. You'll fear neither demons nor plague and you'll find favor in the sight of all." Cf. H. L. Strack and P. Billerbeck, *Kommentar zum Neuen Testament aus Talmud und Midrasch* (Munich: Beck, 1922–28) on Acts 13:9b, pp. 713–715; R. Yose be-R. Haninah in Gen. Rabba 56:11, p. 611, on Abraham and Isaac, and Theodor's citations *ad loc.*

7. Unless otherwise noted, all examples are from Razim.

8. F. Cumont, *Oriental Religions in Roman Paganism* (New York: Dover Publications, 1956), p. 165.

9. Note also Nock, *Essays on Religion,* I, 191.

10. On views of the Amorites cf. the statements by R. Yose and Rabban Simeon ben Gamaliel in T. Shabbat 7:23, 25. On the association of Amorites with fornication, cf. Testament of Judah, 12:2. Note too the combination of fornication, stealing, magic, etc., in Didache 2:2. My suggestion of "metathesis" is of course conjectural only. See J.H. Levy, *Olamot Nifgashim* (Jerusalem, 1960), p. 67.

11. T. Shabbat, chaps. 6–7, ed. S. Lieberman, pp. 22–29.

12. They are encountered in a variety of and even antagonistic cultures.

13. TK, 94 and also n. 20. Note by the way, the "Tale of the Fuller's Wife" in Apuleius, the *Golden Ass*, IX.

14. TK, 85.

15. TK, 82.

16. TK, 83.

17. TK, 88.

18. Shabbat 67a; cf. T. Shabbat 7:21, TK, 102; P. Shabbat 6:9. On Aristides' dream of a bone stuck in his throat, and the cure for that, cf. A. J. Festugière, *Personal Religion among the Greeks* (Berkeley: University of California Press, 1960), p. 101f.

19. *Loc. cit.,* in the names of different sages.

20. TK, 103f. and n. 63.

21. T. Shabbat 4:9, and cf. TK *ad loc.*

22. The language of piety is literal, but may be allowed to be metaphorical; the magician's vocabulary is expected to be strictly literal and precise. Yet the Establishment boasts that what it says is strictly true, but what the magician says is deliberately obscure and full of deceitful double entendres.

23. Shabbat 6:9; note the names in the Babylonian Talmud.

24. Sanhedrin 10:1. People may have preferred spells out of lack of confidence in the ordinary physicians; note even Philo *Special Laws* 1.252f. (LC, VII, 245f.)

25. The rabbis don't hesitate, when it suits their purpose, to put biblical verses in the mouths of Gentiles; see, for example, J. Goldin, *The Song at the Sea* (New Haven: Yale, 1971), pp. 116f.—this is of course haggadic. Now note the anecdote in M. Abodah Zarah 3:4 (see also W. A. L. Elmslie in his edition, Cambridge, University Press, 1911, pp. 47ff.) where a halakic problem is involved.

26. 101a in the name of R. Yohanan; in the Palestinian Talmud in the name of Rab. But see already Tosefta 12:10 (ed. Zuckermandel, p:443). See the delightful anecdote about R. Meir in P. Sotah 1:4.

27. B. Shebuot 15b also.

28. Cf. Rashi in Sanhedrin 101a, s.v. *wbrwqq;* cf. the reference to Galen in J. Trachtenberg, *Jewish Magic and Superstition* (Cleveland: World Publishing Co., 1961), pp. 120ff. and 293, n. 7. On the use of spittle see S. Eitrem, *Some Notes on the Demonology in the New Testament* (Oslo, 1966), pp. 56ff.

29. See briefly Trachtenberg, p. 107 and Yoreh Deah 179:8.

30. PK, 74f. and cf. ibid. for references to parallels.

31. See I. Löw, *Flora der Juden* (Hildesheim: Ohlms, 1967), I.

92, n., "Wutanfall," fir of rage. Cf. Preuss, *Biblisch-talmudische Medizin* (Berlin, 1911), p. 367, who speaks of "der Geist *thezazith.*" In MhG, Numbers (ed. Z.M. Rabinowits, Jerusalem, 1967), p. 325, the editor explains it as spirit of *madness, shetuth.*

32. I think this is intended to suggest: Here is a well-balanced man, not one with a sick mind. However, the meaning may also be: Have you ever had experience in these matters or are you simply being cantankerous and mocking with questions?

33. So the addition in Numbers Rabba 19:8. On the connection of the number seven with the "red heifer", cf. PK, 59. On the order "burn," "beat down"(*ktš*, but in Exod. 32:20 *thn;* cf note however Deut. 9:21, *ktt* and *thn*).

34. Literally, with a reed, but other sources read literally "with straw."

35. This is an oath, by the way; cf. S. Lieberman, *Greek in Jewish Palestine* (New York: Jewish Theological Seminary of America, 1942), pp. 115f. and n. 2. See also M. Greenberg in *Journal of Biblical Literature* 76 (1957), 37, n. 18.

36. *Huqqah*, a commandment to be obeyed though no explanation for it is available. Though we do not have it, note that Philo apparently did have an allegorical explanation in mind. Cf. *Special Laws* 1.269 (LC, VII, 255, and note c).

37. The magician also calls what he does magic (of course not referring to himself as quack; cf. A.D.Nock, *Essays on Religion*, I, 309, 313); perhaps even prefers that his work be regarded as nonconformist or irregular, so that he may continue to fascinate clients. Cf. A. D. Nock, *St. Paul* (London: Oxford University Press, 1960), p. 99. But it's what the authorities declare which brings magic into conflict with the *law.* For the reaction of satirists, see Lucian, "Alexander the False Prophet."

38. *Essays on Religion*, I, 314f.

39. See further M. Smith, *Clement of Alexandria and a Secret Gospel of Mark* (Cambridge, Mass.: Harvard University Press, 1973), pp. 231ff. The magician's task may be more difficult than piety's, for the latter's promises are frequently granted an extension (if the reward or punishment is delayed, there's the future when it will take place); the magician is expected to produce immediate results (or within the time limits he set) if his credibility is not to suffer.

40. See S. Lieberman, *Greek in Jewish Palestine,* p. 92.

41. Ibid., pp. 110f, 114.

42. TK, 94, 95.

43. TK, 102.

44. Lieberman, *Greek in Jewish Palestine,* pp. 104–106.

45. Cf. *Jewish Encyclopedia* (New York, 1901–1905), s.v. "Bibliomancy" for the listing of the verses. See L. Ginzberg, *Legends of the Jews* (Philadelphia: Jewish Publication Society of America, 1913–1938), VI, 468.

46. In spells and charms you refer to a person's mother rather than to the father. You're always sure of the identity of the mother, and in magical formulae you have to be sure. See also E. R. Goodenough, *Jewish Symbols in the Greco-Roman Period,* (New York: Pantheon Books, 1953), II, 196, n. 180. On the triad of Hananiah, Mishael, and Azariah and the evil eye, cf. Genesis Rabba 56, end (611f.) and Ginzberg, *Legends,* VI, 419.

47. B. Shabbat 67a, J. Preuss, *Biblisch-talmudische Medizin,* p. 185. Cf. B. Lewin, *Otzar ha-Gaonim, Shabbat* (Haifa, 1930), 66 (of Responsa) and 28 (explanation, by R. Hai Gaon).

48. MRS, p. 1 and also p. 2, in the name of Eleazar ben Arak. But see also MRS, ed. Hoffman (Frankfurt a. M., 1905), p. 2. See further D. Lieberman in *Tarbiz,* 27 (1958), 186f.

49. Abot de-Rabbi Natan, ed. S. Schechter (Vienna, 1887), 41a.

50. Lauterbach in *Hebrew Union College Annual* 11 (1936), 207–340; and cf. S. Spiegel, *The Last Trial* (New York: Pantheon Books, 1967), p. 65f. and nn. 19–22. See also R.Dalven, "The Yearly Cycle of the Ioannine Jews," in *Conservative Judaism* (Winter 1974), p. 50, for a charming *Tashlik* custom when it rains.

51. M. L. Margolis, *Micah: The Holy Scriptures with Commentary* (Philadelphia: Jewish Publication Society of America, 1908), p. 79.

52. Lauterbach, p. 239.

53. Ibid., pp. 287ff.

54. See for example, the quotation from R. Moses Isserles (1520–1572) in Lauterbach, n. 115: "Even a mere custom (*minhag*) of Israel is Torah. Consider this going to a body of water and reciting, 'Cast all our sins into the depths of the sea.' For from contemplation of the deeps (of the sea) one learns the truth of the creation of the universe—for the deep of the sea is the abyss (*tehom*) and it is the very deepest part of the sea. Now it is of the fundamental nature of the elements that the waters cover the earth, and the earth is the center, and it is at the lowest point of the whole universe. Now then, the earth was intended to serve mankind, all its inhabitants, and this is not independent of the purpose of the

Creator, for it is He who brought the universe into being according to His will and with the aim of having the earth inhabited. That is why we go to a body of water to behold how here (at the shore), He set a boundary to the sea, declaring, Thus far you come, no further (cf. Jer. 5:22 and Job 38:11). Now when we go to the sea, we behold there the omnipotence of the Creator. This is why we go to some body of water on Rosh ha-Shanah, for it is the Day of Judgment when everyone ought to put his mind on the theme of the creation of the universe, and that the Lord, may He be exalted, is King over the earth. There is recited 'Thou shalt cast our sins into the depths of the sea,' for indeed he who puts his mind to the theme of the depth of the sea and recognizes that the world is created, thereby comes to know of the existence of the Lord, may He be exalted, and thereby regrets all his iniquities; and his sins are forgiven. And thus the sins are cast into the depths of the sea."

55. T. Shabbat 6:1, TK, *ad loc.*, and n. 25.

56. Cf. Lauterbach, p 251.

57. Ginzberg, *Legends*, V, 87, n. 40.

58. See for example, the lovely apparition of Isis in Apuleius, *The Golden Ass*, XI.

59. Mekilta, Be-Shallah 1 (I,176). Cf. E.E. Urbach, Hazal (Jerusalem, 1969), pp. 104f.

60. Ginzberg, *Legends,* II, 181 and notes *ad loc.* See also Memar Marqah 1:10 (ed. MacDonald, II, pp. 40 ff.).

61. Rabbi M. M. Kasher, Torah Shelemah, XIV, 16, does reproduce this reading.

62. On a beautiful gold tablet, about 2 inches long and 1 3/4 inches wide, referring to the city of Apqu of the Assyrian Empire, which I had the privilege of seeing and handling thanks to the late Albrecht Goetze and first called to my attention by S. D. Walters, see F. J. Stephens in vol. VII (1953), pp. 73f., of the *Journal of Cuneiform Studies.* Reference to a gold tablet on which a biblical text is inscribed—M. Yoma 3:10. See also Suetonius on Nero, 10 (LC, II, 103). On a gold sheet with instructions for the dead, cf. D. C. Kurtz and J. Boardman, *Greek Burial Customs* (Ithaca, N.Y.: Cornell University Press, 1971), p. 210; see also p. 217. See further Goodenough, *Jewish Symbols,* II, 194 (top of page) and 204; PGM, IV, 1215 (I, 114). On the Mekilta passage cf. also Goodenough, II, 283.

63. See also Yalqut Shimeoni (Salonica, 1526–27) or Exod. 13:19 and MhG, Exodus, ed. Margulies, on the verse.

64. On the dogs, cf. PK, 187f. and Ginzberg, *Legends*, VI, 1, n. 3. Of course there is some significance to the fact that here too "gold" is spoken of. On gold, see also Razim, 66, 102, 105.

65. "Etc.": so the printed text.

66. Midrash Aggadah, Exod., ed. Buber, p. 143, says, "And Moses wrote out the Ineffable Name and cast it into the Nile." Not a word of what he wrote on.

67. Be-Shallah 2; Eqeb 6 is of no help here; nor is Deut. Rabba 11:7, nor Yalqut on Deut. 34:6.

68. On "Ox" (or "Bull") cf. Deut. 33:17. See also BhM, II, 11. As for the reading in the latter *'ly šwr* (rather than *'lh šwr*), Professor Saul Lieberman writes me that it is associated with the reading of Gen. 49:22, *'ale shur*!

In Sekel Tob, Exodus, 170, the reading is, "he took a pebble and threw it into (the Nile) and cried out' 'Rise, O ox, Rise, O ox. . . . '"

Particularly interesting is the reading of the Midrash Shir ha-Shirim (ed. L. Grünhut), 13a-b: "When Moses came to raise (Joseph's) casket, he inscribed and engraved on four silver tablets (plates; cf. below) the image of (the) four living creatures (cf. Ezek.1)—(on one) the image of a lion, (on one) the image of a human being, (on one) the image of an eagle, (and on one) the image of an ox (bull)." (See also the exorcism in Goodenough, *Jewish Symbols,* II, 182.) "He threw the one with the image of the lion (into the Nile) and that place grew turbulent. He threw in the one with the image of the human being, and Joseph's bones assembled. He threw in the one with the image of the eagle, and the casket rose to the surface. In his hand remained only the plate (=tablet) with the image of the ox. And while Moses was occupied with Joseph's casket, he gave that plate to a woman and forgot about it. When (later Israel) gathered the gold to make the (golden) calf, the woman gave the tablet to them and they threw it in the fire and out came that calf (cf. Exod. 32:24). . . . " Cf. Ginzberg, *Legends*, III, 122 and VI, 51f. See also TK ad Megillah, 1218f. And my colleague Professor Jeffrey Tigay calls my attention to the paper by S. E. Loewenstamm in *Biblica* 48 (1967), 481–490, "The Making and Destruction of the Golden Calf."

A *silver* plate for the *golden* calf: is there some textual fusion here?

The engraving of the Ineffable Name does not appear here, but engraving does, and it is picturesquely associated with the vision of Ezekiel, in turn related to the story of the golden calf. At all events, magic has not disappeared from the legend. Nor from the version of the story in MhG, Gen., 887, where Moses writes (=draws images) on pieces of Joseph's cup.

69. Cf. M. Shebuot 3:5.

70. Cf. n. 69 above.

71. See in this connection S. Lieberman in *Jewish Quarterly Review* 37 (1946), p. 46, and on the white cock, pp. 50f.

72. Cf. A.D. Nock, *Essays on Religion*, I, 315: "What then do the ancients mean by *magia?* . . . *the religions belonging to aliens* or on any general ground disapproved." (The italics are mine.)

73. Cf. S. Ganzfried, *Kutsur Shulhan Aruk*, 3:4. On notions of right and left, cf. the references in Goldin, p. 149. See also G. Scholem, *Sabbatai Sevi* (Princeton, 1973), p. 91.

74. For Islam cf. Ibn Khaldûn, *The Muqaddimah*, trans. F. Rosenthal (Princeton: Princeton University Press, 1967), I, lxxii: III, 159ff.

75. Hilkot Abodah Zarah 1:1 (M. Hyamson's translation). Cf. Festugière, *Personal Religion*, p. 117.

76. See, e.g., A.D. Nock, *Essays on Religion*, I, 188f. On Jews famous as magician's, see also E. Braver, *Sefer Magnes* (Jerusalem, 1938), p. 61.

77. All this can be seen in the vocabulary of Razim.

78. On Judaism's awesome attitude toward the Name (and Names) of God, see, for example, M. Sanhedrin 10:1, Abot de-Rabbi Natan, 28b (cf. TK ad Yoma 2:1, 755, n. 14; G. Scholem, *Jewish Gnosticism, Merkabah Mysticism, and Talmudic Tradition* (New York: Jewish Theological Seminary of America, 1960), pp. 46, 54, n. 36, M. Yoma 6:2 (and cf. Albeck in his edition, p. 470). See also Razim, 99.

79. On what papyri reveal of *professional* nature, cf. A.D. Nock, *Essays on Religion*, I, 179.

80. See on this and the following, Razim, Introduction and Text.

81. Cf. Gen. 32:2f.

82. Note especially the brilliant decipherment by Professor Morton Smith in *Sefer ha-Razim*, 12, and similarly brilliant decipherment and interpretation of names and places in Hekalot Rabbati, by J. H. Levy in *Studies in Jewish Hellenism* (Hebrew, Jerusalem, 1960), pp. 259–265.

83. Probably the name of the mother; cf. note 46 above.

84. Razim, 76f. and notes. I might add that the text on the first heaven is the longest in this work and contains more "excitement"

than the other heavens. To me this suggests that the heaven closest to man is the most easily reached, and it is therefore natural to turn to that region.

85. Note, however, S. Spiegel in *Harry A. Wolfson Jubilee Volume* (Hebrew, Jerusalem, 1965), p. 261 (top of page).

86. Cf. E. J. Bickerman, "Faux Littéraires dans l'Antiquité Classique," in *Rivista de Filologia* 101 (1973), 27ff., and especially 31ff. On the great power of Solomon's wizardy "among us to this day" (first cent.), cf. Josephus, *Antiquities*, 8.45–49 (LC, V, 595f.).

87. For additional discussion of the authorship, cf. Razim, 26ff.

88. This is not surprising. Note also the several injunctions to avoid impurity—81, 91, 103—which would be directed only to a man.

89. Cf. Goodenough, *Jewish Symbols*, II, 199.

90. See also Razim, 15. ". . . the proportion of charms containing no Jewish elements at all is so surprisingly small that it is quite apparent that the pagans hold Jewish magic in high honor" (Goodenough, *Jewish Symbols*, II, 206). See also M. Simon, *Verus Israel* (Paris: De Boccard, 1948), pp. 395ff. Cf. M. Smith, *Clement*, p. 233, n. 10, on the frequency of *Iao*.

91. Cf. PGM, IV, 3079 (I,172) and Eitrem, *Some Notes on Demonology*, p. 22. Cf. A. Deissmann, *Light from the Ancient East* (London, 1911), pp. 259–260. Seneca: in St. Augustine, *City of God*, VI, 11.

92. Cf. Philostratus, *loc. cit.* (above, note 2). See also PGM, IV, 400–405 (I, 84f.).

93. Razim, 94 and p. x. On horse racing passion, cf. Philostratus, *Life of Appollonius* 5.26 (LC, I, 521); and cf. A. A. Barb, "The Survival of Magic Arts," in A. Momigliano, ed., *The Conflict Between Paganism and Christianity in the Fourth Century* (Oxford: Clarendon Press, 1964), pp. 119f.

94. Contrast Goodenough, *Jewish Symbols*. II, 194, 200.

95. Cf. Razim, 8.

96. P. 86, line 93 (of second heaven). Perhaps, however, the term *yeshivah* should be understood as high-court/chief-academy as the term in the Genizah documents in later centuries is explained by S. D. Goitein in *Zion* 26 (1961), 177; see also S. Spiegel, *Wolfson Jubilee Volume*, p. 250, n. 4.

97. Of course, in this he is not unique; cf. an eloquent adjuration in Goodenough, *Jewish Symbols*, II, 198, or 182 (for reference to fire).

98. Razim, 95.
99. Razim, 102.
100. Razim, 108. And note an "echo" of PA, beginning, on 66, line 25. He is likewise familiar with a commonplace Aramaic legal formula, 75 (top.). On *piyyut* forms, 27, n. 11.
101. Cf. Goodenough, *Jewish Symbols,* II, 176.
102. Note the lovely image on 108, "suspends the world like a cluster (of grapes)." Professor Shalom Spiegel calls to my attention (the fact as well as the following references) that the figure of speech and image occur already in Ras Shamra—W. F. Albright, *Journal of the Palestine Oriental Society* 14 (1934), 133f.—and appear also in medieval Hebrew poetry, as noted by L. Zunz, *Synagogale Poesie des Mittelalters* (Frankfurt: O. J. Kauffmann, 1920), pp. 510f., and referred to also by G. Scholem, *Einige kabbalistische Handschriften in British Museum* (Berlin: Schocken, 1932), p. 26f.
103. P. 109. Once (109, line 31) *kebodo* rather than *shemo*; but *kabod* here equals *shem.* for the combination *baruk u-mevorak,* cf. H. Yalon, *Introduction to the Vocalization of the Mishna* (Hebrew, Jerusalem, 1964), p. 96.

7: Jesus and the Disciples as Miracle Workers in the Apocryphal New Testament

Paul J. Achtemeier

IT IS OF COURSE IMPOSSIBLE TO CHARACTERIZE IN ANY complete or unified way the widely disparate writings which could be contained under the rubric "apocryphal New Testament." Those writings cover a range of some five or six centuries, and include everything from fragments of sayings to long, novel-like literary pieces. To gain a perspective on this material, we will lay our main emphasis on the mid-second to mid-third centuries, using other materials to indicate continuity where that seems advisable.

Our title will also guide the way we approach the world out of which our material grew and to which it spoke. Because our problem concerns Jesus and the disciples, we must remind ourselves of the canonical roots of our topic. We shall therefore survey, very briefly, the roots of the understanding of Jesus and his followers as miracle workers in the canonical New Testament writings. To gain further perspective, we will look, again briefly and selectively, at the way in which the non-Christian world of the second and third centuries viewed miracles, miracle workers, and magic. The third component in our attempt to lay a groundwork for our study of this problem in the second and third century apocryphal New Testament writings will involve, again very briefly and selectively, an account of the developing line of Christian apologetic with regard to miracles and miracle workers. We will limit ourselves here to Justin, Irenaeus, and Origen. Only against such a background will we be in a position to grapple with the problems involved in our topic, and the final part of our study will be devoted directly to that.

I

It is hardly necessary to point out that the canonical gospels are filled with traditions about the mighty acts of Jesus. The healings, exorcisms, and prodigies (i.e., non-healing miracles) he performed are there amply recorded. There is much that can be said about them: the history of the development of these stories in the pre-canonical period, the use to which the evangelists put them, the various and changing emphases they are given, and the historical problem they present to an age of scientific historiography, but we shall have to forego discussion of such problems here. It is sufficient to recall that Jesus was remembered as one who devoted an important amount of his time to such deeds.

More important for our purposes, as will become increasingly evident, is the fact that the canonical traditions recall that such power was also given to the followers of Jesus. Both at the time of the commissioning and the sending out of the twelve (Mark 6:7 // Matt. 10:1, 8 // Luke 9:1–2; Mark 3:14–15) and of the seventy (Luke 10:9), the power to heal and cast out demons is given.[1] A comparison of Matt. 10:8 and Luke 9:1–2 with Mark 6:7 and 3:15 indicates a growing tradition about the power granted to the disciples. In both instances there is an expansion of the Marcan commission to cast out evil spirits. The further synoptic traditions about the success of the disciples in these matters (Mark 6:12–13 // Luke 9:6; Luke 10:17), along with some other evidence of miracles done, or expected to be done, by Jesus' followers (Mark 9: 28–29, 38–39) point in the same direction.

Corroborative evidence from the same period as the pre-canonical synoptic traditions can be found in Paul. It is clear from his letters that followers of Christ, especially apostles, would perform mighty acts (e.g., Rom. 15:18–19). In fact, Paul apparently thought there were no true apostles who could not and did not do miracles. Such activity was one of the signs of the true apostle (2 Cor. 12:12; in light of that passage, cf. 1 Cor. 2:4–5; 2 Cor. 6:7). One has the further impression that such things could be expected in the normal course of the life of the local church (1 Cor. 12:10; Gal. 3:5); so much so that their presence would be necessary for any who wanted to imitate it (cf. 2 Thess. 2:9).

The many miracles recorded of the apostles in Acts (in addition to those of Peter and Paul, miracles are reported of Stephen, 6:8; Phillip, 8:6; the apostles as a group, 2:43; 5:12; and of Paul and Barnabas, 14:3; 15:12), and the references to such events in Heb. 2:3b-4 are further indication of the pervasiveness of this tradition within the canonical materials. It is interesting to note, along this line, that the only mention of possible miracles in the Coptic Gospel of Thomas concerns the healing activity of the disciples (logion 14).

The problem of the attribution of such acts to magical practices also surfaces in the canonical traditions, a fact which is less surprising when we note that already in the first century, the name of Jesus was understood to have a power of its own (e.g., Mark 9:38; Acts 3:6; 16:8; in a negative context, Matt. 7:22–23; Acts 19:15). Given the tenor of the times, it is further hardly surprising that the author of Acts, on several occasions, gives a negative judgment on magic in relation to the Christian faith (8:18–24: 13:8–12; 19:19; with 19:13–16, cf. Mark 9:38–40).[2]

From such a cursory examination of the evidence in the canonical New Testament, it is clear that mighty acts were a part of the Christian traditions from the earliest stages, that not only was Jesus remembered to have done them, but that such acts were done, indeed expected, by those who followed Jesus. It should not be surprising, therefore, if later, non-canonical traditions share those views.

II

The second element of our survey of the background against which the apocryphal New Testament, and its view of Jesus and the disciples as miracle workers, must be understood concerns the secular (i.e., non-Christian) world within which those writings had to make their way. As will quickly become apparent, forces were at work within that world which would have encouraged the development of traditions about Jesus and his disciples as wonder workers, even apart from the canonical roots we have seen. The Hellenistic world of the second and third centuries, as earlier and later, was enormously interested in wonders and those who did them. Magic was a universal element within that world.

That such interest extended to, and pervaded, the interests of the Jewish population of that world is not to be doubted.[3] Although the more Hellenized Jews living outside the land of Palestine may have been more devoted to magic and allied arts than those of the Jewish homeland in Palestine, there is ample evidence for the fact that these latter also believed in and practiced magic, despite the direct commands to the contrary from Scripture and rabbis.[4] The Talmud, in addition to reporting events assuming widespread magical practices, e.g., the hanging of eighty witches at one time,[5] and numerous accounts of rabbis who practiced necromancy,[6] stipulates that no one could be a member of the Sanhedrin unless he had "a knowledge of sorcery."[7] While this last point of course does not mean its practice was required, it does indicate that such practices were so widespread, and charges regarding them so frequent, that anyone who aspired to judge the people had to be familiar with them.

With interest in the wondrous and the magical so widespread, it is not surprising that beliefs and practices knew no national or ethnic boundaries. That saliva, for example, was effective in cures, especially of the eyes, was widely believed, and the saliva of a fasting man is of greater power.[8] The evil eye was universally feared;[9] iron was universally thought to remain uninfluenced by, even to provide protection against, demons;[10] the name of the Hebrew God was universally thought to be especially powerful;[11] bits of bone stuck in the throat could be helped by putting bits of the same bone on one's head;[12] such a list could be extended almost indefinitely.[13]

That such universality also contained elements of mutual influence is clear enough from the evidence. We have already mentioned the power imputed to the Hebrew God,[14] and if Hellenistic practices and beliefs influenced Jews both in and outside of Palestine, it is also clear that Jews enjoyed a certain reputation among Gentiles as particularly given to magical practices.[15] It is a further corollary of such universality of belief and practice that one is hard put to maintain the uniqueness of one's own system of belief and practice. A common device to that end was to attribute one's own acts to the Deity, those of one's opponents to magic. Such accusations were common among Jews,[16] and while Gentiles were for the most part oblivious to the religious force of monotheism that made such accusations natural, even necessary, to the Jews, they nevertheless leveled, as one of their most serious charges, the accusation of "magician" at their enemies, great and small alike.[17]

There are other elements common to the magical beliefs and practices of the Hellenistic world which are more directly relevant to our attempt to illumine the background of the apocryphal New Testament writings; to those elements we must now direct our attention. The first of these is the power that was believed to accrue to those

who know the name of a deity. Pliny reports that one of
the methods used by the Romans when laying siege was to
summon the deity of the invested town and promise that
deity superior worship in Rome. For that reason, Pliny continues, the name of the tutelary deity of Rome was kept a
carefully guarded secret.[18] Lucian of Samosata refers to the
belief that curses can be accomplished by means of "holy
names;"[19] and Origen has an interesting discussion on the
need to use the indigenous language when using such
divine cognomens.[20] Incantations also frequently accompanied such names, in the belief that this made the
invocation more powerful,[21] and if that incantation could
be in a foreign language, it would be proportionately more
powerful.[22]

It is not surprising that the Jews also regarded the name
of God as powerful;[23] it may be more surprising to note
that the Jews used that divine name in the same way the
Gentiles did in their magic. The Talmud contains instructions for the cure of one bitten by a mad dog; one of the
steps is to prepare an amulet bearing the sacred tetragrammaton.[24] The source of Solomon's power over demons
consisted of a ring on which was engraved the divine
name,[25] and Solomon in turn was so powerful that demons could be driven out in his name.[26] Much later
tradition ascribed Jesus' power, understood as magic, to
his knowledge of the secret divine name.[27] Incantations
were also known and used by the Jews, some of which
were intelligible,[28] some of which consisted of nonsense
syllables,[29] and some of which the contents were not
given, merely mentioned.[30] It is worth noting in passing
that demons, against whom incantations are normally directed, played a large part in the Jewish beliefs recorded in
the Talmud.[31]

A second element to be considered is the great power
attributed to the use of herbs and other materials in
wondrous and magical acts. An Egyptian raises a corpse to
life by, among other things, placing an herb on its mouth
three times and another on its chest.[32] Diogenes Laertius

reports that Empedocles knew "drugs" that would do everything from retarding age and curing ills to altering the weather,[33] and Pliny knows endless tales of the uses of all sorts of materials for all sorts of purposes, many obviously magical in intent.[34] Typically, Lucian of Samosata caricatures such beliefs and practices by carrying them to absurd extreme.[35] The Talmud, too, knows endless ways to use the strangest materials, from the afterbirth of a black she-cat[36] to the heart of a speckled swine (!).[37] The rabbis also knew how to distinguish between magical practices and acceptable customs, e.g., ways to make a pot boil quickly.[38] Josephus knows of roots that will expel demons if they are merely applied to the sufferer[39] and gives an example of another universal practice when he describes the special way the root must be procured.[40]

Another element common to Hellenistic magical beliefs was the power of a magician to turn himself or herself, or someone else, into another form, i.e., metamorphosis. Known to the Greeks since the time of Homer, where the gods repeatedly turn themselves into other forms or appear in the guise of someone else and do the same to mortals, belief in such metamorphoses continued into the Hellenistic period unabated. It was of course the subject of Ovid's work by that name and constituted the major theme of Apuleius' story of Lucius and his adventures in altered form.[41] While it did not capture the Jewish imagination to the extent that some other items from the Hellenistic world did, the Talmud also has a few accounts of metamorphoses, in one case, interestingly enough, of an ass that is transformed, although the story bears no resemblance to that of Lucius.[42]

The final element common in the Hellenistic world to which we want to call attention concerns the fact that Egypt was the origin and home of wonders and of magic. Greek magic books were known as "Egyptian books," apparently because of their point of origin,[43] and time and again, in popular literature, Egyptians appear as magicians, or magical phrases are most powerful when they can be recited in the "Egyptian language."[44] Celsus shares this belief and then uses it in his anti-Christian polemic by maintaining that Jesus learned his ability to do wondrous acts in Egypt. Because of such acts, Celsus says, he then called himself God.[45]

The Talmud also reflects this belief concerning the origin of magic. Nine-tenths of the world's witchcraft descended on Egypt,[46] and the Midrash on Exodus knows that even children of four or five could duplicate the wonder Aaron performed with his staff (Exod. 7:10).[47] Only a fool is not careful when buying anything in Egypt, lest it have a spell upon it,[48] and the demon driven out by Tobit's magic flees to its home, the "farthest parts of upper Egypt" (8:3). Like Celsus, the Talmud also has the tradition that Jesus (= ben Stada) learned his witchcraft in Egypt,[49] and the growing influence of the Christian faith, with its traditions of the miracles of Jesus and of his disciples, appears to have considerably lessened the traditions of wonders and magic done by rabbis, both in number and significance.[50] Although folk-traditions of magic appear to have continued, miracles, after about the year 90 A.D., play a less significant role in the learned traditions and debates of the rabbis.[51] As far as miracle traditions and wondrous acts are concerned, the Christians appear to have won the religious competition with the Jews.[52]

III

The third element in our survey of the background against which to understand the apocryphal New Testament writings of the mid-second to mid-third centuries is the growing apologetic trends as they affect the way wondrous deeds are reported and understood. As was true of the previous reviews, this will also be highly selective. We will limit our treatment to the writings of Justin Martyr and Irenaeus, and to the *Contra Celsum* of Origen.

Perhaps the most striking fact is the relative absence of

references to the miracles of Jesus. Whereas the Apostolic Fathers had virtually ignored such acts of the Lord, the apologists do mention them, but as a rule limit such treatment to summaries. There is no evidence either of a growing tradition of miracles of Jesus, nor are any miracles ascribed to him that were not already reported in the synoptic gospels.[53] That does not mean a corresponding loss of interest in miracles as such, however, nor in their importance. It is quite clear that at the time the apologists wrote, wondrous activity was still very much a part of contemporary Church life. When Irenaeus lists the activities then current in the Church, he includes exorcisms, foreknowledge (through visions), healing the sick, and raising the dead.[54] It is further clear that such acts are done through the power of Jesus. This is commonly expressed by pointing to miracles done by his followers as being done "in his name." Justin refers to the "mighty" deeds even now done through his name,"[55] and Origen, while not always having as his point of emphasis the power of Jesus' name, nevertheless regularly points to contemporary Christian miracles done in that name.[56]

In addition to general healing activity on the part of contemporary Christians, it is apparent that the exorcism of demons still plays a large part in the miracles reported. Justin speaks of the "numberless demoniacs" who have been healed by Christians in the name of Jesus[57] and makes it clear to Trypho that "to this day" demons are being exorcised by that name.[58] Origen similarly mentions the "countless demons" which Christians have expelled in Jesus' name.[59] Such activity points to "Jesus' divinity," although not as the primary evidence; that remains, for Origen, the existence of the Church itself.[60] Origen also speaks of the "spiritual miracles" of Christians, i.e., opening the eyes of those blind in soul, the ears of those deaf to talk of virtue, etc., and refers to them as the "greater works" Jesus promised his followers (John 14:12),[61] but there is little question Origen also intends to report "physical" miracles. In all of this, it is clear that such wondrous activity can be traced in a direct line from contemporary Christians, through the disciples, back to Jesus himself. Clearly, Irenaeus thinks the wonders done in his day are the same kind as Jesus performed.[62]

If, then, miracles are still a lively issue, what are the apologetic themes which emerge when miracles are discussed by the three Fathers under consideration? One such theme centers around the idea that miracles awaken faith in Christ and awaken it legitimately. Justin, in fact, argued that it was by such deeds that Jesus compelled his contemporaries to recognize him.[63] Irenaeus points out that being cured from demon possession has frequently led that person to faith in Jesus,[64] and his allegorical treatment of Jesus' use of clay to heal the blind man (John 9:6) leads to the point that such acts were performed so that those who saw them should be restored to the "fold of life."[65] Origen also points out that miracles were necessary for the faith of those who by custom asked for "signs and wonders,"[66] but he qualifies the point by urging (1) that miracles were more necessary earlier on before man had progressed in intelligence to the point where such things were no longer so necessary,[67] (b) that while the masses need miracles, the elite are better served by teaching,[68] and (c) that it is wrong to deduce from the miracles only that Jesus was divine, without recognizing also his humanity.[69] Despite such qualifications, however, Origen is prepared to argue that without miracles, the disciples' preaching would not have met with success, and that the miracles of Jesus did in fact lead many to the "wonderful teaching of the gospel."[70]

A second theme, allied to the first, consists in the argument that Christian miracles are credible because they are the fulfillment of prophecy. This theme is particularly characteristic of Justin, who uses it to defend Christ against pejorative comparison with healers of classical antiquity,[71] to give added weight to the credibility of the reports of Jesus' miracles,[72] or to defend those acts against claims that they were done by magic.[73] Irenaeus

calls upon prophecy to lend credence to the reality of
Jesus' miracles; they were more than mere appearances.[74]
Origen calls upon prophecy to refute Celsus' claim that
Jesus' miracles were mere sorcery.[75]

A third theme which emerges in the discussion of Jesus'
mighty acts has already been hinted at, namely, the need
to defend Jesus against the charge of having performed his
mighty works by means of sorcery. The apologists were
intent on showing that there was a difference between
Christian miracles and pagan magic. Justin recognizes that
there are contemporaries who appear to be doing the kind
of thing Jesus did and his followers do, e.g., Simon and his
disciple Menander, both from Samaria,[76] but they did
their mighty acts by magic, a claim that is totally false
when leveled against Jesus.[77] Irenaeus also knows of magicians, both former and contemporary, who appear to have
done things similar to those miracles done by Jesus,[78] but
he points out two ways in which such magicians differ
from Christ and from those who perform miracles as his
followers. In the first place, their goal is self-aggrandize-
ment through deceit, and they glorify themselves, charging
fees for their deeds and "doing more harm than good."[79]
In the second place, their deeds are not permanent, they
really do not have the power to heal, and any demons they
cast out they have previously sent into the person.[80] The
fact that Jesus rose from the dead, while these magicians
have not, is proof for Irenaeus that Jesus is not to be
compared with them.[81]

Origen, interestingly enough, argues for the reality of
magic, linking it to his argument for the reality of the
power of names,[82] but he never tires of refuting the claim
that Jesus performed his miracles by magic or as a sorcerer. Celsus misrepresents Jesus when he levels such
claims,[83] for Jesus was neither a boaster nor a sorcerer.[84]
The death he met bore no resemblance, as Celsus claimed,
to those put to death for sorcery,[85] and Origen calls upon
the difference between the deeds of Moses (divine) and the
Egyptians (trickery) to point to and characterize the dif-

ference between Jesus and the "Antichrists."[86] Far from
working by means of demonic power or servant demons,
Jesus brought an end to the power of the demons;[87]
indeed, it was when the magi sensed that their (demonic)
power was weakened that they set out to find the cause
and made the journey to Palestine.[88] But Origen's basic
argument against magic in the Christian context centers on
the kind of men who perform miracles in Jesus' name and
the kind of deeds they do. No magician calls men to moral
reformation by means of his tricks, as disciples do by their
miracles, and no sorcerer is concerned, as were Jesus and
his disciples, with proclaiming the will of God and his final
judgment.[89] It is therefore the lives and moral character of
those who do wondrous acts that show the difference
between sorcery and Christian miracle.[90] Indeed, the disciples risked their lives to proclaim a teaching that itself
forbids magic.[91]

A fourth theme, a corollary of the third, concerns the
ways in which wondrous deeds are done. We have already
seen, from the positive side, that Christian miracles are
done in the name of Jesus. But the apologists also felt it
necessary to defend Christians against the charges of magic
and sorcery by pointing out, in a negative way, the differences between them. Justin points out that while Christians exorcise demons in the name of Jesus alone, both
Jews and Gentiles are forced to use incantations, drugs,
and incense.[92] Irenaeus in similar language points to the
miracles of the Church as happening without incantations
or any other "wicked, curious art."[93] Origen refutes the
charge of Celsus that Christians get their wondrous power
by means of the names of demons or incantations[94] and
brands as a lie Celsus' claim that Christian writings contain
names of demons and magical formulas.[95] Whereas magi
work their wonders by means of the formulas they use to
invoke demons to do their bidding, Christ's coming has
weakened such power.[96] In fact, the most potent invocation seems to be the name of Jesus, which Origen concedes
has been used effectively even by "bad men" to drive out
demons,[97] but any hint of sorcery involved in such use is

eliminated, Origen argues, by the fact that Christ predicted such things would happen. In fact, such activity proves the "divine power" of Jesus.[98]

IV

With the completion of the rapid survey of the New Testament roots of Jesus and the disciples as miracle workers, the view of miracles and magic in the secular world, and the emerging themes of the Christian apologists in the discussion of miracles and magic, we are now ready to turn our attention to the New Testament apocryphal writings of the mid-second to mid-third centuries and discern the way in which they present Jesus and the disciples as miracle workers. As the discussion proceeds, the combination of secular elements and apologetic themes effected in these apocryphal writings will become increasingly clear.

The picture of Jesus as miracle worker in the apocryphal New Testament writings is remarkable for its absence. To be sure, Jesus is still remembered in such terms. When, in a letter quoted by Eusebius, Irenaeus recalls his contacts with Polycarp, and the latter's conversations with the Apostle (?) John, the two things recalled from John's reports are the teachings and the miracles of Jesus.[99] There are also scattered, if remarkably rare, summaries of the miracles of Jesus to be found in these apocryphal writings, a state of affairs duplicated in the remaining Christian corpus, including the Fathers, of this period.[100]

Unfortunately, we do not possess in any degree of completeness the apocryphal gospels from this period. Of those we do possess, in part or complete, I am aware of only three references to miracles of the mature Jesus.[101] Only in a much later writing do we find further miracles reported of the mature Jesus which are completely new and different from those in our canonical gospels,[102] and even then in very limited number.

The situation is quite different in the case of the infancy

gospels, where new and unique miracles of the infant and youthful Jesus abound. The remarkable point here, however, is the kind of miracle reported of Jesus. In the second-century Infancy Gospel of Thomas, [103] there are only three healing miracles, and one of those concerns Jesus' lifting the curse on those he had earlier blinded. By contrast, there are four punitive miracles, in each instance performed by Jesus against those who have irritated or insulted him. There are also six prodigies, ranging in subject matter from reading Hebrew by the power of the Holy Spirit (in contrast to the normal learning process) to stretching a board in his father's carpenter shop. The remaining three miracles concern Jesus' raising the dead. Later variations on the infancy gospel theme restrict themselves almost entirely to prodigies. [104]

The basic tendency, then, of the traditions about miracles of the mature Jesus in the second century and beyond, including the material subsumed under the general heading "apocryphal New Testament," is to ignore Jesus as miracle worker. The reason for this is obscure and the consequences intriguing. [105] We will have some further comments on this puzzle at the conclusion of this study.

When we turn from the figure of Jesus and the apocryphal gospels, to the apostles and the apocryphal acts, the situation is reversed. We have many such accounts of Jesus' disciples, and they are replete with miracles entirely independent of those told in the canonical Acts of the Apostles.

In order to gain a perspective on these apocryphal acts and to understand something of the milieu out of which they came and to which they intended to speak, it is necessary to consider them from the standpoint of the history of literary forms.

One of the contributions of the later Hellenistic period to Greek literature was the novel (= romance). [106] The genre is hard to define, but it had certain characteristics, among them the theme of a couple separated from one another, yet remaining true despite great pressures against such a course of action. This theme, completely foreign to the canonical Acts, appears, in adapted form, with startling regularity in the second- and third-century Acts. In this adapted form, a woman, often highborn, withdraws from marriage with her husband due to an apostle's preaching and lives an ascetic life, despite the persecution and torture instigated by the irate husband (or lover) against both the woman and the apostle. Peter is persecuted by Albinus, Caesar's friend, when Albinus' wife, Xanthippe, follows Peter (Actus Vercellenses, § § 34ff.).[107] Paul is persecuted by Thamyris when his betrothed, Thecla, leaves him to follow Paul (Acts of Paul and Thecla, § § 7–24; the theme of separation and reunion is also carried out with Paul and Thecla in § § 21–24 and then again in § § 26–40). Andrew is persecuted by Aegaetes because his wife, Maximilla, has left him to follow Andrew (Acts of Andrew, § § 4ff.). Thomas is persecuted by Charisius because his wife, Mygdonia, leaves him to follow Thomas (Acts of Thomas, § § 82ff.), and by King Misdaeus when his wife, Tertia, leaves him to follow Thomas (§ § 134ff.). In the acts of John, improper advances to Drusiana, wife of Andronicus, lead to that faithful woman's death (Acts of John, § § 63–86).[108] Obviously, in none of these instances are the apostle and the lady pictured as lovers, yet it is equally clear that the commendable faithfulness of the woman is to the apostle and his teaching, not to the husband. In that way, apostle and woman become the "devoted couple" who remain true (to the doctrines taught by the apostle) despite all the temptations and pressures to the contrary. The repeated theme of "love at first sight" (i.e., the woman is totally taken with the apostle and his teaching from the moment she first encounters him and exhibits symptoms that the distraught husband, or lover, interpret as infatuation) is further indication that we are dealing with motifs adapted from the Hellenistic romance.

Other elements that figure in the novelistic literature of this period—accounts of travel, occasionally including visits to distant and unknown lands; accounts of prodigies, including bizarre events, strange people and stranger customs; accounts of miracles, done and observed by the hero or other characters; trips to Hades to learn various secrets, including future events; wondrous interventions by the gods, especially to lighten and hasten sea travel[109]—are also found in the apocryphal acts. Although some of these elements also appear in the canonical Gospels and Acts—i.e., accounts of journeys, wondrous deliverance from dangers, miracles—the shape they assume in the apocryphal Acts of Thomas will clearly demonstrate the differences between canonical and apocryphal literature on this score.

If it is true, therefore, as seems to be the case, that the authors of the apocryphal acts have adapted literary conventions of the Hellenistic world in the composition and structure of their narratives, and if, as seems equally to be the case, those elements make the acts more "entertaining," and thus more likely to be read, then it would also seem to be the case that the authors had some kind of apologetic and/or missionary intention underlying their work. They appear to have wanted to gain readers for their works and were willing to cast those works in a form currently popular. To that extent, they adapted their understanding of the Christian message to the literary tastes of the second and third centuries.[110]

We must now turn to a consideration of the way in which the apostles were pictured as miracle workers in the apocryphal acts. We shall devote major attention to three compositions that appear to originate in the late second century: the Acts of Andrew, of Paul, and of Peter, and to two that appear to originate in the third century: the Acts of John and of Thomas. [111]

An indication of the direction in which these apocryphal acts are moving in their portrayal of the disciples lies in the fact that while the healing miracles reported of them are not numerous, accounts of people being raised from the dead, both by the disciples and by those temporarily empowered by the disciples to do it, are much more numerous. John has only one episode of healing reported of him: he cures a group of aged women of their diseases (§ 37);[112] Andrew's only healing was the casting out of a demon (Papyrus Coptic Utrecht I, p 14); Paul, although he recites the healing miracles of Jesus (Greek Papyrus of the Hamburg Staats-und Universitätsbibliothek, pp. 7—8; cf. Coptic Papyrus no. 1 in Heidelberg, p. 79) heals only one blind man upon whom he lays his hands (Coptic Papyrus no. 1 in Heidelberg, p. 33). More are recited of Peter and of Thomas, but only four in each case.[113] In addition, Thomas is recognized as the unknown young man who cured an old Roman (§ 154) and dust from Thomas' grave heals a king's son (§ 170).[114] Healing miracles occur with even less frequency in the later apocryphal acts.

Stories of people being raised from the dead, on the other hand, are much more numerous. John raises to life four people (§ 23, 51, 75, 80) and empowers, on three other occasions, another person to do the same (§§ 24, 47, 82f.). Thomas raises two (§ 33, when a serpent at Thomas' command withdraws its poison from a man, who then returns to life; § 81), and empowers a youth to raise a girl the youth had murdered in a fit of jealous passion (§§ 53f.). Peter raises three (§§ 27, 28, and a girl whom he had previously caused to die, Ps.-Titus, de disp. sanct., pp. 83ff.; for the latter, see NTA II, 278f.), and empowers a man to raise a youngster (26). Paul raises a young girl (Coptic Papyrus no. 1 in Heidelberg, p. 42) and a young man (ibid., pp. 53—58). Of Andrew, interestingly enough, none are reported.

There are of course many other miracles reported in these acts in addition to those of healing and raising the dead. During a prayer of John, the altar and temple of Artemis in Ephesus are shattered, killing the priest (§42), and at John's word bedbugs abandon the bed upon which he intends to sleep and then, again at his word, return to it the next morning (§§ 60f.). An adulteress is paralyzed at

Paul's approach (A. Ver. § 2) and his prayer causes rain and hail to quench the fire meant to burn Thecla (Acts of Paul, § § 22f.). At Peter's bidding a dog announces a challenge to Simon (§ § 9, 12), and a baby speaks with the voice of a man (§15). When a demon, leaving on Peter's command, shatters a statue, Peter instructs another on how to cause the statue to restore itself immediately (§11), and to show his power, Peter makes a smoked fish swim and eat (§13). Thomas causes a serpent to tell its story after its bite has killed a man (§ § 31f.), causes a wild ass to speak (§ § 39f.) and summons four wild asses to draw his wagon (§ 70; at his summons the whole herd appears, but Thomas dismisses them after choosing the four largest), and sends one of them into a city to summon forth a demoniac (§ 74).

Punitive miracles are also recorded, though not in great abundance. An unworthy woman was paralyzed when she received the eucharist at Paul's hands (A. Ver. § 2), and an unworthy lad's hands withered when he took the elements from Thomas (§ 51). As a result of slapping Thomas, a man dies, as Thomas had predicted he would (§ 8). Simon is struck dumb when a baby speaks to him with a man's voice, and Simon kills a boy by whispering in his ear (A. Ver. § § 15, 25). At Peter's prayer, the flying Simon falls and breaks his leg in three places (§ 32).

A further indication of the nature of this material consists in the things which happen to the apostles, most often for their benefit, which they are not responsible for producing. Water welled up from the ground to cool the heated metal Thomas was to be forced to walk on, and disappeared just before it threatened to flood the city (§ § 140f.). Thecla, Paul's companion, is repeatedly saved from martyrdom by prodigies: a lioness befriends her in the arena and holds off the other animals to the point of its own death (§33); she is saved from the seals in the pool into which she has dived by a lightning flash and a cloud of fire (§34); she is saved from wild beasts in the arena when they fall asleep, and from being torn apart by wild bulls

when the ropes tying her to the beasts are wondrously
burned through (§ 35). Paul himself is saved from death
by a lion when the lion speaks to Paul and acknowledges
he is the same one whom Paul had earlier baptized, and
Paul is then saved from other beasts when hail falling from
a clear sky kills them (§ 7). Thomas is reminded of his
duty to preach the gospel by a homilitizing wild ass (§ §
78f.), and John is blinded for two years for wanting to
marry (§ 113). Paul, at his prayer, is freed from prison
fetters by a youth appearing from heaven (§ 7), and
Thomas has prison doors open for his freedom three times
(§ § 122, 154, 162) as well as having fetters wondrously
removed (§ 119).

Visions are regularly reported, by the apostles and
others, which foretell the future (A. Thom. § 91; A. Ver.
§ 17), give instructions (A. Ver. § 1; A. Thom. § 29; A.
John § § 18, 48), and allow the recipient to see Jesus (A.
Paul § 10; A. John § § 92, 97; A. Ver. § § 5, 30, 32; A.
Thom. § § 1, 29; A. Andr. § 8, Vaticanus 808), or to see
someone else (a mother her dead daughter, A. Paul § 28;
one blind sees light, hears a voice, Berlin Copt. Pap. 8502,
pp. 136f.; an innkeeper sees Paul, A. Ver. § 6; demons
appear, A. Ver. § 22). Heavenly voices are heard (A. Ver.
§ § 1, 5; A. Thom. § § 121, 158; A. John § 18), another's
thoughts are discerned (A. John § 59), and foreknowledge
is a regular occurrence (A. John § 46, 86; A. Andr.,
Vaticanus 808 § 17; A. Ver. § § 1, 4, 5, 16f., 22, 32; A.
Thom. § § 6, 91; A. Paul § 11).

Another regular feature of this literature is accounts of
metamorphoses, especially of Jesus appearing in another's
form. He appears to a group of widows as an old man, a
youth, and a boy, each form to a different portion of the
group (A. Ver. § 21). He appears to Thecla in the form of
Paul (A. Paul § 21) and to Maximilla in the form of
Andrew (A. Andr., Vaticanus 808 § 14). To Drusiana he
appears in the form of John, and of a young man (A. John
§ 87), to John he appears as an old man, to James, who
was with John, as a youth (A. John § 89), and to a young

married couple on their wedding night he appears as
Thomas (A. Thom. § 11).

The world of the apocryphal acts, in sum, is a world of
miracles and prodigies, of dreams, foreknowledge and visions, of metamorphoses and voices from heaven. It is a
world of wondrous rescues and miraculous punishments, a
world in which men return from the dead, having learned
secrets of the future, and having seen the torments of the
damned while there (A. Thom. § § 22ff., 55), a world in
which demons not only possess people (A. Andr., Pap.
Copt. Utr. I, p. 14; A. Thom. § § 46, 75; A. Ver. § 11),
but are seen and described (A. Thom. § § 43, 46, 64; A.
Andr., Pap. Copt. Utr. p. 10; A. Ver. § 22). It is, in many
ways, the Hellenistic world in which magic and sorcery
were quite at home.

It is no wonder, therefore, that accusations of sorcery
are raised, both against Christ's followers, and by them
against others. The same rule seems to apply which we
observed earlier, namely, one's own deeds are by God's
power, those of others by magic. A praetor in Ephesus
accuses John of sorcery by means of magical devices, and a
magical name (§ 31); Paul is denounced as a sorcerer by
the crowds (A. Paul § § 15, 20; A. Ver. § 4); and Thomas
is regularly called a sorcerer (§ § 16, 98, 99, 101, 102,
114, 116, 117, 128, 130, 134, 138, 162, 163) three places
(§ 32) and a magician (§ § 20, 89, 96, 104, 106). Thomas
is accused of having used a potion to lure the king's wife
away, and he is asked by another to teach him his magic
(§ § 134, 139).

Similarly, the opponents of the disciples are accused of
practicing magic and sorcery. John calls all non-Christian
worship sorcery (§ 43), and the demon whom Andrew
cast out from a young girl had been conjured up by a
sorcerer for the purpose of winning the girl for himself
(Pap. Copt. Utr. I, p. 14). But the great opponent of the
Christian faith is Simon, and he comes to represent, as it
were, the incorporation of the evil powers of magic and
sorcery arrayed against the Christian faith. Jesus in a vision

to Peter identifies Simon as a sorcerer (A. Ver. § 5) and as a magician (§ 17), and all that Simon really can do is deal in appearances and illusions. His attempt to restore a Roman senator (or lad; the story is confused) to life results in slight movements of the corpse, and the mere illusion of life (§ 28), and all of his apparent healings and raisings from the dead are magical tricks (§ 31).

Almost as if to disprove any charge against the apostles as sorcerers or magicians, the apocryphal acts never describe their miracles in such a way as even to hint at the use of herbs or incantations, or magical devices. [115] John is commanded to perform a miracle, appearing naked in the public theater, so that he may hide nothing, and is forbidden to hold anything in his hands or use a "magical name," and, apparently, even under such conditions, he heals the sick who had been brought there for that purpose (§§ 31–37). While this is the most obvious example of anti-magical polemic in the way a miracle is performed, the intention is symptomatic of the other accounts of miracles done by the followers of Jesus. Miracles are regularly performed either by prayer, or in the name of Jesus (occasionally both), when any method of performance is mentioned at all. There is no predictability, however, about the mode in which miracles are performed or reported. Some are done by prayer. Thus, to cite a very few, Paul through prayer restores a man's sight (§ 4), Peter raises a widow's son (§ 27), Thomas raises two women (§§ 80f.), and John does many miracles (§ 106). Some, on the other hand, are done by the power of the name of Jesus, mentioned by way of command. John thus commands Cleopatra to rise by the name of Him "whom every ruler fears" (§ 23) and instructs her to raise her husband by the name of God (§ 24). Peter casts out a demon in the name of Jesus (§ 11), as does Thomas (§ 75), who later expressly affirms that his power is from Jesus, not achieved by magic (§ 140). Combinations of these two elements may be used, i.e., prayer and Jesus' name, and the command by the disciple that the desired end be

accomplished may also be added. Thus, John raised Drusiana by prayer and command (§ 80), Paul restored a man's
sight by prayer and the laying on of hands (§ 4), Peter
raised a senator (or a boy) by means of prayer, command
and touch (§ 27), and a youth raised a murdered girl after
prayer and in the name of Jesus, both at the instruction of
Thomas (§ § 53f.). The disciple's power is thus not limited
to himself. At his command, and in his presence, others are
able to do what the disciple desires, as Marcellus, at Peter's
instructions, restored a shattered statue (§ 11). In fact, the
apostle's command at times is able, by itself, to cause
another to perform a miracle. At John's command, a
young man raises a priest of Artemis, killed when the
temple collapsed upon him, with neither prayer nor the
name of Jesus being mentioned (§ 47). Or the apostle may
himself perform a miracle without prayer or the name of
Jesus, as Peter does when he simply commands a dog to
speak (§ § 9, 12).

In the great majority of cases, however, it is clearly by
the power of Jesus that the disciples are able to perform
their miracles. That would appear to be the manifest
intention of the accounts of miracles performed by the
disciples, as they are told in the apocryphal acts. Yet on
occasion, stories are told which point simply to the apostle
as wonder worker, able to do mighty things by his own
word of command, or to empower others by instructing
them in what to do, as Peter does when he tells Marcellus
to pray, sprinkle water on the broken statue, and command the statue in Jesus' name to be restored (§ 11).
Given the magical potency of water, one is tempted to see
here an invasion of magic into the narrative. Yet clearly
the empowering act is the prayer to, and the name of,
Jesus. An apostle is thus a mighty man of wonders, but
withal he remains the apostle of Christ, indeed, his slave, as
the opening narrative of the Acts of Thomas make
clear. [116]

We must give some attention to at least two other points
made by the miracle stories in these apocryphal acts. The

most important of those is the emphasis on the miracles as
capable of awakening faith. Indeed, they seem to be in-
dispensible to making the Christian message believable.
Perhaps at this point the apologetic intention of the acts to
a Hellenistic world, saturated with magic and belief in the
potency of sorcerers and magicians, becomes clearest.
These men, not themselves magicians, nevertheless outdo
the most celebrated sorcerers and magicians. Therefore
they deserve to be believed.

That such belief not only can, but must be based on
miracles, is made explicit repeatedly in these apocryphal
acts. John, brought into the theater in Ephesus, affirms he
will "convict even your praetor's disbelief" by healing the
ill women John has commanded to be brought to the
theater for the purpose of his display. [117] He tells the
miracles of Jesus to encourage faith in Jesus (§ 93), and
chides the Ephesians for their unbelief despite the miracles
they have witnessed (§ 39; cf. Matt. 10:20-23!). Those
same Ephesians are then converted when a temple col-
lapses, and they cry to God: "We are converted, now that
we have seen thy marvellous works." [118] Those who are
healed by Thomas believe in Jesus (§ 59), [119] a crowd
confesses God is One when Paul raises a dead girl (§ 8),
and Tryphaena believes in the resurrection as a result of
the prodigies that save Thecla from death in the arena (A.
Paul § 39). Andrew claims the people have seen signs that
will not let them disbelieve (A. Andr., Vaticanus 808, §
16). The writing in which this point is most explicitly and
repeatedly made, however, is the Actus Vercellenses,
which recounts the deeds of Peter. Marcellus, who had
been perverted in his faith by Simon, renews his faith in
Christ when he hears a dog speak at Peter's command (§
10), and it is further strengthened when, at Peter's instructions, he miraculously restores a shattered statue (§ 11).
In response to a popular request for another sign, so the
people can believe in God, since "Simon too did many
signs in our presence, and therefore we followed him,"
Peter causes the smoked fish to swim and eat (§§ 12-

13). [120] Peter, in contest with Simon, annunciates the principle that "We must put no faith in words, but in actions and deeds" (§ 17), [121] a principle then validated when Peter's purpose in raising a widow's dead son is achieved: the people believe in Jesus (§§ 26f.). As a result, Peter was venerated as a god, which appears to have been quite proper. Neither he nor anyone else repudiates it (§ 29; cf.Acts 10:25f.!). It is thus, in this one case at least, clear that the line is not always clearly drawn between the apostle working solely by God's power, as indicated by the presence of prayer and the name of Jesus as empowering devices, and working by his own inherent power, as indicated in those instances where he performs the miracle simply by his own command. The apostle has taken something of the divine power into himself.

The second point—and it is closely allied to the first point, that miracles are necessary to make the Christian faith credible—is the emphasis on the ability of the apostle to win contests of miraculous power. If, as seems evident, the crowds follow the one who performs the greatest wonders, then the way to establish the truth of faith-claims is to see who can do just that. Such a view, close to the surface at any time where miracles are understood as a potent argument for the credibility of faith-claims, as is the case in these second- and third-century acts, becomes explicit in the Acts of Peter. Indeed, the core of this writing seems to concern the contest between Peter and Simon in Rome. Simon, driven out of Palestine at an earlier time by Peter, has now captivated Rome, having arrived, apparently, in a flying cloud (§ 4). Peter has been summoned to combat the enormous influence Simon has won through his wonders. After some preliminary sparring, in which Peter's miracles begin to win back the once-faithful, Simon challenges Peter to a contest of miracles (§ 14), and it is agreed that the winner will be believed (§ 23). All of official Rome gathers to witness the contest. Simon kills a lad by whispering in his ear (§ 25), and Peter raises him (§ 26—this was the first contest, its contents proposed by a Roman official). The mother of a dead senator then proposes to both that they raise her son. Simon is able to restore only a semblance of life, but Peter restores him fully (§ 28). Simon, at this point in the contest admittedly enfeebled, proposes as a final test that he will fly "up to my Father" to prove the truth of his claims (§ 32). This he does, but Peter's prayer to Jesus, in which he warns that if Simon is successful, "all who have believed on thee shall now be overthrown, and the signs and wonders which thou gavest them through me shall be disbelieved," asks that Simon fall and break his leg in three places, which then happens. The onlookers react appropriately. "They [the crowd] stoned [Simon] and went to their own homes; but from that time they all believed in Peter." [122] It only remains for a former follower of Simon to pronounce the theological rationale of such a contest: "Simon, if the Power of God is broken, shall not the God himself, whose power you are, be proved an illusion?" He then says to Peter, the winner, "I too desire to be one of those that believe in Christ." [123] Thus Simon, the sorcerer, who performed his wonders by tricks and incantations, was defeated by Peter, the apostle of Christ, who overcomes Simon by prayer and the name of Jesus.

V

We have now completed our brief survey of the view of Jesus and the disciples as miracle workers contained in the New Testament apocrypha of the second and third centuries. Let us, in conclusion, examine the interrelationship of secular and Christian worlds, and of apologetic and apocryphal motifs.

We noted that the world of the second and third centuries is a world in which magic plays a large role. Magic evidently occupied, in one way or another, people from all ranks of social life and intellectual endeavor. From the philosopher or the writer who must defend himself against the charge of magic, to the humblest love-sick swain seeking to bend the amorous interest of some maiden toward himself, magic was part of the cultural milieu in which all shared. This world is reflected in the apocryphal acts we have examined and is reflected in the writings of the three apologists, at which we cast a quick glance. The frequency with which metamorphoses are narrated in the apocryphal acts, along with numerous astonishing prodigies, seems to indicate that the Hellenistic view of magic has been taken over less critically there than by the apologists. Yet both apologists and apocryphal traditions attempt to separate themselves from magic—primarily, it would seem, by denying that Christian miracles involve the usual techniques of magic, e.g., drugs, herbs and incantations, and by affirming that they do involve solely the power of God or of Jesus, applied by prayer or by using the name of Jesus. In this regard, we seem to catch sight of an emerging Christian consensus on the way in which Christian wonders are to be separated from non-Christian magic.

In similar vein, the view that followers of Jesus continue to be capable of performing wonders, a view found in the apologists, is carried forward as a major emphasis in the bulk of apocryphal writings preserved for our examination. The apostles, however much their power may be attributed to Christ, nevertheless occupy center stage in the drama, and references to miracles of the mature Jesus are as rare in the apologetic as in the apocryphal literature. If it could be assumed that interest in the Church loomed as large in the thinking of those who composed and transmitted the traditions contained in the apocryphal acts [124] as it did in the thinking of the apologists, then we could perhaps see here the growth of the idea that the Church is the major miracle, representing God and his power on earth. But, given the Gnostic flavor of the apocryphal acts [125] and the paucity of our knowledge about the conditions of their origin and composition, such an assumption is questionable at best. But for whatever reason, the apostles and followers of Jesus emerged in the late second and early third centuries as the chief workers of miracles.

The assumption, already evident in the apologists, that faith can be awakened and strengthened on the basis of miracles, bursts into full flower in the apocryphal acts, and becomes most explicit in the Acts of Peter. The corollary idea—namely, that of the competition among wonder workers to prove whose faith claims are valid—while it appears with some regularity (at least in implied form) in the apocryphal acts, seems not to have been used by the apologists in relation to the miracles of the apostles and followers of Jesus. Yet the existence of the Church, for Origen the greatest of miracles, seems to play a similar role in the apologists' thought. The triumph of the gospel, rather than of the miracle-working followers of Christ, seems to hold priority of place.

The appeal to prophecy, appearing in the apologists as evidence for the credibility of Christian miracles, comes up only once in the apocryphal acts we have examined and then in somewhat different application. To Simon's sneering charge that the true God can neither be born nor crucified, Peter replies that such things fulfill prophecy (A. Ver. §§ 23f.). Such an appeal, however, apparently did not commend itself to the authors of apocryphal tradition as an important way to defend the differentiate Christian wonders from pagan magic.

There is, finally, an enigma associated with the apocryphal New Testament literature, namely, the virtually total absence of new miracle stories told of the mature Jesus. That is true right through the sixth century. Only the Gospel of Philip and the later Acts of Andrew and Matthias report miracles of Jesus not contained in the synoptic accounts, and they total only three. Miracles reported of the apostles, on the other hand, abound, as we have seen. So do miracles of the period in Jesus' life not covered in the canonical gospels, his childhood. It has been argued that this is an indication of the towering importance of the

original, canonical traditions. [126] But this must be quickly
modified, since Peter and Paul, whose activities are covered
in the canonical Acts, figure prominently in the apocryphal traditions. To say the apocryphal acts fill out gaps in
the canonical tradition is less than entirely accurate; for
example, the Acts of Peter tell mostly of Peter in Rome,
activity not mentioned or even hinted at in the canonical
Acts, and the Acts of Paul give no indication they were
understood to take place after his imprisonment in Rome,
reported in Acts 28.

Again, to argue that the canonical gospels exercised a
greater restraining force on the developing tradition than
did the canonical Acts, and that for that reason no additional miracles are told of the mature Jesus, faces one with
the problem that the canonical traditions of Jesus exercised no such restraining force on the sayings of Jesus.
But why such selective restraint on the part of the canonical traditions? To argue that the sayings of Jesus were
multiplied by Gnostics, who cared little for miracle accounts, is rendered less than convincing by the Gnostic
flavor of the apocryphal acts, where miracle accounts
abound. Nor is there any indication in the canonical
gospels that while Jesus said things not there recorded, all
of his wondrous acts had been set down.

In fact, the situation is quite the opposite. John 20:30 is
an open invitation to the later tradition, an invitation of
the kind rarely passed up, [127] to develop additional miracle stories of Jesus, something one would surely have
expected if the earlier form critics were correct in their
estimate of the origin and direction of the miracle stories
in the canonical gospels. [128] If John 21 be considered the
acceptance of the invitation contained in John 20:30 (a
miracle is reported in John 21:4–8), one has still to reckon
with the same invitation reextended in John 21:25a. Obviously the author of chapter 21 did not feel he had in any
way exhausted that implied invitation. Surely, these two
passages in John represent an impulse to tell more stories
about the miracles of the mature Jesus. That that "invita-

tion" was not accepted by the framers of apocryphal tradition remains a mystery within the development of Christian tradition in the second and third centuries.

NOTES

1. This tradition is limited to the synoptic gospels. John lacks any tradition comparable to the synoptic representation of Jesus choosing the twelve, or any indication they were given power to work miracles. The one exception may be John 14:12, although this does not have to refer to miraculous deeds; cf. R. E. Brown, *The Gospel According to John* (Garden City: Doubleday, 1970; The Anchor Bible series), *ad loc.*; J. H. Bernard, *St. John* (Edinburgh: T. and T. Clark, 1928: ICC series), *ad loc.*

2. The use of περίεργα in Acts 19:19 to designate incantations and spells may mean that one of the difficulties young widows got themselves into according to 1 Tim. 5:13 was magical practices (περίεργοι), perhaps to lure another husband for themselves. Love potions and incantations made up a large share of the common magical practices of this period. A long incantation to induce love, apparently from a Jewish background, is given in Ludwig Blau, *Das altjüdische Zauberwesen* (Berlin: Louis Lamm, 1910²), pp. 97–99.

3. For the sake of convenience, we will on occasion distinguish between Jewish and Hellenistic (i.e., non-Jewish) elements within the Hellenistic world, but that in no way indicates, as we shall see clearly enough, any far-reaching difference in belief or practice along these lines.

4. See Blau, p. 97, and esp. pp. 27, 64.

5. Sanhedrin 45b; see the note in the Soncino translation, *ad loc.* I use this version when quoting from the Talmud. Cf. also Sanhedrin 91a.

6. Shabbath 152b; Baba Mezia 107b.

7. This prescription, attributed to R. Johanan, is found in Sanhedrin 17a, Menahoth 65a.

8. For curative power, cf. Suetonius, *The Lives of the Caesars 7.* 2–3; on the same event, cf. Tacitus, *Histories,* 4.81; for the uses of saliva in general, see Pliny, *Historia Naturalis* 28.7 (§§ 35–39); that the saliva of a fasting person is more effective, see Pliny, *HN* 28.7 (§

35); the Talmud, Shabbath 108b; Sanhedrin 49b; Zebaḥim 95b; see also Blau, pp. 162f.

9. E.g., Talmud, Baba Mezia 107b; Pliny *HN* 7, §§ 13ff.; 28, § 30.

10. E.g., Talmud, Shabbath 67a; Lucian of Samosata, *Philopseudas*, §§ 15, 17; Blau, p. 69; Hopfner, "Mageia" in Pauly-Wissowa, *Realencyclopädie der classischen Altertumswissenschaft*, vol. 27 (Stuttgart: A. Druckenmüller, 1928), col. 326.

11. In addition to the many occurrences of forms of the personal name of the Hebrew God (Ια, Ιαω, etc.) in the magical papyri, see Blau, p. 123; Origen (*Contra Celsum* 4. 33) says that "almost all who deal in magic and spells" use the name of the God of the Jews, especially in spells against demons (quoted from the translation of H. Chadwick, Cambridge: University Press, 1953, *ad loc.*).

12. Shabbath 67a; Pliny *HN* 18, § 49. Blau finds evidence that the Greek origin of this particular practice was known to the rabbis (p. 76).

13. Many others will be found in Blau, pp. 35f. and *passim.*

14. See, in addition, esp. Blau, pp. 129–135.

15. E.g., Juvenal, *Satire* VI, lines 542–547; Pliny, *HN* 30.2 (§ 11), where a whole branch of magic is attributed to "the Jews;" Solomon was also known as a great magician, see *Testamentum Salomonis, passim*; Josephus, *AJ* 8.2.5 (§§ 42–59).

16. What Egyptians do by magic, Aaron does by God in Exod. 7:8–12; God's superiority is demonstrated when Aaron's "rod" swallows the others. A. Guttmann, "The Significance of Miracles for Talmudic Judaism," *Hebrew Union College Annual* 20, (1947), 363–406, points to the same phenomena, p. 365. Cf. also Talmud, Abodah Zarah 55a, against cures in the temples of idols; Berakoth 59a, against a certain necromancer. See also Blau, pp. 30–31, for other examples for the Talmud.

17. E.g., Apollonius of Tyana (see Philostratus, *Vita Apol.* 8.7.2); Apuleius (see his *Apologia*). Hopfner, col. 383–387 gives many other examples.

18. *HN* 28.4 (§ 18); it is supposed the name, in Greek, was ἔρως, which has the Latin equivalent "amor," or "Roma" spelled backwards.

19. *Philops.* § 10

20. *Con. Cel.* 1.24.

21. E.g., Lucian, *Philops.* §§ 11, 35; Plotinus says some nasty things about such practices (*Enneads,* § 14).

22. E.g., Lucian, *Philops* § 31; cf. Origen, *Con. Cel.* 1.25, who rationalizes this by saying demons must be summoned forth in their native language.

23. E.g., Midrash Rabbah Exodus I, 29, where Moses slew the Egyptian by pronouncing God's name against him. While he who used the name ought to use it for moral purposes, it was powerful enough even to effect immorality and murder (so Blau, pp. 138f.).

24. Yoma 84a; cf. Blau, p. 102, who also reports that forms of the tetragrammaton were especially used in amulet formulae found in the magical papyri, p. 103.

25. Gittin 68a, b; this is also the way Solomon controlled the various demons he summons before him in the *Test. Sal.*

26. E.g., Josephus, *AJ* 8.2.5 (§§ 47f.).

27. E.g., in the Toledoth Yeshu (translation in M. Goldstein, *Jesus in the Jewish Tradition* [New York: Macmillan, 1950]).

28. E.g., Pesaḥim 110a-b.

29. E.g., Pesaḥim 111a–112b; cf. also Blau, pp. 84f.

30. E.g., Sanhedrin 68a, where R. Eliezer plants and harvests a field of cucumbers with a "statement," the content of which is not given.

31. E.g., Berakoth 6a: they are numberless; Pesaḥim 111b: each tree has its own demon; for accounts of individual demons, cf. Pesaḥim 112b, Gittin 70a, Kiddushin 29b, and Meʻilah 17b, where a demon, ben Temalion, helps the Jews outwit the Romans.

32. Apuleius, *The Golden Ass* 2. 28f. For the theory behind this kind of practice, i.e., the "sympathy" existing between various elements within the world, cf. Hopfner, col. 311–327, esp. 312–314.

33. *Empedocles* 8, § 59.

34. *HN* 28, as an example.

35. *Philos.* § 7; absurd for us, but perhaps not so strange for Pliny, or a Jew who knew talmudic traditions (see note 37 below).

36. Berakoth 6a.

37. Shabbath 110b; for other such practices, see Shabbath 67a, Gittin 68b–70a.

38. Shabbath 67b; to urinate in front of it is "Amorite practice," i.e., magic; to put a mulberry chip and broken pieces of glass is permitted. Cf. also Sanhedrin 67b.

39. *AJ* 8.2.5 (§§ 46–48); *BJ* 7.6.3 (§ 185); cf. Tobit 6:7–8.

40. *BJ* 7.6.3 (§§ 178–84); cf. Hopfner, col. 322–324 on ways to gather various plants and herbs, so their power is not lost. On the magical uses of plants and herbs generally, see col. 319–326.

41. Ovid's opening line announces the theme: "In nova fert animus mutatas dicere formas corpora." In Apuleius *The Golden Ass,* Pamphile the sorceress changes herself, by means of salves, into an owl (3.21); secretly watching this performance, Lucius decides to duplicate it but, getting the wrong salve, he changes into an ass (3.24). The goddess Isis then brings about his retransformation (11.13). Lucian of Samosota has what I think is a shorter, more original version ("Lucius, or the Ass"), which Apuleius then lengthened into a religious tract for the religion of Isis, but this is no more than a conjecture on my part at this point. Many scholars take Lucian's version to be a compend of Apuleius' longer story.

42. Sanhedrin 67b; in one story an ass becomes a "landing board"; in the other, a sorceress becomes an ass which Jannai then rides into town.

43. So Blau (citing Dieterich, *Abraxas,* p. 155, n. 1), p. 42f. He asserts Egypt was known as the home of magic from Homer to late Hellenism, p. 42. Cf. also the first lines of Pseudo-Callisthenes, *The Life of Alexander of Macedon* (1.1). Strangely, Pliny insists that Persia was the home of magic (= Magi), and cites many "authorities;" *HN* 30.2 (§§ 3–6).

44. Arignotus, for example, has many Egyptian books on magic and exorcises a demon from a house using an imprecation in the Egyptian language (Lucian, *Philops.* § 31).

45. Origen, *Con. Cel.* 1.68; cf. also 1.38, 46.

46. Kiddushin 49b; cf. also Blau, p. 38.

47. Midrash Rabbah Exodus XI, 6.

48. Sanhedrin 67b.

49. Shabbath 104b.

50. So Guttmann, pp. 402–405.

51. Ibid., pp. 384f. Guttmann attributes the refusal to allow a Bat Kol (= voice from heaven) to influence doctrinal decisions to the growing anti-Christian polemic that developed between 90 and 100 A.D., and mentions that R. Eliezer, who was sympathetic to Christians, called upon it to confirm his legal interpretations (pp. 384–386; for the dispute, cf. Baba Mezia 59b).

52. For this view, it was better for a faithful Jew to let a person die than to be healed by a Christian; cf. Abodah Zarah 27b, where a rabbi who does just that is called "blessed."

53. For further evidence on this point, see my article "Gospel Miracle Tradition and the Divine Man," *Interpretation* 26 (1972) 191, esp. the notes.

54. *Adv. Haer.* 2.32.4.

55. *Dial. c. Try.* 35.

56. *Con. Cel.* 1.67; 2.33; 3.24, 28.

57. *Apol.* 2.6.

58. *Dial. c. Try.* 30, 76.

59. *Con. Cel.* 1.25.

60. *Con. Cel.* 3.33.

61. *Con. Cel.* 2.48.

62. E.g., Irenaeus, *Adv. Haer.* 2.31.2.

63. *Dial. c. Try.* 69. This is not so foreign to the NT perspective as has on occasion been argued. Faith based on miracles is regularly reported in Acts (8:9–11; 9:35, 42; 13:12; cf. also 16:30; 19:17), and Paul apparently thought it not only likely, but legitimate, that signs and wonders should lead people to faith in Christ (1 Cor. 2:4; cf. Rom. 15:18–20, where it appears such wondrous acts are part and parcel of "preaching the gospel"). Although the total picture in John is ambiguous, that gospel also implied that faith can be based on mighty acts (e.g., 2:11; 4:53; 6:14; 11:15).

64. *Adv. Haer.* 2.32.4.

65. *Adv. Haer.* 5.11.2; cf. 3.11.5.

66. *Con. Cel.* 2.52.

67. *Con. Cel.* 4.80.

68. *Con. Cel.* 3.21.

69. *Con. Cel.* 3.28.

70. *Con. Cel.* 1.46.

71. *Apol.* 1.22f., 54; *Dial. c. Try.* 69.

72. *Apol.* 1.48.

73. *Apol.* 1.30.

74. *Adv. Haer.* 2.32.4.

75. *Con. Cel.* 2.48; 8.9. A similar appeal to prophecy to bolster the legitimacy and uniqueness of Jesus' miracles is found in the *Clementine Recognitions* 1.41; 3.60. It was probably a more widespread device than our brief treatment has indicated.

76. *Apol.* 1.26, 56.

77. *Dial c. Try.* 69.

78. Simon and Carpocrates, *Adv. Haer.* 3.31.2; Marcus, a contemporary, it appears, *Adv. Haer.* 1.13.1f.

79. *Adv. Haer.* 2.31.2; 3.32.3.

80. *Adv. Haer.* 2.31.2; cf. the account of the demon ben Tamalion, Me'ilah 17b.

81. *Adv. Haer.* 2.32.3.

82. *Con. Cel.* 1.24.
83. *Con. Cel.* 2.48; cf. 50.
84. *Con. Cel.* 2.32; cf. 1.71.
85. *Con. Cel.* 2.44.
86. *Con. Cel.* 2.50.
87. *Con. Cel.* 4.32.
88. *Con. Cel.* 1.60.
89. *Con. Cel.* 1.68.
90. *Con. Cel.* 2.51.
91. *Con. Cel.* 1.38.
92. *Apol.* 2.6; *Dial. c. Try.* 85.
93. *Adv. Haer.* 2.32.5.
94. *Con. Cel.* 1.6.
95. *Con. Cel.* 6.40.
96. *Con. Cel.* 1.60.
97. *Con. Cel.* 1.6.
98. *Con. Cel.* 2.50.
99. Eusebius, *Historia Ecclesiastica* 5.20.6. In the translation by K. Lake (Loeb Classical Library series), those miracles are unaccountably reported as "their miracles" and "their teachings," i.e., as those of the apostles (αὐτοῦ is translated as though the text read αὐτῶν). For the correct translation, cf. H.J. Lawlor and J.E.L. Oulton, eds., *Eusebius* (London: SPCK, 1954) vol. I, *ad loc.*
100. For a list of such summaries, see my article in *Interpretation*, p. 191, n. 83; Walter Bauer, *Das Leben Jesu im Zeitalter der neutestamentlichen Apokryphen* (Tübingen: JCB Mohr, 1909; reprint Wissenschaftliche Buchgesellschaft, 1967), p. 364. To those lists may be added the summary found in the "Epistula Apostolorum" § 5; cf. E. Hennecke and W. Schneemelcher, *New Testament Apocrypha,* Eng. trans. ed. R. McL. Wilson (Philadelphia: Westminster, 1963, 1965), vol. I. This latter work will hereafter be cited as "*NTA* I" or "*NTA* II."
101. The Gospel of the Nazaraeans (cited by Jerome in his *Commentary on Matt.,* Matt. 12:13; cf. *NTA* I, 148), where the man with the withered hand identifies himself as a mason and asks to be cured; The Gospel of Philip, p. 111, § 54 (see *The Gospel of Philip,* trans. R. McL. Wilson [New York: Harper and Row, 1962], p. 39), where Jesus throws seventy-two colors into the vat in Levi's dyeworks, and takes them all out white (a miracle similar to this is found in the Arabic Infancy Gospel; cf. *NTA* I, 400); and in the Coptic Gospel of Thomas, logion 14, where the charge to the

disciples to heal is not necessarily to be interpreted as miraculous power, but in the tradition is probably so to be understood. Perhaps one ought also to reckon here the "longer" ending of Mark (16:17–18), although all but one of the types of miracles there are reflected in the NT (casting out demons: Mark 9:38; Luke 10:17; glossalalia: Acts 2:4, 11; 10:46; 19:6; picking up serpents: Luke 10:17–20; healing: Acts 9:17; 28:8). Only drinking poison unharmed is not reflected in the canonical NT; but cf. Eusebius, *HE* 3. 39. 9.

102. The Acts of Andrew and Matthias, perhaps as late as the sixth century. Here we learn that during his life, Jesus made stone sphinxes walk and talk, who summoned the three patriarchs from Mamre to sepak to the high priests, all in an unsuccessful effort to convince them of Jesus' importance. Other miracles for the same purpose performed in private before the same group are not detailed. For a translation, see *The Ante-Nicene Fathers,* ed. A. Roberts and J. Donaldson, rev. A.C. Coxe (New York: Scribners, 1899), VIII, 517–525. This volume will hereafter be cited as "*ANF* VIII."

103. For a translation, see *NTA* I, 392–399.

104. For translations, see *NTA* I, 399–417; *ANF* VIII, 395–415.

105. If the trend is in the direction of the disappearance of the miracle story about the mature Jesus, can we continue to assume, as Bultmann did, that the miracles are a late addition to the canonical gospel traditions, and that the trend was toward increasing emphasis on the miracles of Jesus? Changes from Mark to Matthew and Luke, with respect to miracle stories, may be due as much to the intentions of the respective evangelists as to any traditional trajectory. Development of this point, however, must await a later time.

106. A convenient, brief summary of this kind of literature, and some of its representatives, can be found in F.A. Wright, *A History of Later Greek Literature* (London: G. Routledge and Sons, 1932) pp. 292–308. There are of course many other such accounts. For a study more directly related to this topic, see Rosa Söder, *Die apokryphen Apostelgeschichten und die romanhafte Literatur der Antike* (Stuttgart: Kohlhammer Verlag, 1969–a reprint of the 1932 edition).

107. Some idea of the pressure on this unknown author to include this motif is indicated by the fact that this becomes the motive for Peter's martyrdom at the hands of Caesar, after Peter had won the approval of the whole of Rome through his prodigy-laden victory over Simon. Peter's death from faithfulness to Christ becomes here his death due to a jealous husband.

108. The novelistic nature of this last instance is heightened by the merely peripheral involvement of the apostle John in this episode. The erotic elements, present in most of the apocryphal acts, are here carried to rather bizarre lengths.

109. These are some of the major motifs Ms. Söder finds in her analysis of novelistic literature. Most of them go all the way back to the Odyssey.

110. Any author, of course, writes to be read. But the continuing and unresolved debate over the possible genre of the canonical gospels indicates that such adaption to current Hellenistic literary tastes was not so great an element in their formation, as in that of the apocryphal acts. The same is true of the canonical Acts, if in somewhat modified degree. Cf. E. Plümacher, *Lukas als hellenistischer Schriftsteller* (Göttingen: Vandenhoeck und Ruprecht, 1972), who sees Luke as dependent on Hellenistic historiography for his model, but never using elements drawn from it to arouse interest or decorate his narrative to make it palatable to Hellenistic tastes (p. 139). It is just this, it seems to me, that the authors of the apocryphal acts are doing.

111. For a discussion of possible dates, cf. *NTA* II, *ad loc.* The remaining acts, e.g., the Acts´of Philip, of Barnabas (as told by John Mark), of Pilate, of the Holy Apostles Peter and Paul, of Andrew and Matthias in the city of the Man-eaters, and the Martyrdom of the holy and glorious Apostle Bartholomew, appear to date from the fourth century and later, and will be referred to only rarely.

112. Paragraph numbers refer to the acts of the respective apostles. The Acts of Peter, called Actus Vercellenses, are hereafter cited as "A. Ver."

113. Of Peter, two healings and a restoration of sight (Berlin Coptic Papyrus 8502, pp. 128–132, 135–41; *NTA* II, 276–278), and a general healing (A. Ver. § 31); of Thomas, two general healings (§§ 20, 59), expulsion of a demon (§§ 42–47) and restoration of withered hands (§ 52).

114. The apostle Thaddaeus heals King Abgar in an account that may have been written in the second or third century, although it is not recorded until later in Eusebius, *HE* 1.13.17, where a general reference to Thaddaeus' healing "every disease and infirmity" is also included (1.13.12).

115. King Abgar is impressed by the fact that both Jesus and Thaddaeus heal without drugs and herbs, an observation that could stand as a motto for the way the disciples perform miracles in these Acts; cf. Eusebius, *HE* 1.13.6 and 18.

116. In §§ 1–3, Thomas, having refused the assignment to evangelize India which was his by lot, is sold by Jesus to a merchant from India. Jesus says to the merchant: "I have a slave who is a carpenter, and I wish to sell him" (*NTA* II, 443).

117. § 33; *NTA* II, 223.

118. § 42; *NTA* II, 237.

119. Oddly, despite the large number of miracles and prodigies in the Acts of Thomas, this is the only instance where faith results from such events.

120. *NTA* II, 295.

121. *NTA* II, 299.

122. *NTA* II, 316.

123. § 32; *NTA* II, 316.

124. It seems appropriate to speak of "traditions" because of indications, contained in the apocryphal acts, of literary compilation and editing. This is indicated—in addition to the episodic nature of the works and the patent insertions, e.g., the "Hymn of the Pearl" into the Acts of Thomas (§§ 108–113)—by the confusion of geography and characters within some narratives, rather clear indication of combination of traditions, or later literary additions. Such indications are: confusion of characters within a story (A. Andr. Vaticanus Ms. 808, §§ 8, 10; an attempt to repair the confusion, § 14; A. John §§ 63–73; A. Ver. § 28); confusion of detail, with events already narrated forgotten (A. Ver. § 32) or changed within the story (A. John §§ 71–76). There appears to be the insertion of a wisdom discourse in the Acts of Andrew, Vaticanus 808, § 9, within another story, §§ 8, 10.

125. Phrases that reflect Gnostic cosmology and beliefs occur with some regularity within the apocryphal acts we have examined, e.g., John reports that Jesus sometimes had a material, sometimes an immaterial body, and left no footprints when he walked (§ 93); a youth cannot praise God because it is not in his "nature" (§ 84); when one understands himself, he understands all (A. Andr. § 6); Paul's opponents affirm that the resurrection of the Christian has already occurred (§ 14); a person must recognize what he was, is now, and that he is to become again what he was (A. Thom. § 15); those who realize that the true meaning of Christ's passion and cross is something other than that which is visible, and who withdraw from the material world, will learn the "whole secret" of their salvation (A. Ver. § 37, *NTA* II, 319). Such instances could be multiplied many-fold. Along with this is a strong ascetic strain present in all the apocryphal acts here examined, and aimed primarily against sexual

intercourse, to the point that a lion, baptized by Paul, refuses to yield himself to the blandishments of a lioness (from a yet-un-published coptic papyrus; *NTA* II, 189). A thorough examination of these motifs lies beyond the scope of our present study.

126. So. H. Schlingensiepen, *Die Wunder des neuen Testaments* (Gütersloh: Bertelsmann, 1933), p. 7f. Although I did not come upon this study until I was far along in my own research, I gladly note the similarity of approach and conclusion in other areas of common investigation.

127. For example, the time of the presence of the risen Lord on earth could be extended to allow for new teaching, as in the *Pistis Sophia,* example of such pretexts for expanding the tradition is to be found in a writing entitled The Acts of Peter and Andrew, where Jesus' saying about a camel passing through the eye of a needle (Matt. 19:24) becomes an actual miracle Peter is forced to perform to pacify an enraged rich man to whom Peter had quoted that saying.

128. See the comments in note 105, above.

Bibliography

Achtemeier, P. "Gospel Miracle Tradition and the Divine Man." *Interpretation* 26 (1972), 174–197.

Axenfeld, K. "Die jüdische Propaganda als Vorläuferin der urchristlichen Mission." In *Missionswissenschaftliche Studien. (Festschrift Warneck)*, pp. 1–103. Berlin: Evang. Missionsgesellschaft, 1904.

Baron, S. W. *A Social and Religious History of the Jews.* 8 vols., 2nd ed. New York: Columbia Univ. Press, 1952–1973.

Bauer, W. *Orthodoxy and Heresy in Earliest Christianity.* Edited by R. Kraft and G. Krodel. Philadelphia: Fortress Press, 1971.

———. *Das Leben Jesu im Zeitalter der neutestamentlichen Apokryphen.* 1909, repr. Darmstadt: Wissenschaftliche Buchgesellschaft, 1967.

Baumbach, G. "Die Mission im Matthäusevangelium." *Theologische Literaturzeitung* 92 (1967), 889–893.

Beare, F. W. "The Mission of the Disciples and the Mission Charge Matthew 10 and Parallels." *Journal of Biblical Literature* 89 (1970), 3–13.

Belkin, S. *The Alexandrian Halakah in Apologetic Literature of the First Century C.E.* Philadelphia: Jewish Publication Society of America, 1936.

Bell, H. I. *Jews and Christians in Egypt.* Oxford: Clarendon Press, 1924.

Benko, S., and O'Rourke, J. J. *The Catacombs and the Colosseum: The Roman Empire as the Setting of Primitive Christianity.* Valley Forge: Judson Press, 1971.

Bergmann, J. *Jüdische Apologetik im neutestamentlichen Zeitalter.* Berlin: Reimer, 1908.

Betz, H. D. *Der Apostel Paulus und die sokratische Tradition.* BzhTh 45. Tübingen: Mohr, 1972.

Betz, O., Haacker, K., and Hengel, M., eds. *Josephus–Studien. Untersuchungen zu Josephus, dem antiken Judentum, und dem Neuen Testament.* Göttingen: Vandenhoeck & Ruprecht, 1974.

Beyschlag, K. *Simon Magus und die christliche Gnosis.* WMANT 16. Tübingen: J.C.B. Mohr, 1974.

Bialoblocki, S. *Die Beziehungen des Judentums zu Proselyten und Proselytentum.* Berlin: J. Nobel, 1930

Bieder, W. *Gottes Sendung und der missionarische Auftrag der Kirche nach Matthäus, Lukas, Paulus, und Johannes.* ThSt 82. Zurich: Zwingli Verlag, 1964.

Blau, L. *Das altjüdische Zauberwesen.* 2nd ed. Berlin: Lamm, 1910.

Bosch, D. *Die Heidenmission in der Zukunftsschau Jesu.* Zurich: Zwingli Verlag, 1959.

Braude, W. G. *Jewish Proselytizing in the First Five Centuries of the Common Era.* Providence: Brown Univ. Press, 1940.

Braun, M. *History and Romance in Graeco-Oriental Literature.* Oxford: Blackwell, 1938.

Bultmann, R. *Primitive Christianity in Its Contemporary Setting.* New York: Meridian Books, 1956.

Bussmann, C. *Themen der paulinischen Missionspredigt auf dem Hintergrund der spätjüdisch-hellenistischen Missionsliteratur.* Bern: H. Lang, 1971.

Campbell, B. "Traces of Thaumaturgic Techniques in the Miracles." *Harvard Theological Review* 20 (1923), 171–181.

Causse, A. "La propagande juive et l'hellénisme." *Revue de Histoire et de Philosophie Religieuse* 3 (1923), 397–414.

Clemen, C. "Die Missionstätigkeit der nicht-christlichen Religionen." *Zeitschrift für Missionskunde und Religionswissenschaft* 44 (1929), 225–233.

Conzelmann, H. *History of Primitive Christianity.* Nashville: Abingdon·Press, 1973.

Cullmann, O. "Eschatology and Mission in the New Testament." In *The Background of the New Testament and Its Eschatology: Studies in Honour of C. H. Dodd,* pp. 409–421. Cambridge: Univ. Press, 1956.

Cumont, F. *Oriental Religions in Roman Paganism.* New York: Dover, 1956.

Dalbert, P. *Die Theologie der hellenistisch-jüdischen Missionsliteratur unter Ausschluss von Philo and Josephus.* Hamburg: Reich, 1954.

Delling, G. *Studien zum Neuen Testament und zum hellenistischen Judentum.* Göttingen: Vandenhoeck & Ruprecht, 1970.

Derwacter, F. M. *Preparing the Way for Paul: The Proselyte Movement in Later Judaism.* New York: Macmillan, 1930.

Edelstein, E. J. and L., eds. *Asclepius: A Collection and Interpretation of the Testimonies.* 2 vols. Baltimore: John Hopkins Press, 1945.

Feldman, L. H. *Scholarship on Philo and Josephus.* New York: Yeshiva Univ. Press, 1963.

——. "Jewish 'Sympathizers' in Classical Literature and Inscriptions." *Proceedings of the American Philological Association* 81 (1950), 200–208.

——. "Abraham the Greek Philosopher in Josephus." *Proceedings of the American Philological Association* 99 (1968), 336–353.

Fiebig, P. *Rabbinische Wundergeschichten des neutestamentlichen Zeitalters.* 2nd ed. Bonn: Marcus & Weber, 1933.

Fischel, H. A. *Rabbinic Literature and Graeco-Roman Philosophy.* Studia Postbiblica 41. Leiden: Brill, 1973.

Fridrichsen, A. *The Problem of Miracle in Primitive Christianity.* Minneapolis: Augsburg Publishing House, 1972.

Friedländer, M. *Geschichte der jüdischen Apologetik als Vorgeschichte des Christentums.* Zurich: C. Schmidt, 1903.

Gager, J. G. *Moses in Greco-Roman Paganism.* SBL Mono. Ser. 16. Nashville: Abingdon Press, 1972.

Geffcken, J. *Zwei griechische Apologeten.* Leipzig: Teubner, 1907.

Georgi, D. *Die Gegner des Paulus im 2. Korintherbrief. Studien zur religiösen Propaganda in der Spätantike.* WMANT 11. Neukirchen-Vluyn: Neukirchener Verlag, 1964.

——. "Forms of Religious Propaganda." In H. J. Schultz, ed., *Jesus in His Time,* pp. 124–131. Philadelphia: Fortress Press, 1971.

——. "The Records of Jesus in Light of Ancient Accounts of Revered Men." In *Proceedings of the Society of Biblical Literature 1972,* II, pp. 527–542.

Gigon, O. *Die antike Kultur und das Christentum.* 2nd ed. Gütersloh: G. Mohn, 1969.

Glover, T. R. *The Conflict of Religions in the Roman Empire*. London: Methuen, 1909.

Goldin, J. *The Song at the Sea*. New Haven: Yale Univ. Press, 1971.

Goodenough, E. R. "The Political Philosophy of Hellenistic Kingship." *Yale Classical Studies* 1 (1928), 55–102.

———. *The Politics of Philo Judaeus*. New Haven: Yale Univ. Press, 1938.

———. *By Light, Light*. New Haven: Yale Univ. Press, 1935.

Grant, F. C. *Hellenistic Religions: The Age of Syncretism*. New York: Bobbs-Merrill, 1953.

Gressmann, H. "Jüdische Mission in der Werdezeit des Christentums." *Zeitschrift für Missionskunde und Missionswissenschaft* 39 (1924), 169–183.

———. "Heidnische Mission in der Werdezeit des Christentums." *Zeitschrift für Missionskunde und Missionswissenschaft* 39 (1924), 10–24.

Grundmann, W. "Die Apostel zwischen Jerusalem und Antiochien." *Zeitschrift für die neutestamentliche Wissenschaft* 39 (1940), 127–135.

Guttmann, A. "The Significance of Miracles for Talmudic Judaism." *Hebrew Union College Annual* 20 (1947), 363–406.

Guttmann, H. *Die Darstellung der jüdischen Religion bei Flavius Josephus*. Breslau: Marcus, 1928.

Habicht, C. *Gottmenschentum und griechische Städte*. 2nd ed., Zetemata 14. Munich: Beck, 1970.

Hadas, M., and Smith, M. *Heroes and Gods: Spiritual Biographies in Antiquity*. New York: Harper & Row, 1965.

Hahn, F. *Mission in the New Testament*. Naperville, Ill.: Allenson, 1965.

———. "Der Apostolat im Urchristentum. Seine Eigenart und seine Voraussetzungen." *Kerygma und Dogma* 20 (1974), 52–77.

Harnack, A. *The Mission and Expansion of Christianity in the First Three Centuries*. New York: Harper Torchbook, 1962.

Hengel, M. "Die Ursprünge der christlichen Mission." *New Testament Studies* 18 (1971/72), 15–38.

———. *Judaism and Hellenism: Studies in Their Encounter in Pales-*

tine during the Early Hellenistic Period. Philadelphia: Fortress Press, 1974.

Hennecke, E., and Schneemelcher, W., eds. *New Testament Apocrypha.* 2 vols. Philadelphia: Westminster Press, 1965.

Hull, J. M. *Hellenistic Magic and the Synoptic Tradition.* Studies in Biblical Theology 28. London: SCM Press, 1974.

Jeremias, J. *Jesus' Promise to the Nations.* London: SCM Press, 1966.

Juster, J. *Les Juifs dans l'Empire romain.* 2 vols. Paris: Geuthner, 1914.

Kasting, H. *Die Anfänge der urchristlichen Mission.* Munich: Kaiser, 1969.

Kennedy, G. *The Art of Rhetoric in the Roman World.* Princeton: Univ. Press, 1972.

Klein, G. *Der älteste christliche Katechismus und die jüdische Propaganda Literatur.* Berlin: Reimer, 1909.

Klein, G. "Der Synkretismus als theologisches Problem in der ältesten christlichen Apologetik." In *Rekonstruktion und Interpretation,* BevTh 50, pp. 262–301. Munich: Kaiser Verlag, 1969.

Krüger, P. *Philo und Josephus als Apologeten des Judentums.* Leipzig: Dürr, 1906.

Kuhn, G. "Das Problem der Mission in der Urchristenheit." *Evangelische Missionszeitschrift* 11 (1959), 161–168.

Lake, K., and Cadbury, H. J. *The Beginnings of Christianity.* 5 vols. London: Macmillan, 1933.

Lerle, E. *Proselytenwerbung und Urchristentum.* Berlin: Evangelische Verlagsanstalt, 1960.

Lieberman, S. *Hellenism in Jewish Palestine.* New York: Jewish Theological Seminary of America, 1962.

Liechtenhahn, R. *Die urchristliche Mission: Voraussetzung, Motive, und Methoden.* Zurich: Zwingli Verlag, 1946.

Lohse, E. "Missionarisches Handeln Jesu nach dem Evangelium des Lukas." *Theologische Zeitschrift* 10 (1954), 1–13.

MacMullen, R. *Enemies of the Roman Order: Treason, Unrest, and Alienation in the Roman Empire.* Cambridge: Harvard Univ. Press, 1966.

Margalioth, M., ed. *Sepher ha-Razim*. Jerusalem, 1966.

Matthews, I. G. "The Jewish Apologetic to the Grecian World in the Apocryphal and Pseudepigraphical Literature." Dissertation, University of Chicago, 1914.

Meeks, W. A. *The Prophet-King*. Leiden: Brill, 1967.

———. "Moses as God and King." In J. Neusner, ed., *Religions in Antiquity*, pp. 354–371. Leiden: Brill, 1968.

———. "The Image of the Androgyne." *History of Religion* 13 (1974), 165–208.

Meinertz, M. *Jesus und die Heidenmission*. Münster: Aschendorff, 1908.

———. "Zum Ursprung der Heidenmission." *Biblica* 40 (1959), 762–777.

Meissner, N. *Untersuchungen zum Aristeasbrief*. 2 vols. Berlin: Kirchliche Hochschule, 1972.

Mott, S. C. "The Greek Benefactor and Deliverance from Moral Distress." Ph.D. dissertation, Harvard, 1971.

Moule, C. F. D. *Miracles: Cambridge Studies in Their Philosophy and History*. London: A. R. Mowbray, 1965.

Nock, A. D. *Conversion: The Old and the New in Religion from Alexander the Great to Augustine of Hippo*. London: Oxford Univ. Press, 1961.

———. *Essays on Religion and the Ancient World*. Edited by Z. Stewart. 2 vols. Cambridge: Harvard Univ. Press, 1972.

Petzke, G. *Die Traditionen über Apollonius von Tyana und das Neue Testament*. Leiden: Brill, 1970.

Pick, B. "Jewish Propaganda in the Time of Christ." *Quarterly Review of the Evangelical Lutheran Church* 23 (1893), 149–172: 24 (1894), 115–131.

Plümacher, E. *Lukas als hellenistischer Schriftsteller*. StUNT 9. Göttingen: Vandenhoeck & Ruprecht, 1972.

Prümm, K. *Religionsgeschichtliches Handbuch für den Raum der altchristlichen Umwelt*. Rome: Päpstliches Bibelinstitut, 1954.

Radin, M. *The Jews among the Greeks and Romans*. Philadelphia: Jewish Publication Society of America, 1915.

Rankin, O. S. *Jewish Religious Polemic*. Edinburgh: Univ. Press, 1956.

Rengstorf, K. H. *Die Mission unter den Heiden im Lichte des Neuen Testaments.* Hermannsburg: Missionshandlung, 1936.

Robinson, J. M., and Koester, H. *Trajectories through Early Christianity.* Philadelphia: Fortress Press, 1971.

Rosen, G., Rosen, F., and Bertram, G. *Juden und Phönizier. Das antike Judentum als Missionsreligion und die Entstehung der jüdischen Diaspora.* Tübingen: J.C.B. Mohr, 1929.

Rostovtzeff, M. *The Social and Economic History of the Hellenistic World.* Oxford: Clarendon Press, 1941.

Sabourin, L. "Helenistic and Rabbinic Miracles." *Biblical Theology Bulletin* 2 (1972), 281–307.

Schille, G. "Anfänge der christlichen Mission." *Kerygma und Dogma* 15 (1969), 320–339.

——. *Die urchristliche Kollegialmission.* AThANT 48. Zurich: Zwingli Verlag, 1967.

Schlier, H. "Die Entscheidung für die Heidenmission in der Urchristenheit." *Evangelische Missionszeitschrift* 3 (1942), 166–182, 208–212.

Schneider, C. *Kulturgeschichte des Hellenismus.* 2 vols. Munich: C. H. Beck, 1967.

Schneider, G. "Urchristliche Gottesverkündigung in hellenistischer Umwelt." *Biblische Zeitschrift* 13 (1969), 59–75.

Schürer, E. *The History of the Jewish People in the Age of Jesus Christ (175BC - 135 AD).* Revised and edited by G. Vermes and F. Miller. Edinburgh: T. & T. Clark, 1973.

——. *The Literature of the Jewish People in the Time of Jesus.* New York: Schocken Books, 1972.

Simon, M. *St. Stephen and the Hellenists in the Primitive Church.* New York: Green, 1958.

——. "Early Christianity and Pagan Thought: Confluences and Conflicts." *Religious Studies* 9 (1973), 385–399.

Smallwood, E. M. *Philonis Alexandrini Legatio ad Gaium.* Leiden: Brill, 1961.

Smith, M. *Clement of Alexandria and a Secret Gospel of Mark.* Cambridge: Harvard Univ. Press, 1973.

Söder, R. *Die apokryphen Apostelgeschichten und die romanhafte Literatur der Antike.* 1932, repr. Stuttgart: Kohlhammer, 1969.

Spitta, F. *Jesus und die Heidenmission*. Giessen: Töpelmann, 1909.

Stearns, W. N. *Fragments from Graeco-Jewish Writers*. Chicago: Univ. Press, 1908.

Talbert, C. H. *Literary Patterns, Theological Themes, and the Genre of Luke-Acts*. SBL Mono. Ser. 20. Missoula: Scholars Press, 1974.

Tarn, W. W. *Hellenistic Civilization*. 3rd rev. ed. New York: Meridian, 1961.

Tcherikover, V. *Hellenistic Civilization and the Jews*. Philadelphia: The Jewish Publication Society of America, 1961.

Thackeray, H. J. *Josephus the Man and the Historian*. New York: Ktav Publishing House, 1968.

Theissen, G. *Urchristliche Wundergeschichten*. StNT 8. Gütersloh: G. Mohn, 1974.

———. "Legitimität und Lebensunterhalt. Ein Beitrag zur Soziologie urchristlicher Missionäre." *New Testament Studies* 21 (1975), 192–221.

Thyen, H. *Der Stil der jüdisch-hellenistischen Homilie*. FRLANT 65. Göttingen: Vandenhoeck & Ruprecht, 1955.

Tiede, D. L. *The Charismatic Figure as Miracle Worker*. SBL Dissertation Series 1. Missoula: Scholars Press, 1972.

Trachtenberg, J. *Jewish Magic and Superstition*. Cleveland: World Publishing Co., 1961.

Vermes, G. "Hanina ben Dosa." *Journal of Jewish Studies* 23 (1972), 28–50; 24 (1973), 51–64.

Vogelstein, H. "The Development of the Apostolate in Judaism: Its Transformation in Christianity." *Hebrew Union College Annual* 2 (1925), 99–123.

Votaw, C. W. *The Gospels and Contemporary Biographies in the Greco-Roman World*. Fb Bibl. Ser. 27. Philadelphia: Fortress Press, 1970.

Wendland, P. *Die Hellenistisch-römische Kultur in ihren Beziehungen zu Judentum und Christentum*. HNT I, 2. Tübingen: J.C.B. Mohr, 1907.

Wilckens, U. *Die Missionsreden der Apostelgeschichte*. WMANT 5. Neukirchen-Vluyn: Neukirchener Verlag, 1963.

———. "Hellenistisch-christliche Missionsüberlieferung und Jesustradition." *Theologische Literaturzeitung* 89 (1964), 517–520.

Wilken, R. "Toward a Social Interpretation of Early Christian Apologetics." *Church History* 39 (1970), 1–22.

Wilson, S. G. *Gentiles and Gentile Mission in Luke-Acts.* SNTS Mono. Ser. 23. Cambridge: Univ. Press, 1973.